*Alexander the Great and the Mystery
of the Elephant Medallions*

Alexander the Great
and the Mystery of the
Elephant Medallions

Frank L. Holt

UNIVERSITY OF CALIFORNIA PRESS

Berkeley   *Los Angeles*   *London*

University of California Press
Berkeley and Los Angeles, California
University of California Press, Ltd.
London, England

© 2003 by the Regents of the University of California

Library of Congress Cataloging-in-Publication Data

Holt, Frank Lee.
   Alexander the Great and the mystery of the elephant
medallions / Frank L. Holt.
      p.   cm. — (Hellenistic culture and society ; 44)
   Includes bibliographical references and index.
   ISBN 0-520-23881-8
   1. Coins, Greek.   2. Coins, Ancient.   3. Alexander, the
Great, 356–323 B.C.—Numismatics.   4. Elephants in
numismatics.   I. Title.   II. Series.
CJ385 .H65   2003

737'.22'0938—dc21

                              2003008772

Manufactured in the United States of America

13   12   11   10   09   08   07   06   05   04

10   9   8   7   6   5   4   3   2   1

For my parents, with love and gratitude

CONTENTS

List of Maps and Illustrations
ix

Preface
xi

1. Man of Mystery
1

2. A Treasure
23

3. Picking a Fight
47

4. Whose Pachyderm, Whole or Halved?
68

5. Another Treasure
92

6. A Closer Look
117

7. A Dark and Stormy Night
139

Appendix A. The Published Elephant Medallions
167

Appendix B. Some Possible Forgeries of the Large Medallion
171

Appendix C. The 1973 Iraq Hoard
173

Select Bibliography
175

Index
191

Plates follow page 67.

MAPS AND ILLUSTRATIONS

MAPS

1. Alexander's empire   12
2. Nineteenth-century Afghanistan   32
3. The battle of the Hydaspes River   51

FIGURES

1. Augustus Franks listening to Schliemann's lecture   28
2. The Franks Medallion   44
3. The Greek monogram (enlarged) as reported by   64
    G. F. Hill
4. Two medieval representations of the elephant   82
5. The reverse of the large medallion   119
6. The obverse of the large medallion   125

PLATES

Plates follow page 67.

1. The Alexander Mosaic from Pompeii, showing Alexander in
    battle against Darius

2. The Franks Medallion (E/A 1)

3. The 1926 British Museum specimen (E/A 2)

4. The American Numismatic Society specimen (E/A 3)

5. The Copenhagen specimen (E/A 4)

6. An American Numismatic Society tetradrachm (E/B 1)

7. A Bank Leu tetradrachm (E/B 2)

8. A British Museum tetradrachm (E/B 3)

9. A tetradrachm formerly in the Wahler collection (E/B 5)

10. An American Numismatic Society tetradrachm (E/B 9)

11. A Bank Leu tetradrachm, now in the Bibliothèque nationale (E/C 1)

12. An American Numismatic Society tetradrachm (E/C 3)

13. A black cabinet forgery (F 9)

14. An American Numismatic Society gold aureus of Marcus Aurelius

PREFACE

I had arrived at this result, for no other hypothesis would meet the facts.

Sherlock Holmes, in *A Study in Scarlet*

This book aims to solve a great puzzle from the ancient past, like some mystery unlocked by the relentless logic of Mr. Sherlock Holmes. Because it is a real and not imaginary case, all of its strands can never be tidied up as neatly as Sir Arthur Conan Doyle might have done; nonetheless, the solution offered here does seem to be the only hypothesis that meets all the facts as we now know them. But let us be fair. While many earlier attempts to resolve this mystery will be examined and found wanting in one way or another, it must be obvious throughout this investigation that progress could never have been made without them. Indeed, the labors of many scholar-sleuths have kept this case moving forward for more than a century. Their names, and sometimes those of their influential peers, will justly echo through the narrative that follows.

Not among them, of course, are the fictional characters Sherlock Holmes and his amiable companion Dr. Watson. Yet, by a strange coincidence of fact and fiction, the mystery pursued in these pages surfaced in the Afghanistan of John Watson and was investigated in the London of Sherlock Holmes. When they were first introduced, Holmes remarked to Watson, "You have been in Afghanistan, I perceive." That astonishing deduction alerted the unsuspecting doctor to the extraordinary methods of observation and analysis employed by the detective, the

chronicling of which would become Watson's true calling. Watson's alleged service in Afghanistan had been a miserable, unheroic affair end-
ing when he was seriously wounded at the battle of Maiwand in July
1880. Conan Doyle did not invent the battle; it was a very real disaster
for the British during the Second Afghan War. Real survivors, like the
imaginary Watson, recuperated from grievous wounds as best they could
in the crowded hospital at Peshawar. As they did so, a strange ancient
medallion—the first in our mystery—also passed through Peshawar,
making its way from Afghanistan to England. Conan Doyle's Watson
nearly died, so weakened by "enteric fever" that he was finally shipped
back home in 1881. Seeking lodgings in London, Watson finally made
the acquaintance of Holmes, who instantly deduced the outlines of his
Afghan experience; meanwhile, in a real-life adventure of its own, the
odd medallion soon found a home nearby in the British Museum.

I first encountered this medallion some ninety years later in many of
the books I was reading about Alexander the Great. Published photographs captured the stirring scene stamped in silver of a bold cavalryman
attacking a retreating war elephant. With flowing cape and couched
spear, the man directs his attack upward against two adversaries astride
the great Indian beast. One enemy meets this peril by grabbing desperately at the cavalryman's spear, while the other aims a javelin at their attacker. The outcome of the ancient battle remains uncertain in this
freeze-frame image, until we see the medallion's other side. There, still
decked in full battle gear, the victorious cavalryman gloriously transcends
the domain of mortals, wielding in his hand (as no human could do) an
unmistakable bolt of lightning, the weapon of Zeus.

A few books mentioned in passing the existence of other elephant
medallions (so called because each variation features an elephant on one
side). These smaller varieties offered exotic scenes that also appeared to
be vignettes from Alexander's adventures in India. Scholars could not
agree on the actual meaning of these medallions, but surely they bore
witness—perhaps, mirabile dictu, contemporary witness—to one of the
turning points in world history. No evidence could be more important—

or inscrutable, for no text beyond a few Greek letters accompanied the images: no names, no mottoes, no mention whatever of when, where, or why they were minted. The mystery naturally tugged at my imagination and tempted my skills as both historian and numismatist, just as earlier generations of scholars had found this same problem irresistible.

I kept this project in the back of my mind while writing other books and articles. In June 1984, I had my first opportunity to examine some of these medallions firsthand while conducting research on other topics at the Bibliothèque nationale (Paris) and the British Museum (London). To hold such artifacts in one's hand brings history to life, and I subsequently pursued the elephant medallions as a secondary endeavor wherever my research trips carried me. Over the years, my own theories about the medallions took shape, and I began to share them with both specialist colleagues and general audiences in the United States and abroad. Finally, as other projects cleared from my desk, I determined to try to write an engaging, accessible narrative of the discovery and ongoing debates about the elephant medallions, concluding with my own resolution of the mystery.

I hope that experts in ancient history and numismatics will find my analysis constructive and convincing. At the same time, I have taken pains to make this work interesting and useful to university students and the general public. Matters that specialists take for granted, I have explained for the benefit of laypeople. It is one thing to blaze new trails, quite another to widen that road so that everyone may follow. I hope that casual readers who hitchhike through history by thumbing the pages of popular books and magazines will take this journey with me. To that end, the book unfolds as a mystery that traverses many lands and touches the lives of many legendary figures, and it often attempts a livelier style than is customary in academic works.

A book must balance as best it can the interests of the author, readers, and publisher. Although I prefer the traditional forms B.C. ("before Christ") and A.D. (*anno Domini*, "in the year of the Lord"), the Press and some readers consider these notations to be culturally biased. I have

therefore consented to adopt the "neutral" descriptors B.C.E. ("before the common era") and C.E. ("common era"), even though this only masks, rather than changes, the religious basis of our Western chronological system: the so-called common era is simply the Christian era by another name, and 323 B.C.E. and 1954 C.E. are patently the same years as 323 B.C. and 1954 A.D. I trust that readers will be neither confused nor offended one way or the other, and that they will excuse the necessity of using one set of abbreviations in my text while preserving the older set where they occur in quotations and titles. Likewise, although I might have wished to include illustrations of every one of the elephant medallions known to date, good pictures can be difficult (and are sometimes simply impossible) to procure and reproduce. Most readers will need only a representative sampling, while specialists will be able to find additional illustrations easily enough in the works cited.

While accepting full responsibility for its shortcomings, I take pleasure in acknowledging that the merits of this book derive from the contributions of many learned friends. Historians and numismatists at many museums and universities have helped me over the years, and I thank them all profusely. Special mention must be made of the staff of the American Numismatic Society, particularly its librarian, Frank Campbell, its curator, Peter van Alfen, its collections manager, Elena Stolyarick, and its former curator Carmen Arnold-Biucchi; of Dominique Gerin of the Bibliothèque nationale; of Andrew Meadows of the British Museum; of Helle Horsnaes of the National Museum in Copenhagen; of the scholarly and collegial numismatists Silvia Hurter, Frank Kovacs, and Harlan Berk; of members of the Institute for the Study of Material Culture of the Russian Academy of Sciences in St. Petersburg; and of Michel Duerr, James Millward, Michael Flower, and Marc Melcher.

I am grateful also to the outside readers of the University of California Press for their useful comments, and to the book's sponsoring editor, Kate Toll, for doing her job so cheerfully and so well. I owe much to the University of Houston, especially its Department of History, for providing a stimulating intellectual workplace. As always, I appreciate most

the support of my family. To my infinite advantage, and that of my readers, my wife Linda types, reads, and responds to every line I write. My daughter Laura has helped immensely with her art. Finally, on this occasion it is my added privilege to acknowledge those who have inspired and encouraged me from the very beginning: I dedicate this book to my parents, Jane A. and Elwood D. Holt, Sr.

Houston, Texas

Man of Mystery

Few men have transcended their moment in history more than Alexander the Great of Macedonia (356–323 B.C.E.).[1] He reigned as king from the time he was twenty, had conquered most of the world he knew to exist by the time he was thirty, came to be seen as a living god, and then died before he was thirty-three.[2] His short life cast a shadow so long that it has eclipsed over one hundred generations of famous generals from Caesar and Charlemagne to Napoleon and Eisenhower. Admired and despised, he has always evoked strong passions. St. Augustine considered Alexander a rogue with a global appetite for plunder; Dante put him in the seventh circle of Hell in the company of tyrants, murderers, and thieves.[3] In

---

1. Alexander was not, as far as we know, called "Alexander the Great" in his lifetime; the sobriquet was conferred upon him by Romans around 200 B.C.E. See Plautus *Mostellaria* 3.2.775.

2. Recommended biographies include Peter Green, *Alexander of Macedon, 356–323 B.C.* (Berkeley: University of California Press, 1991), and A. B. Bosworth, *Conquest and Empire: The Reign of Alexander the Great* (Cambridge: Cambridge University Press, 1988). Lively but less detailed treatments include Michael Wood, *In the Footsteps of Alexander the Great* (Berkeley: University of California Press, 1997), Pierre Briant, *Alexander the Great: Man of Action, Man of Spirit* (New York: Abrams, 1996), and Richard Stoneman, *Alexander the Great* (New York: Routledge, 1997).

3. Augustine *City of God* 4.4; Dante *Inferno* 12.107.

2 / Man of Mystery

1848, Jacob Abbott indicted Alexander for "the most gigantic case of murder and robbery which was ever committed by man."[4] Yet Pope Paul III, Louis XIV of France, and Philip V of Spain all commissioned paintings of Alexander's inspirational deeds to adorn their palaces; Dryden wrote a famous poem about the king ("Alexander's Feast"), and Handel set it to music. The young Sigmund Freud idolized Alexander and lobbied his parents to name his new brother in honor of the hero.[5] In 1810, Thomas Jefferson advised Governor John Langdon that Napoleon's mania for Alexander would most likely lead the Frenchman east in his footsteps, thus sparing America from possible invasion.[6]

Were Alexander alive today, one writer has gushed:

His sprawling holding company, Alexander, Inc., would span a dozen advancing technologies, from supercomputers to bioengineering. Watch him take over NASA's foundering space shuttle program and send a man to Mars by 2010. See him negotiate the opening of a Joint Economic Zone in Hokkaido, where U.S. and Japanese partners would build massive electronics and manufacturing plants to export goods to the United States and the rest of the world. Alexander's philanthropic works might serve as a standard of public-spiritedness for decades, perhaps for generations.[7]

This unlikely creature, an entrepreneurial and managerial Macedonian philanthropist/conqueror, illustrates the lengths to which some will go to

4. Jacob Abbott, *The History of Alexander the Great* (New York: Harper & Brothers, 1848), pp. 208–9.

5. *The Standard Edition of the Complete Psychological Works of Sigmund Freud,* ed. James Strachey, vol. 6: *The Psychopathology of Everyday Life* [1901] (New York: Norton, 1976), pp. 107–9. See also S. L. Warner, "Freud the Mighty Warrior," *Journal of the American Academy of Psychoanalysis* 19, 2 (1991): 282–93. Later in life, Freud most envied the adventurous career of Heinrich Schliemann; see Peter Gay, *Freud: A Life for Our Time* (New York: Norton, 1988), p. 172.

6. Jefferson to Langdon, dated March 5, 1810: see Saul Padover, ed., *A Jefferson Profile* (New York: John Day, 1956), pp. 190–194.

7. Michael Meyer, *The Alexander Complex* (New York: Times Books, 1989), p. 4.

fashion Alexander into the man of their dreams. An envious Julius Caesar wept in Spain at the mere sight of Alexander's statue.[8] Pompey the Great rummaged through the closets of conquered nations for Alexander's 260-year-old cloak, which the Roman general then wore as the costume of greatness.[9] In his zeal to honor Alexander, Octavian (the future emperor Augustus) accidentally broke the nose off the Macedonian's mummified corpse while laying a wreath at the hero's shrine in Alexandria, Egypt.[10] The unbalanced emperor Caligula later took the dead king's armor from that tomb and donned it for luck.[11] The Macriani, a Roman family that rose to the imperial throne in the third century c.e., always kept images of Alexander on their persons, either stamped into their bracelets and rings or stitched into their garments. Even their dinnerware bore Alexander's face, with the story of the king's life displayed around the rims of special bowls.[12] A century later, this obsession had spread far and wide. St. John Chrysostom, the patriarch of Constantinople, complained that many people in his day bound the coins of Alexander to their heads and feet to ward off evil.[13] In the latter stages of imperial Roman history, Alexander's portrait could be found on coins and tokens of all kinds. Napoleon III purchased a stunning set of such artifacts found at Tarsus in

8. Plutarch *Caesar* 11.5; Suetonius *Caesar* 7.1; Dio 37.52.2. See Peter Green, "Caesar and Alexander: *Aemulatio, imitatio, comparatio,*" *American Journal of Ancient History* 3 (1978): 1–26.

9. Appian *Mithridatic Wars* 117. On Alexander in Roman literature, politics, and art, see the essays in Jesper Carlsen et al., eds., *Alexander the Great: Reality and Myth* (Rome: "L'Erma" di Bretschneider, 1993); Gerhard Wirth, "Alexander und Rom," in *Alexandre le Grand: Image et réalité* (Geneva: Fondation Hardt, 1976), ed. Ernst Badian, pp. 181–221; Margarete Bieber, *Alexander the Great in Greek and Roman Art* (Chicago: Argonaut, 1964), pp. 68–81.

10. Dio 51.16.5; cf. Suetonius *Aug.* 18.1. Suetonius *Aug.* 50 also reports that the emperor put Alexander's portrait on his signet ring.

11. Suetonius *Calig.* 52.

12. Scriptores Historiae Augustae *Tyranni triginta* 14.2–6.

13. Chrysostom *Ad illuminando catechesis* 2.5.

the mid–nineteenth century; struck in gold, each specimen bears Alexander's name and a scene from his extraordinary life.[14]

The ancient relics of the king remain important to us today as the prizes of museums and private collections around the world. Some examples underscore the intensity of this infatuation. André Malraux, when French minister of culture, reportedly tried to buy for the Louvre a silk scarf said by his medium to have belonged to Alexander the Great. In her trance, this psychic claimed to see the young warrior cough up a wad of bile and then fall dead upon the sand.[15] The search for those physical remains and the lost sepulcher that held them has long been the Holy Grail of tomb archaeology. Robbed, as we have seen, of various items by overzealous ancient admirers, the grave keeps turning up in the unlikeliest modern places. In 1801, the British captured what they believed to be Alexander's coffin in the filthy hold of a French hospital ship, *La Cause*. Napoleon's men had found the sarcophagus in Alexandria, along with the famous Rosetta Stone. It was rumored that Napoleon planned to be buried in the borrowed coffin of his hero. The sarcophagus, seized by the British, now resides in the British Museum, near the Rosetta Stone, from whose text Jean-François Champollion eventually deciphered Egyptian hieroglyphics, making it possible to read the inscrutable carvings on the "Alexander Sarcophagus"—which turned out to have belonged, not to Alexander, but to Pharaoh Nectanebo II.[16] This revelation reopened the search for the real grave of Alexander the Great.[17]

14. Adrian de Longpérier, "Trésor de Tarse," *Revue Numismatique* 13 (1868): 309–36; cf. Cornelius Vermeule, "Alexander the Great, the Emperor Severus Alexander and the Aboukir Medallions," *Revue suisse de numismatique* 61 (1982): 61–72, esp. p. 62.

15. Thomas Hoving, *Making the Mummies Dance* (New York: Simon & Schuster, 1993), pp. 118–19.

16. Edward Clarke, *The Tomb of Alexander: A Dissertation on the Sarcophagus Brought from Alexandria and Now in the British Museum* (Cambridge: Cambridge University Press, 1805).

17. Achille Adriani, *La tomba di Alessandro: Realità, ipotesi e fantasie* (Rome: "L'Erma" di Bretschneider, 2000). Some believe that Alexander was truly buried

In 1887, another "Alexander Sarcophagus" was unearthed at Sidon (now in Lebanon) and taken to Istanbul. Although its marble sides are decorated with images of Alexander in battle, scholars later determined that it was the coffin of a contemporary Phoenician named Abdalonymos.[18] So the quest continued. The grave remains elusive to this day, even though at least eight announcements of its discovery have been made since 1800—all of them quite false, and some utterly fantastic. Alexander's tomb has been found in Alexandria, Siwah, Central Asia, and even a secret cave in southern Illinois. From the graveyard scene in Shakespeare's *Hamlet* (see chapter 2 below) to Hollywood's blockbuster *Cleopatra* (or the more lackluster 1989 movie *The Serpent of Death*), Alexander's whereabouts still fascinate us.[19] According to popular Greek legend, sailors are still confronted at times by a Nereid who asks, "Where is the great Alexander?" Only one response will satisfy the dangerous creature: "Great Alexander lives and reigns!"[20] The king remains a potent force in modern pop culture: for a mere $10,000 a night, the weary traveler can lounge in the Alexander the Great Suite at the Trump Taj

---

in this "borrowed" sarcophagus: see Andrew Chugg, "The Sarcophagus of Alexander the Great?" *Greece and Rome* 49, 1 (2002): 18–26.

18. On the Sidonian Sarcophagus, see O. Hamdy Bey and T. Reinach, *Une nécropole royale à Sidon* (Paris: Leroux, 1892). The indispensable reference for all such discoveries is now Andrew Stewart, *Faces of Power: Alexander's Image and Hellenistic Politics* (Berkeley: University of California Press, 1993).

19. Cecil B. DeMille's *Cleopatra* (1934) starred Claudette Colbert in the title role; Joseph Mankiewicz's film of the same name (1963) featured Elizabeth Taylor. *The Serpent of Death* (1989) was directed by Anwar Kawadri. For further details, see Frank Holt, "Dead Kings Are Hard to Find," *Saudi Aramco World* 52, 3 (2001): 10–11; id., "The Missing Mummy of Alexander the Great," *Archaeology* 39 (January/February 1986): 80. See also Racine's tragedy *Alexandre le Grand*.

20. On such modern folktales, see Martha Payne, "Alexander the Great: Myth, the Polis, and Afterward," in *Myth and the Polis*, ed. Dora Pozzi and John Wickersham, pp. 164–81 (Ithaca, N.Y.: Cornell University Press, 1991).

Mahal Casino Resort in Atlantic City, New Jersey, perhaps wearing an Alexander the Great World Tour 336–323 B.C. T-shirt (listing major stops in the king's campaigns), sipping an Alexander the Great cocktail, listening to Iron Maiden sing about the youth who "became a legend 'mongst mortal men," and reading about him in Anne Rice's *Servant of the Bones.*[21] At this moment, several new movies and miniseries are in production to meet the public's insatiable appetite for legends of the Macedonian conqueror. While the rest of us wait impatiently for our fifteen minutes of fame, Alexander has already enjoyed his share 82 million times over.

Everything about Alexander evoked awe among his contemporaries and still does so today. In the past forty years alone, experts have published more than 2,000 books and articles in a painstaking effort to solve the fundamental puzzles of his life. There we read that Alexander personally dreamed up the lofty ideal of world brotherhood and paved the way for universal religions of peace and love. We learn, too, that he conquered and killed with epic abandon, unable to sate his lust for innocent blood. He exhibited the noblest virtues of friendship and chivalry, and he butchered his closest companions out of raging insecurities. He was enlightened, intelligent, and temperate; he was insane and addicted to violence and alcohol. These studied portraits of Alexander as both a sensitive youth and a psychopath could not be more controversial and contradictory.

Modern scholars did not, of course, invent this mystery. We have simply inherited the problem from many generations of writers, going all the way back to the fourth century B.C.E. Even then, Alexander emerged upon the world stage, it might have seemed, from the smoke and mirrors of a

21. I thank the management of the Trump Taj Mahal for information about the suite. The T-shirts are sold on eBay; an Alexander the Great cocktail is made with vodka, cream, coffee liqueur, and crème de cacao; Iron Maiden's *Somewhere in Time* album includes a song titled "Alexander the Great"; and he appears briefly in Rice's *Servant of the Bones* (New York: Knopf, 1996), pp. 170–71, 262–63.

magician's trick. With all eyes fixed upon the dazzling reign of his father, King Philip II, no one expected the young Alexander to so upstage his sire. Through war and diplomacy, Philip made himself a difficult act to follow.[22] In 359 B.C.E., Philip had taken the throne of a kingdom in disarray. Macedonia had lost nine monarchs in forty years, at least five of them to assassination, and the latest—Philip's older brother Perdiccas III—to a devastating invasion.

Macedonia was a tough place that bred a tough population. To survive in the midst of so many enemies on the northern fringes of the Greek world, the Macedonians held fast to the heroic warrior code of Homer's *Iliad* and *Odyssey*. They seemed a time warp back to the Trojan War and the bellicose Bronze Age. In battles, brawls, and drinking bouts, the Macedonians measured a man from king to commoner by the implacable standards of Achilles and Agamemnon. Risks ran high among such aggressive egos, and no offense passed unanswered. Even kings could not afford a slip in the company of such warriors; hesitation or error meant speedy elimination. Philip thus led his troops with conspicuous bravado, enduring horrendous battle injuries to his face, arm, collarbone, and leg that left him half-blind and hobbling the rest of his life.[23] These were the legitimizing wounds of a warrior king.

In the eyes of many Greeks outside of Macedonia, Philip and his subjects appeared backward and barbaric—they were like the hard-riding, hard-fighting, hard-drinking cowboys of the lawless American frontier

22. On the reign of King Philip II, consult the following representative works: E. N. Borza, *In the Shadow of Olympus: The Emergence of Macedon* (Princeton: Princeton University Press, 1990); N. G. L. Hammond, *Philip of Macedon* (Baltimore: Johns Hopkins University Press, 1994); N. G. L. Hammond and G. T. Griffith, *A History of Macedonia*, vol. 2 (Oxford: Clarendon Press, 1979); George Cawkwell, *Philip of Macedon* (London: Faber & Faber, 1978); and J. R. Ellis, *Philip II and Macedonian Imperialism* (Princeton: Princeton University Press, 1976).

23. Consult Alice Riginos, "The Wounding of Philip II of Macedon: Fact and Fabrication," *Journal of Hellenic Studies* 114 (1994): 103–19.

to the socialites of nineteenth-century Boston and New York. The women of Macedonia were no less hardened than their husbands.[24] Alexander's mother Olympias (one of Philip's seven wives) savagely murdered her husband's last wife and child, and later she waged what one contemporary called "the first women's war." Macedonian royal polygamy may have been designed to ensure a wide selection of worthy heirs, but it also destabilized the family, court, and kingdom in a winner-take-all world. Yet out of this chaos, Philip II slowly created the most powerful political and military state in all of Greece—surpassing even Athens and Sparta. This alarmed some Greeks and encouraged others. The former, led by the eloquent Demosthenes, warned that Philip would enslave the whole of Greece; the latter, rallying to the rhetoric of Isocrates, had for some time been looking for a leader to unite them against a long-standing foreign enemy, the mighty Achaemenid Empire of Persia.[25] As Philip's power grew, Isocrates called upon him to assume this enormous task. Meanwhile, as his father became the most famous man in Europe, Alexander fretfully absorbed the competitive ethos of his heroic ancestors Achilles and Hercules, studied philosophy under the tutelage of Aristotle, learned the art of war from his father, and challenged himself to change the world when (and if) his chance ever came.[26]

That dramatic moment arrived, appropriately enough, when his father strode at the height of his glory into a crowded theater. In 336 B.C.E., Philip had assembled dignitaries from all over Greece to witness the wedding of his daughter and launch the long-awaited invasion of Persia with lavish fanfare. Then, without warning, Philip fell dead before the

24. The standard reference is now Elizabeth Carney, *Women and Monarchy in Macedonia* (Norman: University of Oklahoma Press, 2000).

25. Pierre Briant, *Histoire de l'empire perse de Cyrus à Alexandre*, 2 vols. (Leiden: Nederlands Instituut voor het Nabije Oosten, 1996).

26. J. R. Hamilton, "Alexander's Early Life," *Greece and Rome* 12 (1965): 117–24. Our knowledge of Alexander's youth rests largely upon the anecdotal account in Plutarch *Alex.* 1–10.

throng—the victim of an assassin's dagger.[27] His son Alexander, barely out of his teens, was hauled from the shadows and hailed the new king of Macedonia. It was an impressive entrance in the opening act of a show that has no equal in history. From that theater, when the dust had cleared, Alexander would guide men as much as three times his age on an epic march that made him master of an unprecedented empire stretching from Olympus to India. Every part of that story is a mystery.

Alexander began with a lightning Balkan campaign that made believers of many who lacked confidence in the untested king. To secure his inheritance and silence his critics, Alexander led the Macedonian army against rebellious tribes as far north as the Danube River and as far west as modern Albania. He then plunged south into the heart of Greece and punished the defiant city of Thebes by pulling down most of its buildings and selling its citizens into slavery. The message was clear. Athens and other cities quickly acknowledged Alexander's right to lead the Panhellenic attack on Persia originally planned by his murdered father. With a coalition army of about 37,000 troops, Alexander launched the invasion in the early spring of 334 B.C.E. Before he was twenty-six, Alexander would defy all odds and defeat the Persians in a series of battles that rocked the cradle of civilization from Egypt to Mesopotamia.[28]

27. The dramatic scene is best described in Diodorus 16.92–95. Interesting modern investigations of the event include Ernst Badian, "The Death of Philip II," *Phoenix* 17 (1963): 244–50; R. D. Develin, "The Murder of Philip II," *Antichthon* 15 (1981): 86–99; J. R. Fears, "Pausanias, the Assassin of Philip II," *Athenaeum* 53 (1975): 111–35; N. G. L. Hammond, "The End of Philip," in *Philip of Macedon*, ed. M. Hatzopoulos and L. Loukopoulos, pp. 166–75 (Athens: Ekdotike Athenon, 1980); and J. R. Ellis, "The Assassination of Philip II," in *Ancient Macedonian Studies in Honor of Charles F. Edson*, ed. H. J. Dell, pp. 99–137 (Thessaloniki: Institute for Balkan Studies, 1981).

28. The military aspects of Alexander's career are the focus of several useful works: J. F. C. Fuller, *The Generalship of Alexander the Great* (New Brunswick, N.J.: Rutgers University Press, 1960); N. G. L. Hammond, *Alexander the Great: King, Commander and Statesman*, 2d ed. (Bristol, U.K.: Bristol Press, 1989); E. W. Marsden, *The Campaign of Gaugamela* (Liverpool: Liverpool University

Exceeding everything ever expected of Philip, Alexander seemed invincible. He came ashore in Asia Minor wearing full ceremonial armor and symbolically cast a spear into the beach to claim the East by right of conquest. At the Granicus River (334), a regional Persian army reinforced with Greek mercenaries tried to stop Alexander's relatively small force. The young king, still earning his throne, was nearly killed in a brash charge into the enemy's lines. But his companions rallied to the cause, crushed the Persian cavalry, and slaughtered the mercenaries. This first victory awakened the Greek and Persian worlds to Alexander's potential for greatness; but, given the many factions that so badly wanted him to fail, every such military engagement had to be a make-or-break triumph. He could not lose and live to fight another day. He had embarked upon a career of conquest so circumscribed by foreign and domestic dangers that it demanded absolute perfection—a statesman's nightmare, a general's torment, a mortal's impossibility. Only a steely survivor of the Macedonian court, with its daily tests of nerve and talent, could stand these pressures and believe so completely in his own star.

From the Granicus River, Alexander turned south to take the Ionian Greek coastal cities of Asia Minor. He faced strong resistance at Miletus and Halicarnassus, but Macedonian siegecraft eventually won the day. Along the march, two highly publicized incidents took place that were embellished to manifest Alexander's unique standing among men and gods. Along the beaches beneath Mt. Climax, the king and his entourage suddenly found themselves blocked by menacing waves crashing across their path. Then, just as quickly, the waters calmed and fell back, as though bowing before Alexander—an apparent sign of his divine power and protection. Later, as the army wintered inland at Gordium, Alexan-

---

Press, 1964); and Donald Engels, *Alexander the Great and the Logistics of the Macedonian Army* (Berkeley: University of California Press, 1978). On Alexander's Persian opponent, Darius III, see Carl Nylander, "Darius III—the Coward King: Point and Counterpoint," in *Alexander the Great*, ed. Carlsen et al., pp. 145–59.

der allegedly solved the intractable problem of the Gordian Knot. By cutting (or unraveling) the rope that held a yoke to the legendary wagon of Gordius, Alexander fulfilled an ancient prophecy that guaranteed divine favor. At the same moment, a display of thunder and lightning signaled Zeus's support for Alexander's drive to conquer Persia.

Meanwhile, Persia's King of Kings, Darius III, prepared to meet this threat by marshaling an imperial army and moving it toward the Syrian coast to intercept his rival. In 333 B.C.E., Alexander fought Darius in a massive battle by the sea at Issus (see map 1). Although outnumbered, the Macedonian king used the terrain to his advantage and put the Persians to flight. Darius escaped inland, while Alexander methodically completed his conquest of the entire coastline of the eastern Mediterranean. During the seven-month siege of Tyre (332), the Macedonians, under withering fire, prevailed in the arduous task of constructing a roadway across open waters to the island. Tyre was destroyed, and Gaza fell later in the same year. Alexander received a hero's welcome in Egypt, where the Persians had never been liked since the day one of their kings had defiled Egyptian religion by slaughtering a sacred Apis bull. For his part, Alexander made a point of paying his respects to this venerated beast and showing his general sympathy for the ageless rites of his new subjects. He also founded one of his greatest cities, naturally named Alexandria, on the Egyptian coast. After a celebrated trek into the Libyan desert to consult the oracle of Zeus-Ammon at Siwah, Alexander's fame and mystique reached new heights. His father, it seemed, must have been greater than even the greatest man in Europe—and so Philip's paternity gave way in legend to that of Zeus. Alexander's exalted status as the son of a god found immediate approval in Egypt, of course, and in some cities of Asia Minor. Bolder steps would follow.[29]

---

29. Ernst Badian, "The Deification of Alexander the Great," in *Ancient Macedonian Studies in Honor of Charles F. Edson*, ed. Dell, pp. 27–71, and his supplemental arguments in "Alexander the Great between Two Thrones and Heaven: Variations on an Old Theme," in *Subject and Ruler: The Cult of the Ruling Power in*

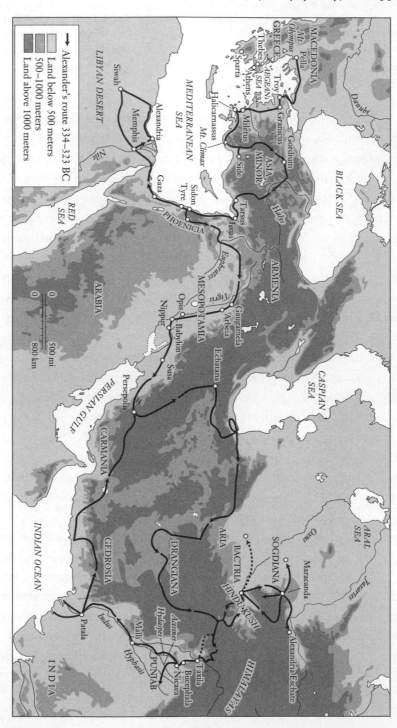

Map 1. Alexander's empire

Alexander's route 334–323 BC
Land below 500 meters
500–1000 meters
Land above 1000 meters

MACEDONIA
GREECE
Mt. Olympus
Pella
Thebes
Athens
Sparta
AEGEAN SEA
Troy
Granicus
Miletus
Halicarnassus
Mt. Climax
Gordium
ASIA MINOR
Side
Tarsus
Halys
Issus
PHOENICIA
Sidon
Tyre
Gaza
MEDITERRANEAN SEA
Alexandria
Memphis
Siwah
LIBYAN DESERT
Nile
RED SEA
ARABIA
BLACK SEA
Danube
ARMENIA
Euphrates
Tigris
MESOPOTAMIA
Nippur
Opis
Babylon
Arbela
Gaugamela
Ecbatana
Susa
Persepolis
PERSIAN GULF
CASPIAN SEA
CARMANIA
ARIA
DRANGIANA
GEDROSIA
INDIAN OCEAN
Patala
Indus
Malli
Hyphasis
Hydaspes
Acesines
PUNJAB
Nicaea
Bucephala
Taxila
HINDU KUSH
BACTRIA
SOGDIANA
Maracanda
Alexandria Eschate
Oxus
Jaxartes
ARAL SEA
HIMALAYAS
INDIA

0
0
500 mi
800 km

Alexander next pushed his way into the heartland of the Persian Empire, where Darius waited again with a gigantic army. At Gaugamela (331), Alexander miraculously defeated his enemy in a battle that decided the course of Middle Eastern history. Darius escaped the debacle, but his fate was sealed: his own commanders killed him the following year. From the plundered treasuries of Persia, Alexander hauled away on the backs of 20,000 mules and 5,000 camels more wealth than the Greek world had ever known, amounting to twelve million pounds of silver.[30] More than human, more than rich, Alexander already ruled the equivalent of ten modern nations (Greece, Turkey, Syria, Lebanon, Israel, Jordan, Egypt, Kuwait, Iran, and Iraq) plus parts of several others. But this was only the beginning.

Never satisfied, Alexander set his sights upon Central and South Asia. From 329 to 327 B.C.E., he campaigned against the obstinate forces of Bactria and Sogdiana, in the tortuous mountains and deserts of present-day Afghanistan, Turkmenistan, Uzbekistan, and Tajikistan.[31] At first, the enemy rallied around a kinsman of Darius named Bessus, formerly the satrap (governor) of Bactria but now claiming the throne of Persia as King Artaxerxes. Alexander countered such claims by right of conquest, and hunted Bessus down as a regicide and usurper. After Bessus had been betrayed by his Bactrian followers, Alexander had him tortured and executed according to Persian custom.[32] Soon afterward, in response to

Classical Antiquity, ed. Alastair Small, pp. 11–26 (Ann Arbor: University of Michigan Press, 1996).

30. The noted economist John Maynard Keynes considered Europe's plunder of the New World to be meager compared to Alexander's despoliation of Persia: see his *A Treatise on Money*, vol. 2 (New York: Harcourt, Brace, 1930), pp. 150–52, 291.

31. Frank Holt, *Alexander the Great and Bactria: The Formation of a Greek Frontier in Central Asia* (Leiden: Brill, 1988).

32. Arrian 3.30.5 and 4.7.3–4 (openly disturbed by the barbarity of Bessus's punishment); Diodorus 17.83.9; Curtius 7.5.40 and 7.10.10; Justin 12.5.11; and Plutarch *Alex.* 43.6.

Macedonian military settlements that threatened the traditional politics, economy, and culture of Bactria and its environs, fresh resistance stirred under the able leadership of a native named Spitamenes. The situation turned catastrophic. Alexander's troops began to tire, and the complaints of some of his closest companions created new tensions that sometimes led to executions. Alexander pressed on through three hard years of guerrilla fighting. Sandstorms and searing heat claimed the lives of thousands; in winter, blizzards literally froze the Macedonians in their tracks. When provisions ran out, the army ate its own baggage animals—sometimes raw. Led by Spitamenes and other tribal chiefs, the enemy used the harsh climate and terrain as a lethal weapon, controlling mountain passes and strongholds to cut off supplies and stage quick but effective ambushes; whenever the Macedonians rallied, the insurgents disappeared into the desert or mountains. As one ancient writer described it, waging war in Bactria was like trying to slay the mythical Hydra—every time one head was severed, others arose in its place.[33] Accepting the challenge, Alexander raided the river valleys, scorched the earth, and sealed off the region with a series of stronger military colonies. The struggle became exceptionally vicious, but the Macedonians persisted. How Alexander drove his men through such hardships is still a mystery of military science, a lesson somehow lost upon the superpowers of the nineteenth and twentieth centuries that dared invade Afghanistan, with tragic consequences. It is yet too soon to know whether the twenty-first century will witness the same result.

In his turn, Spitamenes fell victim to the perfidy of the Bactrians and their allies, who delivered their commander's head to Alexander's camp. This, plus the timely diplomatic marriage of Alexander to Roxane, the daughter of another local chieftain, made it possible for the Macedonians—minus an unhappy occupation force of 13,500 troops—to declare victory and leave Bactria behind. It had taken nearly as long to pacify this

33. Plutarch *Mor.* 341 F.

one province as all the rest of the Persian Empire, and the casualties had never been higher. The strain of these wars erupted from time to time along new fault lines in Macedonia's traditional institutions. Alexander's growing autocracy rankled some senior officers, and even the common soldiers must have struggled with the king's new standing among the gods and his willingness to adopt Persian dress and court practices such as *proskynesis* (ritual obeisance). Plots and protests signaled disaffection, but royal retribution came swiftly. Some very prominent individuals (Philotas, Parmenion, Cleitus, Callisthenes) lost Alexander's favor and their lives.

Alexander, not yet thirty, next led his army across the Hindu Kush mountains and plunged across what is now Pakistan into the monsoons of India.[34] In the midst of so much misery, more than 3,000 miles from home, Alexander's army fought one of its fiercest battles against a resourceful rajah whom they called Porus. In this battle of the Hydaspes River (326 B.C.E.), Porus deployed a dangerous weapon against the invading Greeks: a terrifying corps of trained war elephants, the panzers of antiquity.[35] Alexander outmaneuvered the Indians, crossed the river under the cloak of heavy rain and darkness, and drove straight at Porus's army during a fierce dawn attack. It was a fight the Macedonians would never forget, with elephants trumpeting and trampling in a wild melee. Porus was wounded, defeated, captured, pardoned, and put back on his throne in a unique display of admiration for a worthy adversary. Victorious, Alexander continued his march east, toward what Aristotle had

34. A. B. Bosworth, *Alexander and the East: The Tragedy of Triumph* (Oxford: Oxford University Press, 1996); Johannes Hahn, *Alexander in Indien, 327–325 v. Chr.* (Stuttgart: Jan Thorbecke, 2000).

35. From this battle stemmed the long obsession of the Greeks with elephant warfare: see, e.g., H. H. Scullard, *The Elephant in the Greek and Roman World* (Ithaca, N.Y.: Cornell University Press, 1974); F. E. Adcock, *The Greek and Macedonian Art of War* (Berkeley: University of California Press, 1957), pp. 54–56.

promised were the ends of the inhabited earth. But the king found a different outcome instead, on the banks of the Hyphasis River, where his exhausted army balked at further conquest and put a stop to his search for the world's edge. The men rejoiced at the thought of returning home to enjoy the loot of their labors. Had they known how long that journey would be, and how many of them would never see Greece again, the celebrations might have been aborted altogether.

Frustrated by the first major failure of his life, Alexander turned back and built a fleet near the site of his victory over Porus. When the monsoon abated, he steered his forces down the Indus Valley and cut a swath to the Indian Ocean. The fighting belied all hopes of a leisurely march home. In the assault on one town among the Malli, Alexander noted such lassitude among his troops that he shamed them into action by mounting the enemy's walls and leaping inside all but alone. This startling action invigorated the attack and doomed the town, but not before Alexander fell with a serious wound, from which he barely recovered.

At Patala, in 325 B.C.E., Alexander divided his forces. While his navy explored a sea route between India and the Persian Gulf, the king led a disastrous march across the Gedrosian desert back to Babylon. Weakened by battle injuries and worried that his fleet had been lost, Alexander suffered what some have called a physical and mental breakdown. He lashed out at those who had failed to govern honorably during his long absence in the east. Swelled heads literally rolled as the king investigated abuses of power. The safe arrival of his naval forces seemed to improve the conqueror's mood in Mesopotamia, but the sudden death of his friend Hephaestion plunged the king back into despair.[36]

Meanwhile, in what turned out to be the last months of his life, Alexander wrestled with the enormous problems of his new empire,

36. The classic exposition of this viewpoint is Ernst Badian, "Alexander the Great and the Loneliness of Power," *Journal of the Australasian Universities Language and Literature Association* 17 (1962): 80–91.

while planning boldly for further conquests. The solution to every crisis seemed to provoke another. For instance, the king's so-called Exiles' Decree attempted to rid the empire of a dangerous surplus of homeless mercenaries by allowing them to return to their native cities in Greece. But these soldiers were not wanted back in the places from which they had originally been banished. Angry cities such as Athens saw this act as another example of Alexander's abusive autocracy and threatened to revolt. Resentment still simmered in his own army whenever the king's measures seemed to undermine Macedonian tradition. At Susa, for example, Alexander arranged marriages between important Persian noblewomen and nearly one hundred of his senior officers; the king took two more brides himself. This may have been done to neutralize the power of these women should they wed the wrong people. Nonetheless, this appeared to elevate the status of the enemy and to portend a mixed race that would inherit what ought to be purely Macedonian. The attitude of the Macedonians to these marriages may be gauged by the fact that all (save one) were repudiated as soon as Alexander died. We cannot guess what happened to all of these spurned women, or to the many thousands of camp followers whom the rank and file were forced to marry at the same ceremonies.

Another crisis arose when Alexander unveiled a corps of 30,000 young men recruited from Bactria and Sogdiana, trained in the Macedonian manner and given the alarming title of *Epigoni* ("Successors"). His offer to settle the financial affairs of his veterans and later to send many of them back to Macedonia—once their fondest hope at the Hyphasis River—now aroused fear and resentment. This time, in a mutiny at Opis, the men complained that they were being put out to pasture, while Persians stood ready to replace them. The ringleaders of this sedition were arrested and executed, after which a massive feast of reconciliation calmed—or cowed—the army. Ten thousand were to go home, and a fresh levy of Macedonians was to take their place in an Arabian campaign. It would never begin. At Babylon, Alexander fell ill and slowly lost

his last battle against an uncertain disease.[37] On June 10, 323 B.C.E., he died mysteriously at the age of thirty-two. As suddenly as he had appeared, Alexander vanished again behind the smoke and mirrors of hatred, hype, and hero-worship.

Alexander was incomprehensible to his contemporaries twenty-three centuries ago, unfathomable to eighty-five generations of poets, priests, and politicians in Rome and the Middle Ages, and he remains inscrutable today. What confounds us now is not simply the man's military genius or the magnitude of his achievements, but the surprisingly pitiful state of our evidence about him. The details of his personality and career must be reconstructed on the basis of second- and third-hand accounts; his own records, as well as the many eyewitness histories written by his contemporaries, have all been lost. The earliest available narrative about Alexander's reign was composed 300 years after he died; the best was written nearly two centuries after that.

Our knowledge of Alexander therefore rests on histories produced long after the fact: a late first-century B.C.E. section of a world history written in Greek by Diodorus of Sicily; a Latin *History of Alexander* published by the Roman author Quintus Curtius Rufus in the first century C.E.; a biography in Greek by Plutarch of Chaeronea, also produced in the first century C.E.; a history written in Greek by Arrian of Nicomedia sometime in the second century C.E.; and Justin's third-century C.E. Latin abridgment *(Epitome)* of a lost Greek secondary account by the first-century author Pompeius Trogus. Each of these five narrative treatments of Alexander's reign claims to be a serious work of history or biography, but all five contradict one another on fundamental matters and

---

37. The diagnosis of this disease remains a major controversy among historians and medical experts. See, e.g., David Oldach et al., "A Mysterious Death," *New England Journal of Medicine* 338 (1998): 1764–68, and E. Borza and J. Reames-Zimmerman, "Some New Thoughts on the Death of Alexander the Great," *Ancient World* 31 (2000): 22–30.

cannot be considered absolutely reliable unless somehow corroborated by other evidence. Beyond these texts, we have little except a compilation of legendary material known as the *Greek Alexander Romance*, a wildly imaginative work filled with talking trees and other wonders that later thrilled the medieval world.[38]

In a worst-case scenario, things can go horribly wrong with such different kinds of sources. Consider, for example, the question of what transpired between Alexander and Porus in India. At the dawn of the twelfth century, the Benedictine monk Ekkehard puzzled over this problem while writing a history of the world *(Chronicon Universale)*. Ekkehard, later the abbot of Aura in Bavaria, had traveled to the Holy Land and enjoyed a fine grasp of the sources then available for ancient history. His Latin compilation was one of the first to call attention to some glaring contradictions in that record. In the *Historia de preliis*, derived from a tenth-century translation of the *Greek Alexander Romance*, Ekkehard read (78–79) a haughty exchange of letters between Alexander and Porus not to be found in the historical tradition known best to him through the narratives of Curtius and Justin.[39] Ekkehard found reports (80) that Porus commanded 14,800 scythed chariots and 400 elephants, each beast carrying a tower filled with thirty armed men. Alexander defeated this army and captured Porus's exotic palace (80–81); later, Alexander killed Porus in a David-and-Goliath duel (89). This troubling version could scarcely be reconciled with the famous account of Porus's pardon and subsequent partnership with Alexander. Furthermore, in the *Epistola*

38. English translations of these sources are available in various Loeb and Penguin editions; for Justin, see J. C. Yardley and Waldemar Heckel, eds., *Justin: Epitome of the Philippic History of Pompeius Trogus: Books 11–12, Alexander the Great* (Oxford: Clarendon Press, 1997). *The Greek Alexander Romance* is generally attributed to Pseudo-Callisthenes.

39. Leo, *The History of Alexander's Battles: Historia de preliis, the J1 Version*, trans. R. Telfryn Pritchard (Toronto: Pontifical Institute of Mediaeval Studies, 1992).

ad Aristotelem (Letter to Aristotle) drawn likewise from the *Greek Alexander Romance*, Ekkehard had to deal with another story.[40] In this case, Alexander disguised himself as a common soldier and infiltrated Porus's camp. Alexander tricked Porus into believing his royal opponent would be an old and indolent Macedonian. This whole episode ended in Porus's defeat, but the rajah was spared and allowed to reign as the Macedonian's vassal. What was Ekkehard to make of such *dissonantia hystoriographorum* (discordance of historiographies)? Did Alexander kill Porus or capture and reinstate him? Were the royal letters genuine? Was it possible that Porus's army amounted to so many chariots and elephants? Could Alexander have been a clever spy? Complicating matters, other medieval writers treated these stories as Christian allegories, in which Alexander appeared as Christ and Porus as Satan.[41] Ekkehard warily (or wearily?) chose the Herodotean path, setting forth the contradictory tales and inviting his readers to judge between them.

Nine hundred years later, historians still lament that one of the most important persons and periods in all of history must be studied without the benefit of adequate firsthand testimony. This requires extra caution in our handling of the evidence: we must ask whether the sources at our disposal have been corrupted by myth or political manipulation; whether a secondary author has misunderstood or miscopied a primary one; and whether it is possible to identify and correctly evaluate the lost sources upon which our best extant accounts depend. For example, scholars have determined that a dozen or so contemporaries of Alexander's actually published firsthand records of the reign; these include, among others,

40. Richard Stoneman, ed., *Legends of Alexander the Great* (London: J. M. Dent; Rutland, Vt.: C. E. Tuttle, 1994), pp. 3–19.

41. George Cary, *The Medieval Alexander* (Cambridge: Cambridge University Press, 1956), p. 303. Ekkehard would not have known the Persian *Iskandarnamah*, in which a Muslim Alexander beheads Porus for refusing to accept Islam: Elizabeth Baynham, "Who Put the 'Romance' in the Alexander Romance? The Alexander Romances within Alexander Historiography," *Ancient History Bulletin* 9, 1 (1995): 1–13, esp. p. 11.

Aristotle's relative Callisthenes; Chares, the court chamberlain; Ptolemy, a general and future king of Egypt; Aristobulus, a technical expert; Onesicritus, chief pilot of Alexander's flagship; and Nearchus, admiral of the fleet.[42] Among these, Ptolemy and Aristobulus provided the basis for Arrian's history, although he consulted other primary authors as well.[43] Another contemporary of Alexander's, but probably not an eyewitness participant in the campaigns, was Cleitarchus, whose version of events heavily influenced the so-called Vulgate tradition represented by the extant histories by Diodorus, Curtius, and Justin.[44]

Scholars have wrangled for centuries over the relative merits of these sources, working backward from the five surviving narrative histories (usually discounting the *Romance*) to make useful postulations about those that have disappeared. The idea is to peel back the layers of later prejudice and error in order to reach back to the fragmentary eyewitness accounts. We then infer the past based upon these reconstructed texts. This tedious process cannot be avoided, since historians depend entirely upon their sources: they study *evidence*, not *events*. Short of time travel, the past no longer exists for direct observation. Like those who investigate other singular (rather than recurring) phenomena, such as human evolution or the extinction of dinosaurs, the emphasis in training and research must be on the surviving evidence and how it should be processed into reliable theories about what can no longer be seen.

This holds true, of course, for both literary and material evidence. Ar-

42. The standard reference is still Lionel Pearson, *The Lost Histories of Alexander the Great* (London: American Philological Association, 1960). English translations of these fragmentary works can be found in C. A. Robinson, Jr., *The History of Alexander the Great* (1953; reprint, Chicago: Ares, 1996), vol. 1.

43. Arrian 1.1.1–3.

44. The resulting similarities among these works has given rise to the term "Vulgate Tradition" to distinguish this sometimes harsh version of Alexander's character from the more sympathetic view of Arrian. Some scholars use the term pejoratively, as demonstrated below in chapter 5, but here "Vulgate" is used only as a familiar term of classification, not condemnation.

tifacts, whether dinosaur bones or ancient coins, require the same careful analysis as Arrian's secondary Greek history of Alexander. Of course, we are more likely to discover objects rather than texts that are contemporary with Alexander, so our quest for firsthand evidence naturally excites us about archaeology's potential to put us in more direct contact with the past. Yet we have already seen how difficult and disappointing this prospect can be: Alexander's tomb has tricked us time and time again, our certainties always giving way to doubts the deeper we dig through the layers of evidence. What we can touch or read may not be what it seems. We must ask: how did this text or artifact arrive at this place in this form? Has it been altered along the way? Has it fallen under the power of privileged assumptions that have yet to be noticed and tested?

Much of the literature devoted to Alexander studies has dealt with these issues. We have thus, for example, had the benefit in recent years of entire books devoted to Curtius and his sources and to the mosaic found at Pompeii depicting Alexander's battle against Darius.[45] Every scrap of literary and material evidence deserves this level of intense scrutiny, because the subject is so important and the sources are so few. The chapters to follow undertake such an investigation of one of the most mysterious artifacts ever associated with Alexander the Great and seek to shed light on where, how, when, and why it was made, and what this might tell us about Alexander himself. To reach those conclusions, however, it is necessary to follow the trail of evidence every step of the way. How did it come to be in its unusual place of discovery? By what means did it come into the possession of historians, and what assumptions shaped their evolving theories about it? We can track the growing controversy surrounding this object, and related finds, right up to the present, resolving the mystery and offering an extraordinary glimpse into the psyche of Alexander the Great.

45. Elizabeth Baynham, *Alexander the Great: The Unique History of Quintus Curtius* (Ann Arbor: University of Michigan Press, 1998); Ada Cohen, *The Alexander Mosaic: Stories of Victory and Defeat* (Cambridge: Cambridge University Press, 1997).

TWO

A Treasure

On August 20, 1877, Charles Darwin attended a local excavation on the lands of his good friend Thomas Henry Farrer of Abinger Hall, Surrey. The famous naturalist wished to test his theory that the castings (*ejecta*) of earthworms constantly formed a fresh vegetative surface on the earth, a subject to which he devoted his last book, *The Formation of Vegetable Mould, through the Action of Worms, with Observations on Their Habits* (1881). Through assiduous labors that some still consider beneath the dignity of so great a scientist, Darwin observed and measured the minutiae of the worm-world.[1] At that time, earthworms enjoyed little in the way of scientific interest or popular favor. Non-biologists considered them slimy, clandestine creatures whose main work was the gruesome disposal of the dead. Shakespeare's dying Mercutio had cried out, "A plague o' both your houses! They have made worms' meat of me."[2] In *Hamlet*, the worm-eaten corpse of "poor Yorick" inspired a discourse on

---

1. On this subject, see J. E. Satchell, ed., *Earthworm Ecology from Darwin to Vermiculture* (London: Chapman & Hall, 1983). An interesting defense of Darwin's last book was made on the centennial of his death by Stephen J. Gould, republished from the pages of *Natural History* (April 1982), in *Hen's Teeth and Horses' Toes* (New York: Norton, 1983), pp. 120–33.

2. *Romeo and Juliet* 3.1.111–12.

the fate of even Alexander's decomposed body: "Alexander died, Alexander was buried, Alexander returneth into dust; the dust is earth; of earth we make loam; and why of that loam, whereto he was converted, might they not stop a beer barrel?"[3] From Babylon to a bunghole, the trail of Alexander's remains allegedly passed through the intestines of worms and taught the world a humbling lesson about the transience of all earthly glory.

This was a hard sermon, and it made the maligned earthworm all the more unlikable, even though maggots actually did most of this work. People believed, too, that worms harmed vegetation and ruined crops, a false accusation that gave us the word "vermin" from the Latin *vermis*, meaning worm. Except as bird food or bait, worms seemed totally useless. In Darwin's day, London street vendors sold worms only in small quantities and "very grudgingly," whereas about 2.5 million snails were sold per annum.[4] Against this tide of ill will and ignorance, Darwin pursued his investigations of the worm's true benefit to mankind. He calculated, among other things, that earthworms bring to the surface of Britain's soil about 10,516 kilograms (more than eleven tons) of castings per acre per year.[5] This process undermines objects and causes them to sink as a fresh "vegetable mould" simultaneously grows above them. Given enough time and worms, everything once on the surface will settle deeper and deeper underground. Darwin concluded:

> Archaeologists are probably not aware how much they owe to worms
> for the preservation of many ancient objects. Coins, gold ornaments,

3. *Hamlet* 5.1.231–35. Loam, a mixture of clay and sand, was fashioned into plaster and sometimes employed to seal the spout of a beer barrel (called a bunghole).

4. Henry Mayhew, *London Labour and the London Poor,* vol. 2 (London: Griffen, Bohn, 1851), p. 80.

5. Charles Darwin, *The Formation of Vegetable Mould, through the Action of Worms, with Observations on Their Habits* (London: Murray, 1881; reprint, New York: D. Appleton, 1896), p. 305 (and cf. p. 165).

stone implements, &c., if dropped on the surface of the ground, will infallibly be buried by the castings of worms in a few years, and will thus be safely preserved, until the land at some future time is turned up.[6]

That is why Darwin himself turned up at Abinger, to observe firsthand what worms had done with a Roman villa "probably ruined and deserted 1400 or 1500 years ago."[7] This site, discovered accidentally during work in a field on the southeast side of Farrer's new residence, yielded considerable quantities of pottery, tiles, tesserae, and coins. These Roman artifacts naturally aroused the interest of local antiquaries, and the British Archaeological Association later dispatched several members to measure, record, and report on the findings. For different reasons, Darwin also inspected the excavations and published a useful stratigraphic diagram. The resourceful Darwin even imposed upon Mr. Farrer to keep a diary of the worms' activities for the next seven weeks: the attentive squire counted worm tracks and burrows on the exposed floor of the villa's atrium, measured the castings, and even agreed to follow up on the creatures after a three-year interval.[8] In this way, Darwin accumulated the data he needed to extol the benefit of worms to those of us living a little higher on the evolutionary ladder.

Archaeologists, who blithely peel away the protective layers deposited by worms upon the artifacts they seek, should be among the most grateful to them, Darwin reiterated.[9] And in Darwin's lifetime (1809–1882),

6. Ibid., p. 176.

7. Ibid., p. 179. See "Roman Villa at Abinger, Surrey," *The Times* (London), Wednesday, February 18, 1878, p. 7, for an account of the excavation at Abinger.

8. Summarized in Darwin's *Formation of Vegetable Mould*, pp. 178–89. Darwin also enlisted the aid of his sons and other helpers in gathering such information from various sites in Britain.

9. Ibid., pp. 308–9.

there was surely no greater name in archaeology than that of Heinrich Schliemann (1822–1890).[10] A controversial man then and now, Schliemann gave the world an inspiring rags-to-riches story based on strenuous labor, sensational luck, and shameless self-promotion.[11] With his hard-earned fortune, Schliemann took up archaeology in 1868 as no more than a naïve dilettante who traveled widely and believed in the literal truth of Homer's *Iliad* and *Odyssey*. He searched in Ithaca for the very tree from which Odysseus had made his marriage bed, and he was the sort of amateur whose personal collection of artifacts included a jar of salt sold to him as the remains of Lot's wife. Later in life, he tried his hand at locating the tomb of Alexander in Egypt—but failed. His reputation as an archaeologist rests instead upon his discoveries of great Bronze Age remains at Troy, Mycenae, and other sites immortalized by Homer. For this he became front-page news, and in 1877, William Gladstone—four times prime minister of Britain—dropped what he was doing in order to write a thirty-six page preface to one of Schliemann's publications.

In the nascent field of archaeology, men like Schliemann and Darwin discovered a common (under)ground for the pursuit of their disparate passions. They, and the general public that followed their work so fervently, stood at the threshold of an exciting new science of historical inquiry. Schliemann expended his fortune seeking the lofty warriors who had built Mycenae and Troy; Darwin expended his energies on the lowly worms that had buried all such relics of earlier times. Great minds, great energies, and great fortunes called forth an age of the grandest expecta-

10. Schliemann wrote eleven books (one of them partly autobiographical), 60,000 letters, 150 excavation notebooks, and eighteen diaries (now in the Gennadion Library in Athens), from which many biographies have derived the intimate and extraordinary details of his life. A very readable example is Caroline Moorehead's *Lost and Found: The 9,000 Treasures of Troy* (New York: Penguin Books, 1994).

11. The darker side of Schliemann's career has been the subject of several recent studies, including David Traill's *Schliemann of Troy: Treasure and Deceit* (New York: St. Martin's Press, 1995).

tions. The ancient world beneath our feet had never seemed so close and alluring as it did in 1877.

While Darwin studied his worms in Surrey, Schliemann passed nearby on a grandiose round of banquets, speeches, and honors that commenced with a dazzling appearance before the Society of Antiquaries in London. A large, cheering crowd of notables listened to Schliemann's long lecture, followed by an enthusiastic oration from Gladstone himself.[12] The lionized Schliemann received honorary membership of the society on the spot. The *Illustrated London News* preserved the scene in a woodcut that shows Schliemann standing among the learned throng, reading a report on his remarkable discoveries through his pince-nez. A bearded gentleman hovers directly behind the speaker, listening intently (see fig. 1). This man, Sir Augustus Wollaston Franks, a wealthy official of the British Museum and an archaeological scholar of at least the second rank in that illustrious gathering of intellectuals, would soon have his part to play in a mysterious discovery worthy of an eventful year in archaeology. For at that moment, far away in Central Asia, the rushing waters of the Oxus River (the modern Amu Darya) were hauling away with Schliemannic zeal the millennial accretions of Darwin's worms from atop a most astonishing treasure.

Like the Nile, the Oxus had a potent influence on the imaginations of men in the nineteenth century. It was rumored, for example, that rich deposits of gold lay unmolested along its banks, and that the actual descendants of Alexander the Great lived near its upper reaches. William Moorcroft of Lancashire lost his life in becoming the first Englishman to look upon its waters, and Captain John Wood of the Indian Navy led a dangerous mission in search of the river's source.[13] From its icy head-

12. "Dr. Schliemann at Burlington House," *The Times* (London), March 23, 1877, p. 10. Joan Evans's official *A History of the Society of Antiquaries* (Oxford: Oxford University Press, 1956), p. 339, reports, however, that Gladstone was not there.

13. On the much-traveled Moorcroft, see Garry Alder, *Beyond Bokhara: The Life of William Moorcroft, Asian Explorer and Pioneer Veterinary Surgeon* (London:

Figure 1. Augustus Franks listening to
Schliemann lecture. Drawing based upon a
woodcut in *Illustrated London News* (1877).

waters high in the Pamir Mountains, the Oxus plunges down precipitous
cliffs toward the Turkestan desert, drinks up huge tributaries such as the
Vakhsh, Kokcha, and Qunduz, and finally completes its 1,500-mile
odyssey on the shores of the Aral Sea.[14] Its middle course still defines the
northern borders of Afghanistan (ancient Bactria), in an area once heav-

---

Century, 1985). On Wood, see his memoir *A Journey to the Source of the River Oxus*
(London: John Murray, 1872).

14. Actually a lake (once the world's fourth largest), the Aral has been dry-
ing up at an alarming rate, with grave consequences for Central Asian populations.

ily colonized by Alexander's Greeks, who noted that the turbulent river's burden of silt made its water unfit to drink.[15]

In 1877, a roiling surge near an ancient Greek settlement unearthed a vast hidden treasure of silver and gold from the banks of the Oxus. Over a period of four years, as the water did its work, local villagers gathered up thousands of coins, cups, rings, bracelets, bowls, plaques, and figurines. They sold what they could to passers-by, giving vague accounts of exactly where the hoard had been found in order to safeguard their continuing harvest of artifacts.[16] As those valuables trickled into the eager hands of European collectors by way of Peshawar and Rawalpindi, the old tales of the so-called Oxus Treasure quickly became the stuff of legend.

In 1880, three Muslim merchants from Bukhara bought a huge share of the hoard from the villagers and hurried to Peshawar to reap their rewards. Unfortunately, they were not fast enough. Wazi ad-Din, Ghulan Muhammud, and Shuker Ali had often traversed this perilous terrain carrying great sums of money into India, where they normally bought tea, silk, and other commodities to be hauled back for sale in Samarkand or Khiva.[17] In 1880, this was a particularly dangerous way to make a living. Afghanistan was the center of the giant Central Asian chessboard on

15. Polybius 10.48.1–8; Curtius 7.10.13. See also Frank Holt, *Alexander the Great and Bactria* (Leiden: Brill, 1988), pp. 19–20, with notes.

16. The director of Indian State Railways, Alexander Grant, proved to be especially helpful in passing along information and artifacts. See Percy Gardner, "New Coins from Bactria," *Numismatic Chronicle* 19 (1879): 1–12, and "Coins from Central Asia," *Numismatic Chronicle*, 3d ser., 1 (1881): 8–12.

17. The following account of their adventures is based upon a deposition filed with British authorities in May 1880 and subsequently reported in O. M. Dalton, *The Treasure of the Oxus* (1905), 3d ed. (London: British Museum Press, 1964), pp. xiii–xv. Other useful materials are to be found in John Curtis, "Franks and the Oxus Treasure," in *A. W. Franks: Nineteenth-Century Collecting and the British Museum*, ed. Marjorie Caygill and John Cherry, pp. 228–49 (London: British Museum Press, 1997).

which the so-called Great Game between czarist Russia and the British in India was afoot, as immortalized by Rudyard Kipling.[18] Secret jealousies in London and St. Petersburg played havoc with the lives of spies and other personnel in Central Asia as nations competed for control of new imperial frontiers. Trapped in the middle were the warring tribes of Central Asia and the notorious emirs, khans, slavers, and shahs who vied for power among them. In 1839, the First Afghan War had erupted when the British invaded Afghanistan in order to replace one native ruler (Dost Muhammed) with another (Shah Shuja).[19] One prescient knight on the chessboard, Sir Alexander "Bukhara" Burnes, warned from Kabul that the Afghans would not tolerate an army of occupation.[20] He was right. In 1841, an angry mob hacked Burnes and his brother to pieces, then attacked the British garrison just outside Kabul. Of the thousands who tried to fight their way back to India through the narrow passes near Seh Baba and Jagdalak, only one Englishman—a doctor named William Brydon—survived the bloody retreat.

Nonetheless, the Great Game continued. In 1878, fearing Afghan overtures to the Russians, the British dispatched 35,000 troops to intervene again. Another knight, Sir Pierre Louis Napoleon Cavagnari, hold-

18. The Great Game has been the subject of many historical treatments, including Karl Meyer and Shareen Brysac, *Tournament of Shadows: The Great Game and the Race for Empire in Central Asia* (Washington, D.C.: Counterpoint, 1999); Peter Hopkirk, *The Great Game: The Struggle for Empire in Central Asia* (New York: Kodansha International, 1992); and, emphasizing explorers, Kenneth Wimmel, *The Alluring Target: In Search of the Secrets of Central Asia* (Washington, D.C.: Trackless Sands Press, 1996).

19. Good general histories of this war include John Waller, *Beyond the Khyber Pass* (New York: Random House, 1990); James Norris, *The First Afghan War, 1838–1842* (Cambridge: Cambridge University Press, 1967); Patrick Macrory, *The Fierce Pawns* (Philadelphia: Lippincott, 1966). For William Brydon's eyewitness account, see *Lady Sale: The First Afghan War*, ed. Patrick Macrory (Hamden, Conn.: Archon Books, 1969), pp. 160–68.

20. On Burnes's colorful career, consult James Lunt, *Bokhara Burnes* (London: Faber & Faber, 1969).

ing the position of British Resident in Kabul for the first time since the murder of Burnes, was similarly attacked and killed. This Second Afghan War (1878–81) scarred the proponents of British imperialism and scared them into supporting an unlikely new emir.[21] Early in 1880, Abdur Rahman left his exile in Samarkand and, with Russian support, invaded Afghanistan to claim his inheritance. Meanwhile, his cousin Ayab Khan hoped to take the throne instead, and later in July inflicted a humiliating defeat on the British at the battle of Maiwand near Kandahar. By then the British had gambled upon the lesser of two evils and acknowledged Abdur Rahman as emir, hoping thus to escape Kabul less bloodied than in the first war. As the cousins fought it out, Russia and England backed quietly from the board—at least for a short while. It was in the midst of this turmoil that the three merchants from Bukhara entered Afghanistan on their way to India.

When they crossed the Oxus River south of Khobadian near Takht-i Kuwad, the merchants learned that Abdur Rahman was camped just ahead at Qunduz. There the future emir was taxing all travelers and merchants in order to raise funds for his army. This news naturally alarmed the Bukharans, since they were carrying at least 80,000 rupees in cash. They cast about, therefore, for some merchandise easier to smuggle past any toll collectors they might encounter. The Oxus Treasure was just what they were looking for. They negotiated the price and then sewed the antiquities into leather pouches to be packed on mules and passed off as something far less valuable. It was a clever plan that almost worked.

The saddlebags passed unmolested through the territories controlled by Abdur Rahman.[22] In Kabul, still—reluctantly—garrisoned by the

---

21. On this conflict, see Brian Robson, *The Road to Kabul: The Second Afghan War, 1878–1881* (London: Arms & Armour Press, 1986). For an eyewitness account of the war by Major General Sir Charles MacGregor, see William Trousdale, ed., *War in Afghanistan, 1879–80* (Detroit: Wayne State University Press, 1985).

22. Other shipments of treasure were in fact intercepted at Kabul by Rahman's collector of customs, who confiscated coins and then sold them to British

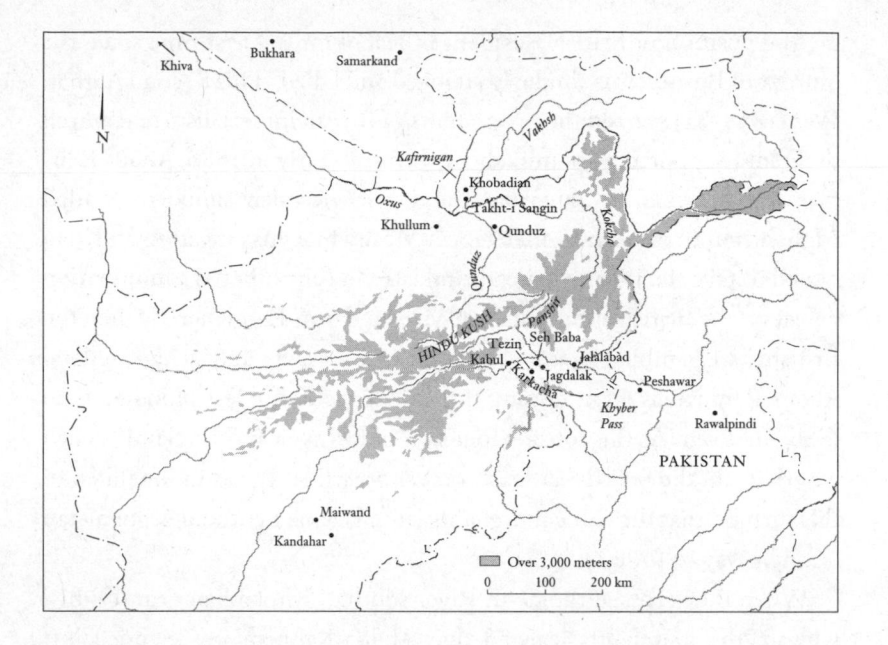

Map 2. Nineteenth-century Afghanistan

British, the merchants contemplated their next move. The most danger-ous stretch of their journey lay directly ahead. The British barely held the lines of communication between Kabul and Peshawar, that vital corridor between Central and South Asia through which every traveler had to pass. Along this mountainous trail, there were numerous defiles that af-forded local tribes unlimited opportunities to ambush merchant caravans and military convoys. This had been the wretched killing ground during the British retreat from Kabul in the First Afghan War. In 1880, the same Ghilzai clans lurked in the hills and looked down upon everything and everyone trying to reach safety in Peshawar. More than 16,000 British troops occupied a series of forts along this route, and two mobile

collectors. See Alexander Cunningham, "Relics from Ancient Persia in Gold, Sil-ver, and Copper," *Journal of the Asiatic Society of Bengal* 50 (1881): 151–86, esp. p. 185.

columns patrolled the passes. Even so, the Ghilzais wreaked havoc. Their attacks around Seh Baba, Jagdalak, and Jalalabad were particularly notable at the time the Bukhara merchants faced the final challenge of running this gauntlet to Peshawar.[23] No one took such a trip lightly. In fact, the inability of the British to guarantee this lifeline to India played an important part in their decision to support Abdur Rahman as a first step toward getting themselves out of Kabul.

In May, the merchants arranged to join a convoy with a military escort. All went well at least as far as the British post at Seh Baba, three days' march out of Kabul. There the relatively open ground rose into steep folds of enclosing hills, and the danger of attack grew sharply. It was at this critical moment that a series of blunders came to haunt the three merchants and their dreams of immense wealth. Apparently, these men had not kept their secret during the preparations in Kabul, thus allowing some word of their cargo to slip out. Then, ten miles short of the next British camp at Jagdalak, the merchants unwisely broke from their caravan and pressed ahead of its military guard. Perhaps fearing thieves among their fellow travelers, the merchants dashed ahead of the column with their mules and—as it turned out—a very loyal and resourceful servant.

Watching from the hills were about 180 Ghilzai raiders from the Khurd Kabul who had heard rumors of the treasure. They had planned an attack earlier in the march but had been thwarted by the presence of the military escort. Before the three merchants could reach Jagdalak, the bandits swooped down. Quickly cutting the saddlebags from the mules, the Ghilzais carried them off, along with the merchants and their servant. By the time the convoy caught up to the abandoned mules, the robbers had disappeared into the mountains. They escaped through the Tesinka Pass to a perfect hideaway among the Karkacha caves (near the sites of camps and caves later used by Osama bin Laden and his terrorist net-

---

23. Robson, *Road to Kabul*, pp. 184–209, provides details of troop deployments, attacks, and casualties.

work). There the thieves spread the leather pouches from the saddlebags on the floor, ripping them open to dump out and divide the contents. The gold and silver treasures that spilled out were not easily apportioned among the bandits except by weight. Greedy beyond caring, the Ghilzais began to carve the artifacts into convenient pieces, and at least one "silver idol" was thrown into a melting pot.

Distracted by all of this hacking and haggling, the bandits lost track of an important item—the merchants' servant. Making his escape from the cave, the latter fled back down to Seh Baba under cover of darkness. There, at 9:00 P.M., he reported the attack to the British authorities. On that May evening in 1880, the political officer for the Tezin Valley was Captain Francis Charles Burton, an accomplished linguist, dashing soldier, and close friend of Kipling, who featured Burton's wife in some of his stories as "Mrs. Hauksbee" ("the most wonderful woman in India").[24] Burton responded to the alarm immediately, taking two orderlies in a daring rescue of the hostages and their possessions. Around midnight, Burton's small party burst upon the bandits inside the cave. It was a scene worthy of an Indiana Jones movie. The cave was littered with leather packets, allotments of booty, and four bleeding Ghilzais who had lost arguments over their shares. Burton persuaded the robbers to surrender at least part of the treasure; but, lacking firepower, he could do little more. He and the liberated merchants gathered what they could and departed. Warned that the bandits would try another ambush, the British officer and his compatriots hid in the mountains until daybreak.

When Burton reached Seh Baba the next day, he made it known that he was organizing a punitive expedition. Quickly, the nervous Ghilzais turned over another large portion of the treasure, holding back and hiding enough to repay their efforts.[25] Under the grim circumstances of

24. Curtis, "Franks and the Oxus Treasure," p. 248 n. 51. I take the quotation from Kipling's story "Kidnapped," in *Plain Tales from the Hills*.

25. Some have argued that this lost portion of the Oxus Treasure was rediscovered in 1993 and eventually sold to the Miho Museum in Japan: see, e.g., Igor

1880, this satisfied all parties. The three merchants and their servant had been saved, and a substantial amount of their property restored; Captain Burton had done his duty with élan; and the thieves were neither arrested nor left empty-handed. The Bukharans were deposed on the whole affair. Grateful to Burton, they allowed him to purchase one of the remaining artifacts: a gold armlet, which in 1884 passed into the collection of the South Kensington Museum (now the Victoria and Albert Museum) for £1,000. The rest of the hoard, minus the lot hidden by the highwaymen, made it safely to Jalalabad and then down through the Khyber Pass to Peshawar. Finally out of danger, the merchants finished their adventure in Rawalpindi, where they hawked their ancient merchandise. Using local jewelers from the bazaar as intermediaries, as many smugglers still do, they managed to sell the last of about 200 gold artifacts and 1,500 gold and silver coins. Most of the buyers, like Burton, were British officials anxious to acquire collections worthy of the Great Game they were playing.

Where had so much treasure originated? Russian archaeologists now argue that the Oxus Treasure was buried in ancient times by the priests of a Zoroastrian temple located nearby at a place now called Takht-i Sangin ("The Throne of Stone").[26] This temple, laboriously excavated in re-

---

Pichikyan, "Rebirth of the Oxus Treasure: Second Part of the Oxus Treasure from the Miho Museum Collection," *Ancient Civilizations* 4 (1997): 306–83. Others argue that this material derives from a different great hoard at Mir Zakah. On the flood of Bactrian hoards in this period, see Osmund Bopearachchi: "Grand trésors récents de monnaies pré-sasanides trouvés en Afghanistan et au Pakistan," *International Numismatic Newsletter* 24 (1994): 2–3; id., "Récentes découvertes de trésors de monnaies pré-Sassanides trouvés en Afghanistan et au Pakistan," *Cahiers numismatiques*, September 1994: 7–14; and id., "Découvertes récentes de trésors indo-grecs: Nouvelles données historiques," *Comptes rendus de l'Académie des inscriptions et belles-lettres*, April–June 1995: 611–29.

26. Elaborated most fully in Boris Litvinsky and Igor Pichikyan, *The Hellenistic Temple of the Oxus in Bactria (South Tajikistan)*, vol. 1 (Moscow: Vostochnaya Literatura, 2000), pp. 13–29 (in Russian). Some cautions have been registered by Paul Bernard, "Le temple du dieu Oxus à Takht-i Sangin en Bactriane:

cent years by the South Tajikistan Archaeological Expedition, yielded many artifacts related to those found by the villagers in the Oxus Treasure. It became obvious, however, that while the Oxus Treasure itself consisted primarily of gold objects and precious coins, the excavated temple artifacts were mostly offerings of bronze and ivory, with just a little gold. This fact convinced the archaeologists that at some moment of dire military emergency, perhaps the invasion of nomadic tribes ca. 150 B.C.E., the priests had quickly gathered up their most valuable gold objects and coins in order to hide them nearby until the danger had passed. For some reason, this great hoard was never recovered by the priests and remained safe in the underground world of Darwin's worms until the artifacts finally began to wash from the riverbank in 1877.

Thus, the materials spirited to eager buyers in Peshawar and Rawalpindi may have constituted the most prized possessions of an ancient Zoroastrian temple that once stood on a hill overlooking a caravan route beside the Oxus River. The Persian religion of Zoroastrianism featured temples in which priests tended an eternal flame, and these rites were apparently respected by Alexander the Great and his successors in Bactria.[27] According to Russian excavators, the temple at Takht-i Sangin was actually built by Greeks, and along with Persian offerings, it possessed a great number of Greek votive objects, including coins, artwork, ornate weaponry, and an altar inscribed in Greek.[28] These represented an extraordinary synthesis in Central Asia between the very different beliefs

---

Temple du feu ou pas?" *Studia Iranica* 23 (1994): 81–121. Bernard's concerns would weaken the connection between the Oxus Treasure and the temple at Takht-i Sangin.

27. The view that Zoroastrians reviled Alexander for his outrages against their religion rests upon a much later literary tradition, dating from the ninth and tenth centuries C.E. In Bactria, Zoroaster's homeland, the Greeks obviously took an active interest in Zoroastrian rituals.

28. Frank Holt, *Thundering Zeus: The Making of Hellenistic Bactria* (Berkeley: University of California Press, 1999), pp. 41 and 177 (inscription no. 10).

held by former enemies. And among these special offerings selected to be safeguarded by the priests in their hidden cache was an extraordinary item destined to fall into the hands of Sir Augustus Wollaston Franks, the man behind the great Schliemann at the meeting of the Society of Antiquaries in 1877.

As sometime director of the Society of Antiquaries and full-time keeper of the Department of British and Medieval Antiquities at the British Museum, Franks (1826–1897) took a keen interest in artifacts of all kinds.[29] Gregarious and well educated, he associated with the leading thinkers of his time, including Charles Darwin. He used his professional position and personal fortune to acquire many rare prizes for the museum, among them the royal gold cup of the kings of France and England, the finger-ring of Queen Aethelswith of Mercia, and the so-called Franks Casket, presumably from Anglo-Saxon Northumbria. He also published books and articles on such diverse subjects as Roman pottery, Chinese painting, Indian sculpture, heraldry, history, megaliths, manuscripts, pilgrims' badges, bookplates, and much more.[30] Franks was at his prime as a collector and curator when the Oxus Treasure spilled into the bazaars of Peshawar and Rawalpindi, and he spared no effort to acquire as much as he could of the hoard. He bought out a rival, the great collector (General Sir) Alexander Cunningham who—unaware, of course, of the temple later discovered at Takht-i Sangin—thought that the Oxus Treasure had belonged to some ancient baronial family of Bactria that had buried it near Khullum (one of the earliest reported find spots of the hoard). Franks bequeathed his large portion of the Oxus Treasure to the British Museum in 1897.[31] Further benefactions by others added more

29. David Wilson, *The Forgotten Collector: Augustus Wollaston Franks of the British Museum* (London: Thames & Hudson, 1984); *A. W. Franks*, ed. Caygill and Cherry.

30. Wilson, *Forgotten Collector*, pp. 14–30.

31. Dalton, *Treasure of the Oxus*, pp. xiii–xvii.

coins said to be from the same hoard, so that a miscellany of numismatic material in the British Museum may be linked to this find. Unfortunately, it is not always possible to be sure.[32]

When all of these artifacts finally entered the museum's vaults, they passed beyond the worlds of worms and thieves into a pampered and productive existence as the objects of numismatic study. This branch of knowledge focuses upon coins and related materials, such as medals and tokens, artifacts that many people might not readily appreciate as valuable historical evidence. Deceptively, coins today seem hopelessly mundane in their usual function as money: they constitute a convenient store of wealth, to be dispensed as needed. This practice has become so routine that although we haul them around in our pockets and purses, we are barely conscious of their larger role as a product and reflection of our history and culture. Albeit barely noticed, the designs on coins are nevertheless carefully chosen to make them (like the Constitution or the Declaration of Independence) representative documents of our society.

Recent history is so rich in various kinds of sources that we habitually overlook coins as important clues about our culture. But for earlier eras lacking documentary evidence, the eloquence and durability of coins come to our rescue. To understand an ancient king's finances, scholars can track the production of royal mints and the distribution patterns of coinage in excavated sites and recovered hoards. To investigate political aims and propaganda, experts try to analyze the designs on coins: what titles and images appear on the state's money, when, and why? Scholars probe this evidence for telltale signs of important new policies, of deliberate ties or breaks with earlier traditions, of regional variations in the economy, and of personal religious beliefs. Ever since the Renaissance, coins and medals have been used to unlock the secrets of the past. Scholars such as Petrarch (1303–1374) championed the study of numismatics as invaluable historical evidence about the art, economics, religion, and

32. A. R. Bellinger, "The Coins from the Treasure of the Oxus," *American Numismatic Society Museum Notes* 10 (1962): 51–67, esp. p. 67.

politics of ancient Greece and Rome.[33] Important research collections of coins and medals grew in response to this movement, first privately and then publicly in great royal and national cabinets that still exist today.[34]

There was no greater period in the advancement of numismatic science than the nineteenth century, particularly during the lifetimes of Schliemann and Franks, who themselves took an active interest in the subject. In 1836, premier scholarly journals were established in London *(Numismatic Chronicle)* and Paris *(Revue numismatique)*; and thirty years later, the American Numismatic Society in New York began publishing its *American Journal of Numismatics*. In time, photography and laboratory analysis allowed greater precision in numismatic studies. In 1873, the British Museum began the publication of its huge collection of Greek coins. And in 1885, Stanley Lane-Poole announced that numismatics was no longer an ancillary science; it now ranked among the independent branches of knowledge no longer fathomable by a single mind, no matter how gifted.[35] He was right. In the case of Alexander, for example, it would require legions of brilliant numismatists just to begin cataloguing and studying the coins minted in his name that flooded by the tens of thousands into museums around the world.[36]

In the midst of that flood, in 1887, Franks donated a large silver medallic coin, with magnificent but mysterious images stamped upon it, to the British Museum.[37] According to the old identification ticket long

33. See Philip Grierson, *Numismatics* (Oxford: Oxford University Press, 1975).

34. For information on collections and related matters, consult Elvira Clain-Stefanelli, *Numismatic Bibliography* (Munich: Battenberg, 1984).

35. Stanley Lane-Poole, *Coins and Medals: Their Place in History and Art* (London, 1885), p. 2.

36. See, for examples, Alfred Bellinger, *Essays on the Coinage of Alexander the Great* (New York: American Numismatic Society, 1963), and Martin Price, *The Coinage in the Name of Alexander the Great and Philip Arrhidaeus* (London: British Museum Press, 1991), vols. 1 and 2.

37. Experts still do not entirely agree whether to call this object a coin or a medal. The two may look similar and are manufactured in approximately the

kept under the medallion in its guarded tray in the museum, it was "found at Khullum Bokhara."[38] Thus, while this artifact is never mentioned in early discussions of the Oxus Treasure, the time and place of its finding, and the donor, persuade some experts that it was part of the hoard that came to light near Khullum in about 1880 and was carried by the three Bukharan merchants to India, where Franks bought it along with the other coins and artifacts.[39] We have no idea what Franks thought of it, or of where it ranked on his "button scale" (according to Joan Evans, the daughter of the archaeologist Sir John Evans, Franks's close friend, the buttons on Franks's waistcoat "served as a barometer of en-

---

same fashion. The difference lies primarily in what their intended purpose was: coins serve as a medium of exchange, whereas medals have no monetary function. The latter normally are made of nonprecious metals and commemorate some event, such as a heroic act or military victory. In some cases, the distinction between coin and medal may be blurred: see, e.g., Cécile Morrison, *La numismatique* (Paris: Presses universitaires de France, 1992), p. 8. Such is the case here, where a large precious-metal object of monetary value also has a special commemorative purpose. Such coin-medals are sometimes called "medallions," a term discussed by Grierson, *Numismatics*, pp. 172–73, and employed in that special sense (and *not* as a synonym for medal) throughout this investigation. Other correct terms include "presentation coin," "medallic coin," and "monetary medal." The term "commemorative" is also appropriate, since it applies equally to coins and medals: see James Mackay, *Key Definitions in Numismatics* (London: Frederick Muller, 1982), pp. 19–20. The words "coin" and "medal," set off by quotation marks, will be used to emphasize a particular scholar's opinion that the artifacts in question are really one or the other.

38. This is item 1887–6–9–1 in the British Museum numismatic inventory. See App. A, E/A 1 and pl. 2.

39. Paul Bernard, "Le monnayage d'Eudamos, satrape grec du Pandjab et 'maître des éléphants,' " in *Orientalia Iosephi Tucci Memoriae Dicata*, ed. G. Gnoli and L. Lanciotti (Rome: Istituto italiano per il Medio ed Estremo Oriente, 1985), 1: 65–94, esp. pp. 91–92, citing E. Zéjmal; also Robin Lane Fox, "Text and Image: Alexander the Great, Coins and Elephants," *Bulletin of the Institute of Classical Studies* 41 (1996): 97.

thusiasm. If he were looking at an object which he liked very much indeed, he fingered the top one; if very much, the next; if moderately, the next, and so down the scale").[40]

The medallion almost certainly placed higher than might be expected from recent studies of his collecting career, where this artifact has been surprisingly ignored by many experts. Of course, the broad range of his activities and acquisitions makes it all too easy to overlook one gift among so many; it is believed that Franks donated about 7,000 objects to the British Museum, including the Oxus Treasure.[41]

Our best evidence is that Franks indeed purchased the medallion during the buying frenzy set off by the Oxus Treasure, and that it was reported (or assumed) by him to have come from the hoard. Nothing now known would make this attribution unlikely, but this interesting connection might nevertheless be completely illusory. The medallion could have been found elsewhere in or near Afghanistan and just happen to have been caught up in the commotion surrounding the Oxus Treasure. Franks knowingly purchased fakes and intrusive artifacts in order to acquire everything of potential value from the antiquities dealers.[42] In such situations, old inventories and odd pieces are naturally hawked as part of the treasure in demand, and the tag "found at Khullum" might therefore have been attached to nearly everything in the shops. Muddled hoards such as this can never be reconstituted with absolute certainty.[43] But what matters now is that, right or wrong, the first experts to study the medallion *assumed* (as some still do) that it came from the Oxus Treasure. Since this hoard seemed to have been buried near the Oxus River around the

40. Evans, *History of the Society of Antiquaries*, p. 346.

41. Marjorie Caygill, "Franks and the British Museum," in *A. W. Franks*, ed. Caygill and Cherry, pp. 51–129, at p. 95.

42. Dalton, *Treasure of the Oxus*, pp. xv–xvi.

43. As noted, e.g., by Margaret Thompson, Otto Mørkholm, and Colin Kraay, eds., *An Inventory of Greek Coin Hoards* (New York: American Numismatic Society, 1973), p. 264 (no. 1822).

second century B.C.E. (based upon some datable objects found in it), scholars therefore put the *manufacture* of the medallion in precisely that same context, with unfortunate consequences.

In 1887, two articles in respected numismatic journals initially brought this unique artifact to the attention of scholars on both sides of the Atlantic. In New York, an anonymous entry appeared in the *American Journal of Numismatics:*

> *A rare Bactrian decadrahm.* [sic]
>
> Mr. A. W. Franks has presented to the British Museum a most remarkable coin, lately received from India. It is a decadrachm of the Bactrian series, the first ever met with, and bears on the obverse a horseman with his lance charging an elephant, on whose back are two warriors; and on the reverse a king or Zeus, standing, holding a thunderbolt and a spear; in the field is a monogram composed of the letters A B. The obverse records some victory of the Greeks over the barbarians, and the reverse may be a representation of Alexander the Great. The coin evidently comes from the district of the Oxus, and was struck about the middle of the second century B.C.[44]

This first published description identifies the artifact as a decadrachm coin minted in Bactria in ca. 150 B.C.E., a deduction based (as we have seen) on the double assumption that it was part of the Oxus Treasure and was therefore produced at about the time and place the hoard was buried. The second inference need not be true even if the first one is: hoards often contain valuables from much earlier periods and from very distant regions. In truth, many coins from the Oxus Treasure and other

---

44. *American Journal of Numismatics,* October 1887, p. 40. A decadrachm is a large silver denomination weighing 42.0 grams (about 1.5 oz) on the popular Attic (Athenian) standard of measures; the object in question weighs slightly more (42.20 gr). In numismatics, the term "obverse" refers to what we might call "heads," and "reverse" indicates the opposing side, or "tails."

Bactrian hoards were minted far away and sometimes centuries before they were finally buried.[45]

The second publication of the "coin" in 1887 demonstrates just how dangerous this double assumption could be, since, in this case, these inferences shaped the author's entire analysis into a rather fantastic theory about the elephant and its riders. Percy Gardner (1846–1937), at that time the Disney Professor of Archaeology at Cambridge University, was a prolific and polished author on many aspects of Greek coinage, and he knew the British Museum collection intimately.[46] His illustrated article in the British publication *Numismatic Chronicle* reports the medallion's find spot ("Khullum, in Bokhara") and purchaser ("Mr. A. W. Franks"). He then describes the object, "a most interesting and wonderful decadrachm," noting that the standing king, as Zeus with thunderbolt, on one side (see fig. 2), must be the deified conqueror Alexander the Great. Nonetheless, Gardner attributed the medallion to a Bactrian mint of the second century B.C.E., long after the death of Alexander, but deliberately close in time and place to the burial of the Oxus Treasure. Based on circumstantial evidence, probably supplied by Franks, Gardner concluded that the elephant battle must also have taken place in Bactria during the second century B.C.E. This inference he supported on grounds of style and physiognomy, claiming that given their full beards and "coarse and

45. See Raoul Curiel and Daniel Schlumberger, *Trésors monétaires d'Afghanistan* (Paris: Klincksieck, 1953), esp. pp. 46–49, on the Oxus Treasure.

46. Percy Gardner contributed immensely to the publication of the museum's vast Greek collection, including the volumes devoted to Sicily, Thrace, Syria, Thessaly, Peloponnesus, and, most important in the present context, *The Coins of the Greek and Scythic Kings of Bactria and India in the British Museum* (1886; reprint, Chicago: Argonaut, 1966). A list of 205 of his publications on archaeological/numismatic subjects (he also wrote extensively on religion) appears in his book *New Chapters in Greek Art* (Oxford: Clarendon Press, 1926), pp. 356–62. This list shows that Gardner was not the author of the unsigned note on the medallion published in the *American Journal of Numismatics*.

Figure 2. The Franks Medallion. Drawing based
upon a sketch in the *Numismatic Chronicle* (1887).

brutal" features, the two men riding the pachyderm must be barbarian
nomads fighting against some Greek cavalryman. But who? Gardner
knew that this region had been ruled from about 250 to 150 B.C.E. by a
series of Greek kings who followed in the footsteps of Alexander the
Great. From coins and a few ancient texts, it was deduced that waves of
invaders—the Yueh-Chi tribes—attacked and took over Bactria during
the reigns of King Eucratides the Great and his son Heliocles the Just.
This catastrophe could well have caused the burial of the Oxus Treasure
from whence the Franks medallion had apparently come. Gardner therefore expressed "little doubt that this remarkable decadrachm was struck
on the occasion of some notable victory won by a Greek king of Bactria
over the invading hordes of Yueh-chi in the second century B.C." He
therefore guessed that the horseman on the medallion was either Eucratides or his son Heliocles, celebrating a success against their foes (albeit too soon).[47]

Today, scholars scoff at Gardner's suggestion that desert nomads invaded Bactria on the backs of Indian elephants. But at the time he wrote,
Gardner was under the powerful influence of circumstantial evidence

47. Percy Gardner, "New Greek Coins of Bactria and India," *Numismatic
Chronicle* 7 (1887): 177–81, quotations from pp. 180–81. The drawing is accurate
in most respects, except the extended ground line ("exergue") beneath the horse's
feet—a matter of some importance later in this investigation.

about the Oxus Treasure, as well as other finds of remarkable Bactrian coins. Only a few years before the discovery of the Oxus Treasure, another medallic coin of different design—considerably larger and made of gold, with Eucratides' name stamped plainly upon it—had been found in Bukhara.[48] This medallion, the largest ever minted in the ancient world, made its way to Europe hidden in the armpit of a murderer. After killing five men to gain possession of the artifact, the Bukharan had sewn it into a leather pouch that fitted snugly in place beneath his undershirt. No one suspected a thing as he roamed across continents in search of a wealthy buyer.[49] On July 18, 1867, special instructions from Emperor Napoleon III provided for the purchase of this rarity, which remains today in the Bibliothèque nationale in Paris.[50] Anyone who has held this beautiful artifact will agree that doing so is a thrill that sends "something like an electric shock" through the senses.[51] Gardner may himself have felt this sensation, and at the very least he—like all numismatists of his day—certainly knew of the Eucratides medallion, which he drew attention to in his publication of Bactrian coins.[52] Thus, while the gold and silver medallions are very different, it may have seemed reasonable at the time to think that Eucratides had minted both.

As for Gardner's view that Alexander's deified image appeared on one side of a "coin" allegedly created much later for Eucratides, we must consider the influence of other discoveries made in Gardner's lifetime. In precisely the period when the Oxus Treasure came to light (but appar-

48. On this incredible gold masterpiece (weighing 169.2 grams), see Anatole Chabouillet, "L'Eucratidion," *Revue numismatique*, 1867: 382–415; Vincenzo Cubelli, "Moneta e ideologia monarchica: Il caso di Eucratide," *Rivista italiana di numismatica e scienze affini* 95 (1993): 251–59.

49. The details are supplied in an anonymous article: "A Coin of Eucratides," *American Journal of Numismatics* 14 (1879): 18–20.

50. Osmund Bopearachchi, *Monnaies gréco-bactriennes et indo-grecques: Catalogue raisonné* (Paris: Bibliothèque nationale, 1991), p. 202.

51. As related in "Coin of Eucratides," p. 19.

52. Gardner, *Coins of Greek and Scythic Kings*, p. 165.

ently unrelated to it), a Bactrian coin was found that proved that one of Eucratides' contemporaries—the rival king Agathocles—had paid homage to Alexander by putting the hero's portrait on silver coins.[53] In fact, Percy Gardner was the first to publish this specimen in 1880.[54] This medal, as he called it, probably made it seem much less strange that Alexander should appear on a concurrent issue of Eucratides'. All of these circumstances of discovery conspired to make Gardner believe too boldly in his unusual theory about the elephant battle depicted on the Franks medallion.[55] No one, however, has ever doubted the identification of the godlike figure standing on the other side—it must surely be Alexander the Great.

53. Frank Holt, "The So-Called Pedigree Coins of the Bactrian Greeks," in *Ancient Coins of the Graeco-Roman World*, ed. W. Heckel and R. Sullivan, pp. 69–91 (Waterloo, Ont.: Wilfrid Laurier University Press, 1984), esp. p. 70.

54. Percy Gardner, "Coin of Agathocles, with Types of Alexander," *Numismatic Chronicle* 20 (1880): 181–91. It was at that time unique, but at least a dozen examples of this particular issue are now known (four of which are almost certainly fakes).

55. The impact of Gardner's views may be seen, e.g., in Alfred von Sallet, *Munzen und Medaillen* (Berlin: W. Spemann, 1898), pp. 39–40. As late as 1965, A. N. Lahiri still found merit in Gardner's attribution of the "coin" to Eucratides or Heliocles: see Lahiri, *Corpus of Indo-Greek Coins* (Calcutta: Poddar Publications, 1965), pp. 37–38.

THREE

Picking a Fight

Percy Gardner, who considered himself "one of the prophets of Schlie-mann,"[1] missed the famous meeting of the Society of Antiquaries in 1877 in order to travel with Sir Charles Newton to examine Schliemann's finds in the Aegean world firsthand. Thus, while Schliemann lectured on these discoveries in London, Gardner was studying them in Greece. For Gard-ner, a future professor of archaeology at both Cambridge and Oxford, this "little expedition to Greece" had special meaning. His enthusiastic reports won him the gratitude of Schliemann, and through him the ac-quaintance of Gladstone. It also opened his eyes to the delights of dig-ging up what Darwin's worms had buried. On this journey, Gardner wit-nessed a German excavation at Olympia and wrote excitedly: "I realized something of the keen delight which excavators feel when there gradu-ally reveals itself to them in the ground the outline of a great work of art, which has been for ages hidden from the world and now comes back from the grave to take its place among historic monuments, and to reveal to the modern world something of the art and the history of a great by gone

1. Percy Gardner, *Autobiographica* (Oxford: Basil Blackwell, 1933), p. 59. Gardner published several obituaries of his friend Schliemann, including one in *Macmillan's Magazine*, April 1891, pp. 474–80.

[sic] civilization."[2] Charles Darwin—of whom Gardner wrote proudly as a fellow Cambridge man—was feeling something of this same joy at the excavation of Abinger in Surrey in 1877.[3]

Gardner surely ranks as a great scholar of ecumenical learning in an age of almost daily breakthroughs in archaeology and science. He acquainted himself with the leading authorities in all such fields, and he focused that enthusiastic illumination into the dark corners of numismatics. He wrote in his autobiography: "The scientific study of Greek coins in relation to history was then taking shape, and to watch its development year by year, and to be constantly working on its problems, and discussing them, not only with my colleagues, but with highly accomplished men in other countries, constituted an introduction to the world of learning and science which could hardly have been matched."[4]

And yet, on the question of the Franks medallion, Percy Gardner struggled mightily against a compelling connection between numismatics and history. When he associated the elephant battle on the Franks medallion with an invasion of nomads during the reign of Eucratides or his son, this line of argument required the total rejection of a more obvious historical attribution. Gardner admitted: "Looking for the first time at this extraordinary coin, or rather medal—for it is clearly a historical monument—everyone will be tempted to exclaim, 'Alexander and Porus!' "[5]

Resisting that temptation, Gardner picked another fight and thus turned his back on perhaps the most famous elephant battle in history—certainly the most celebrated involving the ancient Greeks and, espe-

2. Ibid., pp. 33–34; cf. David Traill, *Schliemann of Troy: Treasure and Deceit* (New York: St. Martin's Press, 1995), p. 166. Although a professor of archaeology at Cambridge and then Oxford, Gardner was obviously not himself a digger.

3. Gardner, *Autobiographica*, p. 11; see p. 36 for his view on "the Darwinian tendency in history."

4. Ibid., p. 26.

5. Percy Gardner, "New Greek Coins of Bactria and India," *Numismatic Chronicle* 7 (1887): 178.

cially, the army of Alexander the Great. Porus and his elephants were to the Greeks what Hannibal and his elephants became to the Romans: legendary symbols of an all but overwhelming alien power. Rajah Porus remains to this day a "great hero of the Panjab" who combined "instinct with Herculean vigour and patriotic fervor."[6] In comic books and movies across the Indian subcontinent, he has merited an enduring celebrity akin to Alexander's in the West. After all, the struggle between these epic figures has an inherently stirring quality, like that of the Homeric duel pitting Ajax against Hector.[7]

Porus ruled the Pauravas (hence his name), and as such he dominated the Punjab region between the rivers Hydaspes (modern Jhelum) and Acesines (modern Chenab).[8] His realm may once have been part of the Persian Empire, but even before Darius's defeat and death, the various Indian tribes had assumed local independence. We have no reliable evidence that Porus answered a summons to fight for Darius at Gaugamela, and he certainly refused to acknowledge Alexander's authority. In fact, Porus had embarked upon his own campaigns to conquer neighboring rajahs to the east and west. Those plans were interrupted in May of 326 B.C.E. by the advance of Alexander's large Macedonian army into the Indus valley. Against this force and Alexander's determination to reach the world's end, Porus had no chance but for two "home field" advantages. First, the Hydaspes River blocked Alexander's path. This considerable waterway had already begun to rise and broaden from the snowmelt of the Himalayas. Second, the seasonal weather also favored Porus, since the rains of the monsoon guaranteed that the Hydaspes would remain in flood for several months, and in the meantime, the

6. Buddha Prakash, *History of Poros* (Patiala: Punjabi University Press, 1967), p. 92.

7. *Iliad* 7.181–310, in which Ajax prevails but nonetheless honors his worthy opponent with suitable gifts.

8. Prakash, *Poros*, is very uncritical about the sources, for which see Helmut Berve, *Das Alexanderreich auf prosopographischer Grundlage* (Munich, 1926; reprint, Salem, N.H.: Ayer, 1988), vol. 2, no. 683.

monsoon would drench the demoralized Macedonian army if it stayed in camp.

Capitalizing upon these natural allies, Porus brought up his army to guard the riverbank, hoping no doubt that Alexander would forgo the risks of forcing a passage or of remaining idle until the rains abated in September. It seemed quite unlikely that the Macedonians could accomplish a contested crossing, especially given the celebrated range and accuracy of the Indian archers, the mobility of the Indian four-horse chariots and cavalry, and, of course, the resolute wall provided by the terrifying Indian war elephants.

Alexander met the challenge.[9] He established a base camp, either near modern Haranpur or Jhelum town, from whence he sent out reconnaissance parties, skirmishers, and diversionary columns. These kept Porus on edge and forced the Indians to respond to a relentless game of cat and mouse that divided their attentions and drained their energy. In time, Porus took these feints less seriously and relaxed his guard, confident that

9. For what follows, see Louis Dupree, "Einige Bemerkungen zur Schlacht am Jhelum (326 v. Chr.)," in *Aus dem Osten des Alexanderreiches: Völker und Kulturen zwischen Orient und Okzident: Iran, Afghanistian, Pakistan, Indien*, ed. Jakob Ozols and Volker Thewalt, pp. 51–56 (Cologne: DuMont, 1984); Rudolf Schubert, "Die Porusschlacht," *Rheinisches Museum für Philologie* 56 (1901): 543–62; Georg Veith, "Der Kavalleriekampf in der Schlacht am Hydaspes," *Klio* 8 (1908): 131–53; Aurel Stein, "The Site of Alexander's Passage of the Hydaspes and the Battle with Poros," *Geographical Journal* 80 (1932): 31–46; Georges Radet, "Alexandre et Porus: Le passage de l'Hydaspe," *Revue des études anciennes* 37 (1935): 349–56; C. Pearson, "Alexander, Porus and the Panjab," *Indian Antiquary* 34 (1905): 253–61; E. Cavaignac, "À propos de la bataille d'Alexandre contre Porus," *Journal asiatique* 203 (1923): 332–34; James Abbot, "Some Account of the Battle Field of Alexander and Porus," *Journal of the Asiatic Society of Bengal* 17 (1848): 619–33; id., "Addendum on the Battlefield of Alexander and Porus," *Journal of the Asiatic Society of Bengal* 18 (1849): 176–77; A. M. Devine, "The Battle of Hydaspes: A Tactical and Source-Critical Study," *Ancient World* 16 (1987): 91–113; Miroslaw Kulak, "Bitwa Aleksandra Wielkiego z Porosem nad Rzeka Hydaspes," *Meander* 43 (1988): 229–41; and J. R. Hamilton, "The Cavalry Battle at the Hydaspes," *Journal of Hellenic Studies* 76 (1956): 26–31.

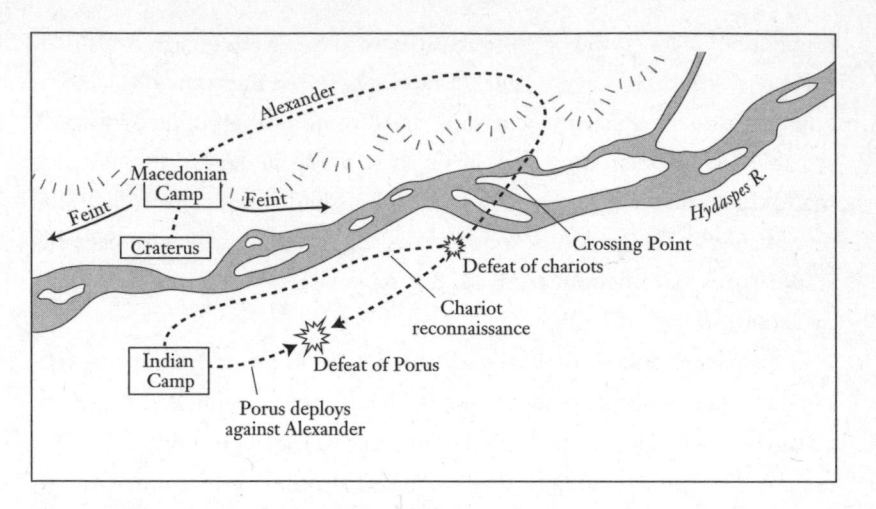

Map 3.   The battle of the Hydaspes River

rain and river would indeed hold back the enemy. All the while, Alexander secretly prepared a crossing point about seventeen miles upriver. Given the long monsoon, and the likelihood that other rajahs might reinforce Porus if the Macedonians delayed, Alexander pressed ahead.[10] Boats were assembled and hidden, a select attack force marshaled, and the timing set for an overnight operation to catch the Indians as much by surprise as possible.

During a particularly severe thunderstorm, Alexander led his turning force across the dangerous Hydaspes. The outcome of more than just a battle hung in the balance. Had fate sunk Alexander's own boat, he—and three future kings—might have perished in this bid to outflank Porus.[11] By dawn, however, about 15,000 Macedonians and allies, with at least 5,000

10. Porus till the end counted upon the arrival of Abisares, who ruled the territory of Kashmir, but this ally was either incapacitated by illness or unwilling to risk the war: Diodorus 17.87.2; Curtius 8.14.1.

11. Arrian 5.13.1. The future kings were Ptolemy (Egypt), Lysimachus (Thrace), and Seleucus (Syria). Also in this vessel was Perdiccas, Alexander's major (nonroyal) successor.

horses, had reached the opposite riverbank. They were met by an Indian force of chariots and cavalry, but Alexander defeated them and prepared to engage Porus's main army. The rajah thus found himself in dire straits. A sizeable Macedonian army still at the base camp under Craterus's command threatened to cross against him if he turned completely aside to intercept Alexander. Seeking a solid stretch of ground on which to make his stand, Porus identified Alexander as the main danger and deployed for battle accordingly.

The Macedonians naturally dreaded the elephants, which terrify horses unaccustomed to them. Alexander therefore launched a cavalry charge in a sweeping maneuver still unclear to us, but undoubtedly successful. The fighting became desperate and at times undisciplined due to the mud, rampaging elephants, and crowded lines of opposing infantry. The Macedonians, veterans of so many campaigns, prevailed and turned the struggle into a rout and then a slaughter. Fresh manpower, crossing eagerly from the base camp, finished the job. Porus himself, wounded and weak, fled on his elephant but could not escape. Nature had proved no match for Alexander's strategy and tactics. Endorsing D. G. Hogarth's opinion that this must "rank among the most brilliant operations of ancient warfare," J. F. C. "Boney" Fuller, a pioneer of modern tank warfare, called it the "most famous of Alexander's campaigns" and "his most skillfully fought battle." He likened the river crossing to Hannibal's maneuver at the Rhône in 218 B.C.E., suggesting that Alexander provided the model for Hannibal's success.[12] Other grand comparisons have been suggested, including the crossings of the English Channel by William the Conqueror in 1066 and the Allied invasion of Normandy in 1944.[13]

12. J. F. C. Fuller, *The Generalship of Alexander the Great* (New Brunswick, N.J.: Rutgers University Press, 1960; reprint, New York: Da Capo Press, 1989), pp. 180, 294; 186 n. 1.

13. Norman invasion: Fuller, *Generalship*, p. 188; Allied invasion: A. R. Burn, *Alexander the Great and the Hellenistic World*, 2d ed. (New York: Collier Books, 1962), p. 153. Arther Ferrill notes a comparison with Wolfe's Quebec campaign of 1759 in "Alexander in India," *Military History Quarterly* 1 (1988): 80. Devine,

What followed on the opposite bank of the Hydaspes was no less than "Alexander's most bloody and complete victory, and designedly so."[14]

It would be natural, therefore, for anyone inspecting the medallion for the first time to exclaim, "Alexander and Porus!" After all, the godlike figure of the Macedonian king on one side might easily correspond to the heroic Macedonian horseman on the other, engaged in personal combat with his noble adversary on the elephant. But Gardner could not escape the circumstantial evidence of the Oxus Treasure, so he left it to others to accept the manifest connection between the two sides of the medallion. The first to do so was Barclay Vincent Head, a close friend of Percy Gardner's, an active researcher and writer, and Keeper of Coins and Medals at the British Museum when the nineteenth century gave way to the twentieth. In 1887, the year of Gardner's study of the medallion, Head published his *Historia Numorum* ("History of Coins"), one of the standard reference works in Greek numismatics, in which he surveyed nearly a thousand years of Greek history and coinage from Spain to Syria, inland to Bactria and India, then back again to Egypt and westward to Mauretania. The book was an encyclopedic sketch that remains indispensable today "of nearly every city, king, or dynast, known to have struck coins throughout the length and breadth of the ancient world."[15] The first edition did not, however, mention the Franks medallion.

In 1906, the year of his retirement from the British Museum, Head published an important paper that finally touched upon the subject of the mysterious elephant medallion in his care.[16] He reported that:

"Battle of the Hydaspes," pp. 96–97, draws attention to Napoleon's campaign across the Danube in 1809.

14. N. G. L. Hammond, *Alexander the Great: King, Commander and Statesman* (Park Ridge, N.J.: Noyes Press, 1980), p. 210.

15. Barclay V. Head, *Historia Numorum* (1887), expanded 2d ed. (1911; reprint, London: Spink & Son, 1963), p. xix.

16. Barclay V. Head, "The Earliest Graeco-Bactrian and Graeco-Indian Coins," *Numismatic Chronicle* 6 (1906): 1–16; this article was later reprinted as a pamphlet by Ares Publishers in Chicago.

After a careful study of the fabric [i.e., appearance] of the famous unique dekadrachm, showing on one side a Macedonian horseman driving before him a retreating elephant with its two riders, and on the other side a standing figure of Alexander holding a thunderbolt and wearing the *Persian* helmet . . . I have come to the conclusion that it belongs to Alexander's own time, and that it records the historical event of his invasion of the Punjab in 326 B.C., and that it was probably intended for a medal for presentation to Macedonian officers rather than for use as current money. I am convinced that Professor P. Gardner was mistaken in assigning this large coin or medal to so late a period as the reign of Eucratides (second century B.C.).[17]

This reattribution to the reign of Alexander marked a significant breakthrough in the study of this artifact. Finally, after twenty-six years, the false *chronological* connection between the manufacture of the medallion and the burial of the Oxus Treasure had been broken. Later discoveries would prove Head absolutely right on this point, and we must admire his clarity of thought all the more given the evidence available at the time. But just five years later, Head was on the wrong trail again.

In the second edition of his *Historia Numorum*, Head proposed a new interpretation of the battle scene (pp. 832–33). He no longer believed that the horseman was spearing the warrior on the back of the elephant; instead, he proposed that the rearmost elephant rider was jabbing his lance at the approaching horseman. This "essential point" allowed Head to do what many others would also attempt with varying degrees of success, namely, match the scene on the "medal" to specific statements in the surviving accounts of Alexander's reign. When Head could not find a source describing what he had originally seen on the "medal" (the horseman wielding the spear), he simply changed his mind about the image in order to accommodate a passage in Arrian that would suffice *if* the elephant rider were attacking the pursuing horseman, and *if* this horseman were someone other than Alexander. By reversing the action and chang-

17. Ibid., pp. 8–9.

ing one of the combatants, Head finally matched a text with the "medal" to his satisfaction:

> The details of the type correspond so closely with the account, as handed down by Arrian (v.xviii.9–11) of the retreat on his elephant of the wounded king Porus, after his defeat at the Hydaspes, and of his pursuit on horseback by Prince Taxiles, that I can hardly hesitate to regard this piece as a medal struck in the name of Alexander, and perhaps by Taxiles himself at his capital city Taxila, in commemoration of that episode.[18]

Taxiles, the regnal name of a prince probably known as Omphis or Ambhi before he assumed the throne, ruled the territory between the Indus River on the west and the Hydaspes River on the east. As Porus's traditional enemy, Taxiles readily became Alexander's vassal and provided food, entertainments, and lavish gifts to the invading Macedonian army. To Alexander himself, Taxiles reportedly gave 3,000 oxen and 10,000 sheep to be sacrificed before the battle with Porus. Alexander also received 200 talents (5.7 tons) of silver, thirty elephants, and 700 cavalry from Taxiles' army.[19] The Vulgate tradition claims that Taxiles presented Alexander with an additional eighty talents (2.28 tons) of coined money at a feast in Taxila where gold crowns were bestowed by the Indians upon the Macedonian king and his companions.[20] Clearly, Taxiles desperately wanted to please the invaders and hence to profit from their war against his enemy Porus across the Hydaspes.

When, later in that war, Porus had retreated from the battlefield, Arrian reports the incident cited by Head:

18. Head, *Historia Numorum*, p. 833. The citation of Arrian, to be discussed below, should read 5.18.6–7.

19. Arrian 5.3.5–6.

20. Curtius 8.12.15. Not to be outdone in lavish generosity, Alexander in turn gave Taxiles back his money plus another *thousand* talents (28.4 tons): Curtius 8.12.16–17; Plutarch *Alexander* 59.5; Strabo 15.1.28. These large sums of coinage will play a part in subsequent theories about the elephant medallion.

Alexander, observing that Porus played a significant and courageous role in the battle, desired to spare him. First, he sent the Indian Taxiles to Porus. Riding up as close to Porus' elephant as he thought safe, Taxiles ordered Porus to stop the beast, since escape was futile, and to listen to Alexander's message. But Porus, seeing this man Taxiles as an old enemy, turned his elephant and charged in order to spear him. If Taxiles had not turned his horse away in time, Porus might have slain him.[21]

This perfectly matched the scene on the medallion, Head argued. But it does not, in my opinion, because here my own translation of the Greek differs from Head's on a critical point. Like most classicists, I understand the passage to say that Porus turned his elephant and attacked Taxiles, which is not at all what we see on the medallion, where the elephant continues to flee from the approaching horseman. Head, on the other hand, construed the passage to mean that Porus turned *himself* around on the elephant, and that this "turning or twisting round of Porus on his elephant in order to spear his enemy—ἐπιστρέφασ ἀνήγετο ὡς ἀκοντίοων—is rendered to the life on this remarkable medallion."[22]

This sort of disagreement over the proper translation of a few ancient words characterizes much of classical scholarship, and it tends to annoy the nonspecialist. But these are not inconsequential trifles. As Darwin wrote in the Introduction to his study of worms: "The subject may appear an insignificant one, but we shall see that it possesses some interest; and the maxim 'de minimis lex non curat,' does not apply to science."[23] Nor does this phrase ("The law does not concern itself with trifles") apply to history, archaeology, or numismatics. Much hung in the balance,

21. Arrian 5.18.6–7. When Taxiles failed in his mission, Alexander sent another Indian, named Meroes, who, as an old friend of Porus's, finally succeeded.

22. Head, *Historia Numorum*, p. 833.

23. Charles Darwin, *The Formation of Vegetable Mould, through the Action of Worms, with Observations on Their Habits* (London: Murray, 1881; reprint, New York: D. Appleton, 1896), p. 2.

and Head's own interpretation gained wide acceptance in prominent places.[24] Thus, we must—as responsible scholars—review his handling of this evidence.

What, then, did Arrian mean when he used the Greek word ἐπιστρέφασ to describe Porus's actions? Just two sentences earlier (5.18.5), Arrian used this very word unambiguously to state that Porus *wheeled his elephant around* in order to flee. It was clearly this same action that occurred minutes later when Porus turned back around to charge at Taxiles. In cases of this sort, it also helps to survey how other ancient authors employed this same verb to describe episodes in battle. For instance, Diodorus chose just this word to describe how Alexander turned his horse to meet an attack, and then charged at the enemy.[25] In another instance, we read that a commander was being pursued by hostile forces, so he wheeled around (ἐπιστρέφασ) and attacked, driving away the enemy with a sudden charge.[26] Diodorus, Plutarch, and the soldier and writer Xenophon all used this same Greek verb to narrate the process by which a retreating horseman, army, or fleet stops, turns about, and counterattacks pursuers—precisely the action that I understand Arrian to mean when Porus turned and charged at Taxiles.[27] Fleeing armies and fleets do not drive away their pursuers by firing back as they continue in flight; they wheel around and counterattack. This very important trifle stands squarely against Head's special interpretation of Arrian's text, and negates its correspondence to the scene on the medallion.

24. For the impact of Head's theory, see as a notable example E. R. Bevan, "Alexander the Great," in *The Cambridge History of India*, ed. E. J. Rapson, vol. 1 (Cambridge, 1922; reprint, Delhi: S. Chand, 1962), p. 329. In the same volume, however, Dr. George McDonald doubted whether Taxila could be the mint city given the find spot at Khullum (p. 349).

25. Diodorus 17.20.3, describing the battle of the Granicus River (334 B.C.E.).

26. Diodorus 16.68.3, recounting an action in Sicily (345 B.C.E.).

27. Diodorus 12.70.3; Plutarch *Aristides* 14.4; Xenophon *Hellenica* 6.4.9. This verb is also used to describe ships swinging around to drive at the enemy in naval battles: see, e.g., Diodorus 13.77.5 and 13.50.3.

To be sure, the existing accounts of Porus's surrender are quite at odds given the overall state of our sources. Curtius, for example, claims that Porus fought conspicuously until loss of blood from nine wounds compelled him to flee. In this account, Alexander pursued him, but his injured horse (the famous Bucephalus) collapsed and died. On a fresh mount, Alexander renewed his chase of Porus's elephant. Meanwhile, Taxiles' *brother* had been dispatched to advise Porus to surrender. When Porus heard the man's voice, he shouted, "I recognize the brother of Taxiles, that traitor to his crown and country." Porus thereupon hurled his last spear, which struck Taxiles' brother with such force that it passed clean through his chest. Then Porus fled again at greater speed, until his wounded elephant began to falter. After another stand to fight, Porus finally began to slip from the beast—whereupon his mahout (elephant handler) ordered the elephant to kneel for an easier dismount. Since all of the other elephants were trained to follow the lead of the rajah's own, the entire fighting corps likewise knelt and was captured by the Macedonians. Then followed the chivalrous meeting of the rival commanders where Porus asked to be treated "like a king" and was forthwith restored to power by an obliging Alexander.[28]

Compared to Arrian, this account replaces Taxiles with his brother, who is actually killed by Porus. Head might as easily have surmised that *this* is the episode pictured on the medallion—Porus slaying the advancing horseman with his last spear, a moment that might be commemorated by Taxiles in honor of his fallen sibling. If we seek a match between text and medallion to solve the mystery, will *any* such text suffice? How do we choose between these competing histories? After all, these extant accounts are far removed from the actual event; indeed, our only firsthand source is the medallion itself, until we can isolate a version of the surrender clearly taken from a reliable contemporary author.

When Curtius so casually quotes verbatim what Porus shouted to Taxiles' brother before killing him, we must ask: who could be the ulti-

28. Curtius 8.14.32–44.

mate source for this information? Did Porus later report this, or did Curtius make it up? To what extent might the whole account be sensationalized? If we decide that Curtius's history appears tainted by melodrama, does that entitle us to trust Arrian instead? The choice of truths is not nearly so simple. We have an instructive anecdote about this problem from the writings of Lucian of Samosata, a witty author of the second century c.e. In his treatise *How to Write History*, Lucian says that while sailing down the Hydaspes River a few months after this battle, Alexander was entertained by Aristobulus, who read aloud from the history he was writing.[29] When Aristobulus read his passage describing the battle, which included a personal duel between Alexander and Porus, the king suddenly snatched the manuscript and tossed it into the river, saying angrily, "You should be thrown overboard as well, Aristobulus, for composing such duels for me to fight and having me kill an elephant with a single spear-thrust."

This passage has (as we shall see) been discussed a great deal in studies of the Franks medallion. For the moment, however, we need only to see it as a reminder of how our eyewitness historians (Aristobulus was one of Arrian's main sources) may themselves have exaggerated and distorted what really happened at the Hydaspes for dramatic effect. Little wonder, then, that we end up with contradictory versions among our extant sources, since every author in the chain of information—beginning with the firsthand sources—could warp the story to heroize or villainize whomever he chose. Within a basic, "true" narrative framework, writers found ample room to express their own ideas about what might have been said or thought, what else might have occurred, who else might have been involved in the action, and so forth. We dare not presume that any one of these accounts is literally true, much less all of them, any more than we can consider the medallion (our only surviving firsthand evidence) to be a snapshot of some actual moment in history. One major alternative against which Head did not provide is that texts and medallion

29. Lucian *Quomodo historia conscribenda sit* 12.

may all be propaganda, symbolism, sensationalism, or even myth, in various and sometimes incongruous forms. Should we ever find a match between ancient texts and the medallion, we may have discovered not—in Head's words (p. 833)—the first numismatic object "to represent pictorially a particular contemporaneous event," but rather a common step in the deliberate distortion of that event for some purpose other than historical veracity.

A number of "trifles" therefore oppose themselves to Head's interesting theories about the fight portrayed on the elephant commemorative. There were, however, no real objections at the time to his proposals—not even to the curious notion that Taxiles would choose to commemorate the very moment in the battle that caused him to flee like a coward, glorifying Porus at his own expense. Indeed, Taxiles cannot have been very happy about the whole affair. His lavish investment as Alexander's ally paid off poorly compared to Porus's reward for being Alexander's enemy. According to Curtius (9.3.22), tensions between the two Indians remained high in spite of a marriage alliance forced upon them after the battle. Still, to Head's enduring credit, he correctly placed the medallion in the time of Alexander's reign and, on the key question of who wielded the spear, wisely admitted (p. 833): "We must wait for the discovery of a better-preserved specimen for a final decision as to which description is correct." In 1914, an ominous year in world history, Head died without ever seeing a second example of the medallion. Not until 1926 did fresh evidence finally appear.

The origins of the second known medallion remain even more obscure than those of the first. Purchased by special subvention for the British Museum, this specimen (Appendix A, E/A 2) apparently came from somewhere in Iran.[30] The honor of publishing the medallion fell to Sir George Francis Hill, soon after his election to Franks's noble old

---

30. On the find spot, see R. B. Whitehead, "The Eastern Satrap Sophytes," *Numismatic Chronicle*, 6th ser., 3 (1943): 70 n. 21.

gathering, the Society of Antiquaries in London.[31] Hill called attention to some notable differences between this and the earlier specimen (see plates 2 and 3).[32] The new example weighed 2.54 grams less, a deficiency explained by Hill as "no doubt chiefly due to wear."[33] On the battle scene, the Greek letter *xi* (Ξ) appears clearly in the field (open area) above the horse. The forward rider on the elephant stands out more clearly, and it can be observed that he holds two reserve spears (?) in his left hand. Unlike Head, Hill had no doubt that the horseman holds the lance and is striking a blow at the Indian on the back of the elephant.[34] He felt equally certain that the horseman must be Alexander rather than Taxiles or someone else. This assurance rested in part on the fact that the figure on horseback wears the same headdress as the "deified" Alexander standing on the other side. Indeed, on this side of the new "coin," the king's regalia are preserved in much better detail, showing "that he wears a helmet combining the Greek crest with the Persian Kyrbasia, and bearing tall upright plumes beside the crest."[35] Hill took this as proof that Alexander, when he had conquered the Persian Empire, combined Greek and Persian headgear in this distinctive new way, a notion that would enjoy a long run in later commentaries.[36] Even more dramatically, the new

31. On February 4: Joan Evans, *A History of the Society of Antiquaries* (Oxford: Oxford University Press, 1956), p. 396.

32. Sir George Francis Hill, "Decadrachm Commemorating Alexander's Indian Campaign," *British Museum Quarterly* 1 (1926–27): 36–37, and "Greek Coins Acquired by the British Museum," *Numismatic Chronicle*, 5th ser., 7 (1927): 204–6.

33. Hill, "Decadrachm," p. 37.

34. In fact, even before this new specimen came to light, Hill thought the first medallion showed plainly enough that the horseman couches the lance against the Indian (*contra* Head): *Catalogue of Greek Coins in the British Museum: Arabia, Mesopotamia, Persia* (London: British Museum Press, 1922), p. 191.

35. Hill, "Greek Coins," p. 205.

36. E.g., Eduard Neuffer, "Das Kostüm Alexanders des Grossen" (diss., Giessen, 1929), pp. 29 and 37; see also chapter 4 below.

specimen revealed the presence of a second figure with the king. Flying above Alexander's head, the goddess Victory (Nike) could finally be seen reaching out to place a wreath upon the conqueror's helmet.

Manufactured slightly off center, the first medallion had concealed from view these very significant clues. In numismatics, surprises of this type frequently arise and compel the scholar to adjust all earlier conjectures. If it could now be proven that the medallions pictured Alexander on horseback, attacking Porus at the Hydaspes, then Head's analysis involving Taxiles and Arrian's text must be abandoned. Hill, of course, still faced the problem that no ancient accounts seem to portray exactly the same engagement as found on the medallions. To this he replied: "the artist instructed to commemorate Alexander's victory could hardly, in the space at his command, have suggested it otherwise."[37] Thus, the representation was deemed symbolic rather than precisely true to life.

It is always instructive, as Hill intimates, to consider the unseen processes that have shaped our observable evidence. Exactly *how* did the medallions come into existence? We can only infer the stages of manufacture based upon the appearance of the artifacts themselves, along with information drawn from related cases. Modern minting methods rely heavily upon machines, but ancient coins and medals were "mass-produced" by hand. As Hill himself reconstructed the process in one of his numismatic books,[38] a pre-weighed piece of metal (the blank, or planchet) must be mashed between two engraved dies (obverse and reverse) in order to impress the chosen designs upon the resulting coin or medal. To do so, a die cutter, or die sinker, had first to engrave the necessary dies. Using basic tools such as awls and tiny chisels, this person dug out the design for the coin or medal from the prepared surface of a hardened die. This had to be done within the confined space of the object's chosen denomination: a circle with a diameter of about 35 mm

37. Hill, "Decadrachm," p. 37.

38. Sir George Francis Hill, *Ancient Greek and Roman Coins: A Handbook* (London, 1899; reprint, Chicago: Argonaut, 1964), pp. 143–60.

(about 1.4 inch) for a decadrachm, 26 mm (about 1 inch) for a tetradrachm, and 16 mm (about 0.6 inch) for a drachm. Furthermore, to produce a coin or medal with raised features (high relief) and correct orientation, everything had to be executed backwards, or in mirror image, on the die: right had to be engraved left, letters and such backwards, and the higher the relief of a desired shape, the lower it had to be cut into the die. The negative-image die stamped out a positive-image coin or medal.

This tedious commission had to be performed in turn for each die, obverse and reverse. In the case of the medallions, the artist had to carve out the battle scene with the elephant and horse moving to the left on the die. The elephant could stand only 14 mm (0.55 of an inch) high, and the details of the horse's trappings and the warriors' faces had to be much smaller still. Likewise, for the other die, the standing king had to be depicted in tight precision with ornately plumed and crested helmet, flowing cape, dangling sword, and jagged thunderbolt; Alexander's face is clearly depicted as youthful and beardless, staring to the right on the die. Above, the goddess Victory had to fit into the scene, crowning the conqueror. Quite unlike most ancient coins and medals, there are no words on either die to trip up the artist.[39] The single letter *xi* (Ξ) on the obverse posed no problem, since it could not be accidentally engraved backwards. On the reverse, however, the die cutter had to cut a two- or three-letter monogram. Head read this as BA, meaning perhaps *B*asileus (king) *A*lexander. Hill saw BAB, which he understood to designate the mint *Bab*ylon (see fig. 3). Gardner had argued much earlier that the trace of the second B after the A might be a mistake that the engraver had tried to correct with a reverted B *before* the A. We cannot be sure why this would matter to the die cutter, since Greek coin monograms were often

39. On the challenges of engraving coin inscriptions, see Frank Holt, "Mimesis in Metal: The Fate of Greek Culture on Bactrian Coins," in *The Eye Expanded: Life and the Arts in Greco-Roman Antiquity*, ed. Frances B. Titchener and Richard F. Moorton, Jr., pp. 93–104 (Berkeley: University of California Press, 1999).

Figure 3. The Greek
monogram (enlarged)
as reported by G. F.
Hill.

designed with letters facing right or left (or even upside down). The
point is, given the confusing way that letters had to be engraved backwards, it remains possible that part of the monogram represents the ves-
tiges of an initial error made by the die cutter. Various kinds of correc-
tions in the preparation of a die can be documented in other ancient
mintages. For example, on the large gold medallion of Eucratides mentioned in chapter 2, it can be observed that the Greek inscription was initially set in one fashion but then partially erased and engraved differ-
ently.[40] As a useful exercise, curious readers might trace the circular
outline of a quarter, cent, or dime, and then draw there the coin's design
in mirror image along with its various retrograde inscriptions. This paper
and pen simulation is, even so, much less demanding than engraving
everything into hardened metal.

In this complex fashion, two dies were prepared. One (the obverse)
was set into an anvil, the other into a punch. A prepared planchet was
placed upon the anvil and its die. Next, a workman gripped the punch
(reverse die), positioned it on top of the planchet, and with his other hand
brought down a solid blow against the punch with a hammer or mallet.
Numismatists thus speak of coins and medals being "struck." The hand-

40. Anatole Chabouillet, "L'Eucratidion," *Revue numismatique,* 1867: 385–87.

made result leaves behind many useful hints about the unseen processes of manufacture. Sometimes, for example, several blows had to be struck, each leaving a ghostly impression as the planchet mashed out with each successive compression. We can determine whether any care was taken to align the dies in consistent fashion, either with the naked eye or by means of notched or hinged dies. Experts note the relative positioning of the dies using arrows or clock-face numbers. If both sides of a coin or medal (when spun on a vertical axis) have their designs right side up, then we describe the die alignment as ↑↑, or 12:00. If the reverse die were inverted relative to the obverse, then the die axis is ↑↓, or 6:00. If the alignment remains constant, then the dies were "fixed." Thus, current U.S. coinage has a fixed die axis of 6:00 (↑↓). The first-known elephant medallion had a 5:00 axis (↑↘), the second, a 12:00 axis (↑↑). These two examples suggest little concern for consistent mintage: the punch was simply held in whatever orientation came to hand. We can also observe that the manufacturers of these commemoratives took few pains to position the planchets carefully between the dies. That is why, for example, so much of the reverse design failed to be transferred onto the first medallion (Appendix A, E/A 1). Nor were the blows struck evenly, since parts of the design appear fainter than others. These facts may prove decisive when deciding, for example, whether these medallions could be the products of certain established mints.

A few other observations bear mentioning. Hill, and some later investigators, believed that these medallions were "overstrikes"—that is, struck using older coins or medals as the planchets.[41] This process sometimes leaves faint traces of the original design (the undertype) visible on the second (the overtype). This becomes especially important if the undertype can be identified and dated, thus establishing the earliest time after which the overtype had to be made. And finally, die linkage also provides chronological clues. When employed to strike many coins or

41. Hill, "Greek Coins," p. 205.

medals, dies wore out or broke and had to be replaced. Since these dies were cut by hand, each one was as distinctive as a fingerprint. Thus, it is often possible to identify among surviving samples of the same types of coins or medals those that were made from the very same dies—such coins or medals are said to be "die-linked." For example, the first and second specimens of the elephant medallion were both struck from the same obverse die, but not from the same reverse die. Enough disparities exist in the reverse designs (e.g., how the sword crosses the shaft of the upright spear or scepter) to show that, while nearly identical, the reverses were not struck from the same die.

Numismatists have determined that, in general, ancient reverse dies had to be replaced more frequently than obverse dies—probably because the latter were securely anchored and protected in the anvil, while the former suffered greater stresses from the hammer and punch. A characteristic pattern resulted: coins or medals were struck using obverse die Obv1 and reverse die RevA until RevA wore out and was replaced with RevB; there followed a series of coins or medals using dies Obv1 and RevB until RevB wore out and die RevC was introduced, producing coins or medals from dies Obv1 and RevC. When Obv1 was finally replaced by Obv2, artifacts with Obv2 and RevC resulted. This die linkage exhibits a telltale pattern: Obv1/RevA → Obv1/RevB → Obv1/RevC → Obv2/RevC → Obv2/RevD, and so on. If enough specimens of this mintage survive, experts can place any given coin or medal into its proper spot in the sequence. As a general rule, the more closely a sample is die-linked, the smaller the number of coins or medals produced was.

Numismatists have therefore learned to trace the size and sequence of a mintage based upon die linkage. With but one specimen, this cannot be done. With two examples, such work can just begin. What investigators sorely need are additional finds, the more the better. For the elephant medallions, however, additional examples were painfully slow to appear. In 1937, numismatists reported that two additional specimens of

the elephant-battle type had been found at Niffer (ancient Nippur) in Mesopotamia.[42] This promising discovery, allegedly made around 1890 at the time of Schliemann's death, proved to be a complete misunderstanding of the material unearthed.[43] There were no new medallions . . . yet.

42. Sydney Noe, *A Bibliography of Greek Coin Hoards,* 2d ed. (New York: American Numismatic Society, 1937), p. 195 (no. 741, reported by E. S. G. Robinson).

43. Margaret Thompson et al., eds., *An Inventory of Greek Coin Hoards* (New York: American Numismatic Society, 1973), p. 248 (no. 1750). The coins were actually decadrachms of Alexander's regular type (Herakles/Zeus), not elephant medallions.

Plate 1. The Alexander Mosaic from Pompeii, showing Alexander in battle against Darius. © Copyright Alinari/Art Resource, N.Y.

Plate 2. The Franks Medallion (E/A 1). © Copyright The British Museum.

Plate 3. The 1926 British Museum specimen (E/A 2).
© Copyright The British Museum.

Plate 4. The American Numismatic Society specimen (E/A 3).
Courtesy of The American Numismatic Society, New York.

Plate 5. The Copenhagen specimen (E/A 4). Courtesy of The
National Museum, Denmark.

Plate 6. An American Numismatic Society tetradrachm (E/B 1). Courtesy of The American Numismatic Society, New York.

Plate 7. A Bank Leu tetradrachm (E/B 2). Courtesy of Leu Numismatics, Zurich, Switzerland.

Plate 8. A British Museum tetradrachm (E/B 3). © Copyright The British Museum.

Plate 9. A tetradrachm formerly in the Wahler collection
(E/B 5). Courtesy of Frank L. Kovacs.

Plate 10. An American Numismatic Society tetradrachm
(E/B 9). Courtesy of The American Numismatic Society,
New York.

Plate 11. A Bank Leu tetradrachm, now in the Bibliothèque
Nationale (E/C 1). Courtesy of Leu Numismatics, Zurich,
Switzerland.

Plate 12. An American Numismatic Society tetradrachm (E/C 3). Courtesy of The American Numismatic Society, New York.

Plate 13. A black cabinet forgery (F 9). Courtesy of Frank L. Kovacs.

Plate 14. An American Numismatic Society gold aureus of Marcus Aurelius. Courtesy of The American Numismatic Society, New York.

FOUR

Whose Pachyderm,
Whole or Halved?

The mystery of the elephant medallions consumed the energies of more and more investigations during the tumultuous twentieth century. At mid-century, the matter was addressed at an international numismatic congress held in Munich. D. E. Stauffer expressed the opinion that the medallions had been minted at Babylon in 324 B.C.E. and probably bore the designs of Alexander's master gem-engraver, Pyrgoteles.[1] Stauffer pressed further, identifying an expansive range of topics for which he considered the medallions a significant primary source; these included Alexander's political ideology, mythology, apotheosis, policy of fusion, military organization, war aims, portraiture, religion, and so on. This was, he said, the extraordinary legacy of the world's first "historical coin."[2]

Stauffer expanded the inquiry into as many areas as he could imagine, but others remained stuck on certain trains of thought. For example, Dr. J. N. Banerji of Calcutta University tried again in 1950 to match the battle scene to a specific passage in ancient literature. Unlike Head, he

1. D. E. Stauffer, "Die Londoner Dekadrachme von 324 und die Indeen-politik Alexanders," *Jahrbuch für Numismatik und Geldgeschichte* 2 (1950–51): 132.

2. Ibid.: "Sie ist die erste 'historische' Münze der Antike" (p. 132), referring to the battle scene on the obverse.

adopted Curtius's description of Porus's surrender, because it mentions that Alexander had in some fashion pursued the enemy rajah. That brief "historical" moment, before the collapse of Alexander's horse, Banerji thought, must be the view shown on the medallion. He presumed, without any real justification, that the die cutter must have followed *one* of the written versions, and Banerji selected Curtius as the most likely.[3] But the choice insisted upon by Banerji was a false one and only served to hamper the case. He had not provided against the possibility that the medallion might stand on its own merits as an independent source. The design may unavoidably resemble some general features of the recorded battle (by picturing elephants and cavalry) but do so symbolically, or with emphasis upon something not commensurate with its treatment in the texts.

In the early days of Schliemann's work at Troy and Mycenae, it had been the fashion of archaeologists to subordinate every monument and artifact to privileged texts, whether Homeric, biblical, or classical. Schliemann set out to find objects that might illustrate events, such as the Trojan War, in the historical reality of which he already firmly believed. Nothing he excavated was therefore treated as independent evidence; it all derived its identity and value from the poetry of Homer and the plays of Greek dramatists: Schliemann found *Priam*'s treasure, the tomb of *Clytemnestra*, the mask of *Agamemnon*, and so on. But modern archaeologists know that it is a mistake to think of artifacts merely as convenient illustrations of texts, and numismatists should be similarly concerned about limiting their inquiries in an antiquarian fashion. Those who would place a picture of the medallion's obverse next to a quotation from Curtius (or Arrian) as a corroborative, factual depiction would not dream of using the medallion's reverse for this same purpose. Few would accept the "historical moment" shown there, with Alexander clutching an actual bolt of lightning while a winged goddess hovers above his head.

In 1959, a third medallion finally came into public view (see plate 4).

3. J. N. Banerji, "The Obverse Device of Some Decadrachms with Alexandrian Association," *Journal of the Numismatic Society of India* 12 (1950): 118–20.

Of uncertain provenience, it entered the collection of the American Numismatic Society in New York as a gift from the noted collector Burton Y. Berry (Appendix A, E/A 3). Berry had lived for many years in the Middle East, where he caught the collecting bug in 1935.[4] His first numismatic purchase, a tetradrachm of Alexander the Great, was followed by hundreds of other valuable coins found in shops across Greece, Turkey, Italy, Egypt, Lebanon, and neighboring countries. In 1958, ready to relinquish the hobby, Berry generously allowed the American Numismatic Society to select any rare coins it desired from his collection for its museum. Apparently, this third-known example of the elephant medallion was among the more than 1,500 specimens chosen. This new medallic coin is die-linked by obverse and reverse to the 1926 British Museum specimen, and thus by obverse alone to the Franks medallion. The American Numismatic Society specimen weighs just 38.71 grams, and has a die axis of 11:00 (↑↖). Parts of the designs do not fit on the planchet used. This new piece therefore conforms to the patterns already noted for the production of these medallions: they were poorly hammered on planchets with erratic weights and unfixed die axes, and it seems that the reverse dies indeed wore out more frequently than the obverse.

With three medallions available for scrutiny (two in London, one in New York), scholars pressed ahead energetically with their various investigations. Following Stauffer's lead, experts tried to fit this evidence into the larger picture of Alexander's life. In the early 1960s, various experts took pains to analyze the god-like image of Alexander on the medallions in relation to similar depictions in other media, drawing broad conclusions from the exercise. In 1961, for example, Ernst Kantorowicz included the medallions in his study of "Gods in Uniform"; a

---

4. Berry recounted his collecting career in a privately published book, *A Numismatic Biography* (Lucerne: C. J. Bucher, 1971), which curiously makes no mention of the elephant decadrachm. The coin is inventoried at the American Numismatic Society as 1959–254–86. Berry dispersed the remainder of his collection as gifts to Indiana University, the Art Institute of Chicago, and various individuals.

year later, Wilhelm Kaiser studied the king's regalia as represented on the medallions, with particular comparisons to the famous mosaic at Pompeii showing Alexander on horseback battling the Persian king Darius, and to the ancient Neisos gem engraved with a nude Alexander clutching a thunderbolt in a pose reminiscent of the medallion's reverse.[5] Agreement still was rare. Whereas Kantorowicz described the king's helmet as Persian, Kaiser concluded that it was neither Persian nor a combination of Greek and Persian styles, as many had assumed, but rather was plainly Homeric.

In a subsequent study of "The Religiosity of Alexander" by Lowell Edmunds of Harvard University, Kaiser's view took root.[6] Edmunds documented Alexander's passionate belief in mythical heroes and his growing desire, on the eve of the Indian campaign, to become a hero-god himself. A deeply religious man, Alexander claimed descent from Hercules and Achilles. The king's emulation of such figures did not arise from Machiavellian deceit or dreamy romanticism; Edmunds perceived in the sources, literary and numismatic, a sincere effort by Alexander to reenact mythology as a living hero-god. In Kaiser's description of Alexander's helmet as "Homeric," Edmunds found some support for his idea that the king wished to be seen as heroic, Achillean, and dynamically engaged in epic face-to-face combat with his foes.[7]

Meanwhile in India, the worldwide endeavor to understand the medallions took a curious turn. After Banerji's article appeared in 1950, other scholars on the subcontinent simply ignored the evidence or argued it away. As late as 1967, a book by Buddha Prakash devoted to a painstaking investigation of the scant surviving sources for Porus's reign (in particular, his battle against Alexander) took no notice whatever of the

5. Ernst Kantorowicz, "Gods in Uniform," *Proceedings of the American Philosophical Society* 105 (1961): 368–93, esp. p. 373; Wilhelm Kaiser, "Ein Meister der Glyptik aus dem Umkreis Alexanders des Grossen," *Jahrbuch des Deutschen Archaeologischen Instituts* 77 (1962): 227–39.

6. Published in *Greek, Roman and Byzantine Studies* 12 (1971): 363–91.

7. Ibid., p. 373.

medallic coins.[8] A few years later, a rather nationalistic attempt was made to remove the medallions altogether from Indian history. The well-known numismatic expert Deena Pandey presented this case to the *Journal of the Numismatic Society of India* in 1971.[9] In its pages, Pandey argued that the medallions must commemorate Alexander's defeat of the Persian King Darius at Gaugamela, not Porus at the Hydaspes River.

The battle of Gaugamela in October 331 B.C.E. was the third and final fray between Alexander and the imperial forces of Persia. Darius, trying hard not to repeat his earlier mistakes, prepared the battlefield and marshaled on it a force as much as five times larger than his opponent's.[10] In front of his lines, the Persian king stationed 200 special chariots equipped with scythed wheels, and a small screen of fifteen elephants.[11] The chariots opened the engagement with a wild and wholly ineffective charge into the unfazed ranks of Alexander's army; the elephants, if they even stayed for the actual fighting, are not mentioned again in our sources except as captives at the end of the battle.[12] As the engagement developed in the choking dust of Gaugamela, Darius tried but failed to encircle the right wing of the Macedonian army, where Alexander commanded his elite cavalry. This allowed the Macedonians to exploit a gap in the enemy line and plunge through toward the Persian center. As Alexander's

8. Buddha Prakash, *History of Poros* (Patiala: Punjabi University Press, 1967). Like Prakash, B. C. Sinha, in *Studies in Alexander's Campaigns* (Varanasi: Bhartiya Publishing House, 1973), believed that Porus had not lost the battle against Alexander.

9. Deena Pandey, "The Hydaspese-Battle Commemorative Medal of Alexander the Great—A Fresh Approach," *Journal of the Numismatic Society of India* 33 (1971): 1–7. Pandey takes some of his views from Prakash, *Poros*, e.g., p. 78.

10. E. W. Marsden, *The Campaign of Gaugamela* (Liverpool: Liverpool University Press, 1964). The fight took place about seventy miles from Arbela (modern Arbil), which sometimes gives its name to the battle.

11. According to Arrian 3.8.6, the elephants came from the *western* side of the Indus and therefore were *not* from the territories ruled by Porus.

12. Arrian 3.15.6.

aged general Parmenion fought desperately to hold back Darius's right wing, Alexander himself pushed hard in pursuit of the Persian king who—as at Issus—eventually lost heart and fled the field.[13] Persian casualties were high, but surely not the 300,000 reported by Arrian (3.15.6). A cabal of Darius's own satraps murdered him the following year, putting an end to the Achaemenid dynasty.

It was therefore the decisive victory over Darius at Gaugamela that sealed Persia's fate and opened the way for Alexander's campaigns in Central and South Asia. For Deena Pandey, the elephant medallions undoubtedly celebrated the defeat of Darius in Mesopotamia. His conclusion, while admirably exploring the possibility of an alternative to the battle of the Hydaspes River, rested here upon emotion rather than evidence. Pandey avowed that Porus and his Indian army had never been beaten by Alexander, and that the medallions could thus not possibly commemorate that particular battle in India:

> What we know from the quoted narrative of Arrian it is not to be accepted that Porus was really defeated in the battlefield. We have references in Greek writings that Alexander offered many times the term of truce in which at the last Merose [Meroes] succeeded in convincing Porus. After this the story runs depicting Porus and Alexander as friends. It is impossible to believe that an undecided battle was taken to be depicted on the medal and Alexander who was really not crowned by Nike in the battlefield has shown himself as being crowned by the goddess of victory. [*sic*][14]

Because Pandey believed that Porus had not lost this battle, the medallions must by default celebrate a Macedonian victory over Darius and the Persians. This remarkable solution warrants closer scrutiny.

13. A. M. Devine, "The Battle of Gaugamela: A Tactical and Source-Critical Study," *Ancient World* 13 (1986): 87–116; and id., "The Macedonian Army at Gaugamela," ibid., 19 (1989): 77–80.

14. Pandey, "Commemorative Medal," p. 7 n. 2.

Did Alexander really fall short of victory over Porus and offer a truce to the unbeaten rajah? Pandey's preferred text, that of Arrian, answers the question quite strongly. The Macedonians outmaneuvered the Indians and managed to ferry across the river a strike force of archers, infantry, and cavalry. Against them, Porus dispatched a probe of cavalry and chariots. Arrian reports (5.14.3–6) that this Indian force consisted either of 60 chariots commanded by Porus's son (as recorded by Aristobulus) or (as recounted by Ptolemy and preferred by Arrian) of 120 chariots and 2,000 cavalry led by Porus's son.[15] Alexander routed this force, whatever its size, and pressed on to face Porus's main army.[16] In that subsequent engagement, the struggle centered around the elephants. Arrian describes (5.15.4–18.4) an unprecedented battle against these beasts, one that was hard-fought on both sides but ended in an overwhelming Macedonian victory. The Indians were slaughtered in large numbers until the remnants of the rajah's army turned and fled. Arrian lists 310 Macedonian casualties, compared to Indian losses of 23,000 dead (including all of Porus's generals, two of his sons, and other notables), the destruction of all the Indian chariots, and the capture of all surviving elephants. Although, again, some numbers are surely exaggerated, it is scarcely any wonder that most modern scholars refer to this battle as a "complete," "overwhelming," "shattering," and "most decisive" victory for Alexander. A. B. Bosworth, a leading expert on Arrian, laments the "killing ground" created by Alexander, which led to "a total, crushing victory."[17] Wherever our sympathies may lie, the Indians undoubtedly suffered a horrendous defeat at the Hydaspes.

Arrian relates (5.18.4–5) that Porus "witnessed the slaughter of his cavalry, saw some of his elephants lying dead and others wandering in

15. Arrian 5.14.4 reports, but rejects, other accounts that claim Alexander was wounded (and his horse killed) in personal combat with Porus's son.

16. Arrian 5.15.1–3, mentioning 400 Indian casualties including Porus's son.

17. A. B. Bosworth, *Alexander and the East: The Tragedy of Triumph* (Oxford: Oxford University Press, 1996), pp. 19–20.

distress without their riders, [and] realized [that] most of his infantry had perished." Unlike Darius, however, he fought on "so long as any of his troops kept formation." But in time, wounded, he also wheeled his elephant around and fled. At this point, even Porus had lost hope, and the rout was complete. We can find no hint whatsoever in Arrian's account that Alexander offered a truce in the midst of an undecided battle. Arrian states (5.18.6) that the Macedonian king admired Porus's bravery during the conflict and wished to spare the fleeing rajah's life. Taxiles, and then Meroes, were sent to Porus to call on him to halt his retreat, since flight was hopeless. This can mean nothing other than total surrender, and the subsequent meeting of the kings clearly indicates that Porus was Alexander's captive. Arrian leaves no doubt that Alexander considered this a Macedonian triumph, reporting (5.19.4) that Alexander founded a city named Nicaea (Victory) on the battlefield in honor of his triumph (*nikē*) over the Indians. Notably, too, he "sacrificed to the gods the prescribed thanksgivings of victory" (Arrian 5.20.1). We therefore have no reason to think that a Macedonian victory medallion would be inappropriate for the battle of the Hydaspes River.

While Pandey's arguments *against* the Hydaspes have no merit, we must still consider his arguments *for* Gaugamela. There can be no mistaking the Indian elephant on the medallic coins, but is it possible that Darius sits upon it? Pandey writes that Darius at Gaugamela was guarded by a group of archers, cavalry, and elephants brought by Porus from India.[18] Whereas our main sources (Arrian, Plutarch, Curtius, Diodorus, and Justin) do not mention Porus at Gaugamela and pay little or no attention to the Indians and elephants that fought with Darius, Pandey presents a very different picture. He insists that Porus's Indians played the pivotal role in this battle, serving as Darius's bodyguard and fixing the course of the whole engagement. He concludes that Darius must have fought on the back of an elephant, and that it is thus the Persian King of

18. Pandey, "Commemorative Medal," pp. 5–6.

Kings whom we see depicted on the medallions as Alexander's defeated foe.[19]

Strangely, Pandey here ignores the main Alexander texts (even Arrian) in order to anchor his case in some very unsatisfactory sources. For example, Pandey cites the *Shah Nama* of Firdausi to support his notion that Porus fought alongside Darius at Gaugamela. This delightful Persian epic poem, composed more than thirteen centuries after Alexander's reign, hardly stands scrutiny as a reliable historical account of the battle. At the other chronological extreme, Pandey cites Herodotus, who died a century *before* the battle he allegedly describes.[20] And finally, the *Alexander Romance* is used to show that Porus had indeed been summoned to help Darius in the west. The dubious value of this source has already been noted above; suffice it to recall that the *Romance* also reports that Alexander personally killed Porus in India. This information is patently false, so much so that even medieval monks commented on the contradictory, unreliable nature of the *Romance*, especially when it came to matters involving Porus.[21] We simply do not have acceptable ancient evidence to support Pandey's view that Indian forces dominated the battle of Gaugamela and that Darius fought on the back of one of Porus's elephants.

Even so, others have also surmised that the medallions commemorated Alexander's victory over Darius rather than Porus. The British nu-

19. Regarding the conspicuous absence of elephants in our main narratives of the battle, see H. H. Scullard, *The Elephant in the Greek and Roman World* (Ithaca, N.Y.: Cornell University Press, 1974), pp. 64–65. Scullard speculates that the beasts were withdrawn from Darius's lines and took no part in the fighting at Gaugamela.

20. Pandey, "Commemorative Medal," pp. 5–6.

21. For the fictional story that Alexander "slew the giant, arrogant King Porus," see A. M. Wolohojian, *The Romance of Alexander the Great by Pseudo-Callisthenes* (New York: Columbia University Press, 1969), p. 120. On the medieval commentators, consult George Cary, *The Medieval Alexander* (Cambridge: Cambridge University Press, 1956), pp. 71–72 and 340. For a useful analysis of part of the tradition, see Lloyd Gunderson, *Alexander's Letter to Aristotle about India* (Meisenheim am Glan: Anton Hain, 1980).

mismatist Michael Mitchiner assumed that the medallions were struck in Bactria *before* the Indian campaign, arguing that the battle of the Hydaspes was "an insignificant oriental episode when compared with the battle of Gaugamela (331 B.C.) in which Alexander defeated the Persian Emperor himself."[22] This approach tries to couple the most important battle with the most extraordinary battle memorial. Mitchiner follows a dangerous method here: regardless of what is shown on the artifacts, he allows himself to decide which battle *should* be commemorated. We cannot base such judgments on what we now think is important, ignoring altogether what Alexander and his contemporaries may have believed. The fact that from a modern perspective, the battle of Gaugamela might seem more vital simply does not matter in any investigation of the elephant medallions. What really matters is the mind-set of Alexander and his troops. We have already seen that many modern historians do consider the battle of the Hydaspes far more than "an insignificant oriental episode." Some reckon it among the greatest battles of ancient times. More significantly, Alexander did, too.

Alexander did defeat Porus, and this was considered no less an achievement than the Macedonian victory at Gaugamela. In fact, the only reference in Arrian's history to a victory celebration by Alexander's army is to that which took place following the battle with Porus, not Darius.[23] This does not mean that sacrifices were not made after other battles (as recorded in the Vulgate sources), but Arrian and other writers clearly recount the special significance to Alexander of the victory in India. Later authors in the West continued to dwell upon the commemoration of this battle. Some of their accounts are quite unbelievable, but their very existence proves that the battle against Porus remained a popular subject in Greece and Rome for many centuries. In Philostratus's bi-

22. Michael Mitchiner, *Indo-Greek and Indo-Scythian Coinage* (London: Hawkins, 1975), 1: 8–9 and 20.

23. A. B. Bosworth, *A Historical Commentary on Arrian's History of Alexander*, vol. 2 (Oxford: Clarendon Press, 1995), p. 316. The passage is Arrian 5.20.1.

ography of the widely traveled holy man Apollonius of Tyana, written in
the third century c.e., we read that Apollonius visited India and saw many
memorials of the battle of the Hydaspes River. Some 350 years after the
battle, Apollonius was shown an elephant—still alive—that had allegedly
fought with Porus against the Macedonians. This beast was reported
to have gold bands around its tusks inscribed in Greek: "Alexander the
son of Zeus dedicates Ajax to the sun."[24] Alexander, we are informed,
had named this elephant in honor of the renowned Trojan War hero
Ajax.[25]

Philostratus also describes an unusual temple allegedly seen by Apollonius at Taxila:

> Bronze plaques were hung on its walls, each engraved with pictures
> showing the exploits of Porus and Alexander. The images were fashioned from brass, silver, gold, and black bronze, depicting elephants,
> horses, warriors, helmets, and shields. The spears, javelins, and
> swords were made of iron. The entire composition exhibited a masterful style like that of Zeuxis, Polygnotus, and Euphranor. . . . Porus
> dedicated this artwork, after Alexander had died, to show the Macedonians in victory and the subsequent reinstatement of Porus,
> wounded in battle, as Alexander's gift.[26]

On the old battlefield itself, Apollonius supposedly viewed commemorative monuments and statues not unlike the memorials seen today at Gettysburg and other battle sites.[27] Archaeology has not yet confirmed the
existence of such shrines and monuments near Taxila, and no one expects
the bones of the long-lived elephant Ajax to be unearthed, but even the

24. Philostratus *Life of Apollonius* 2.12. One of the Greek myths regarding elephants, originating with Alexander's own men, was that these animals could live
for centuries: Strabo 15.1.43.

25. Curiously, in *Troilus and Cressida* 1.2.20–21 and 2.3.2–3, Shakespeare
twice describes the Greek hero Ajax as an elephant.

26. *Life of Apollonius* 2.20.

27. Ibid., 2.42.

invention of these stories by a writer of the Roman Empire shows a keen awareness of the battle's import and its enduring relevance to his readers.[28]

The battle of Gaugamela may have "changed the political axis of the ancient world,"[29] but history also hung in the balance at the Hydaspes. It serves no purpose to debate which battle better *deserves* to be featured on the elephant medallions. Alexander won both and made light of neither. His celebrations in India prove that he did not reckon his victory there as insignificant in any way, and later writers as far away as Rome seem to have upheld that judgment.

In spite of the theories of Pandey and Mitchiner, numismatists and historians have overwhelmingly maintained the view that these three medallic coins commemorated Alexander's successful campaign against Porus. The impressive pachyderm on the medallions seemed a signpost pointing to India, where Alexander's only major confrontation with war elephants occurred. These beasts awed the Greeks, and this may be their earliest portrayal in Hellenistic art. Authors such as Arrian express much more sympathy for the plight of these animals than for the Indians slaughtered in battle.[30] Porus's own elephant appears remarkably human in several accounts, especially Plutarch's. We are told that this huge animal possessed keen intelligence and a deep devotion to Porus; that it defended the rajah in battle; and that it gently set its wounded master upon the ground and tenderly pulled the spears from his body with its trunk.[31]

28. See now Paul Bernard, "Greek Geography and Literary Fiction from Bactria to India: The Case of the Aornoi and Taxila," in *Coins, Art, and Chronology: Essays on the Pre-Islamic History of the Indo-Iranian Borderlands*, ed. M. Alram and D. Klimburg-Salter, pp. 51–98 (Vienna: Österreichischen Akademie der Wissenschaften, 1999).

29. J. F. C. Fuller, *The Generalship of Alexander the Great* (New Brunswick, N.J.: Rutgers University Press, 1960; reprint, New York: Da Capo Press, 1989), p. 180.

30. Bosworth, *Commentary*, 2: 301–2.

31. Plutarch, *Alex.* 60.13 and *Mor.* 970D; cf. Aelian *De natura animalium* 7.37 and Strabo 15.1.42. One is reminded of Darwin's *The Expression of the Emotions*

In the Vulgate tradition, this elephant defended Porus to the death, acting to the last as the loyal servant of its royal rider, just like Alexander's beloved horse Bucephalus, which also perished at the Hydaspes.[32]

It is difficult today to imagine just how surreal such an elephant seemed to the Greeks of Alexander's day. Schooled as we are in circus acts and neighborhood zoos, the elephant has become all too tame and familiar. In an age that can magically bring extinct dinosaurs to life, we have mentally reduced our largest living land animal in scale and significance. But prior to Dumbo and Dinomation™, not much could astonish us more than an elephant. The Greeks knew of ivory (elephas/ ἐλέφας) long before they had seen the animal that produced it. Herodotus in his travels to Egypt and elsewhere met with the crocodile and hippopotamus, but apparently not firsthand with the elephant. The earliest reliable information about elephants did not reach the Greeks until Alexander's invasion of the East. Aristotle, researching and teaching in Athens, produced such clear documentation of the elephant's habits and anatomy that many scholars assume the philosopher must have examined an actual specimen.[33] In the period after Alexander's death (the so-called Hellenistic Age, 323–30 B.C.E.), Greek kings and commanders became inordinately fond of war elephants, developing large herds of them as part of a preindustrial arms race. The Romans, of course, learned about these elephants by fighting the Greeks and, more

---

in Man and Animals (1872; 3d ed., Oxford: Oxford University Press, 1998), p. 168.

32. Curtius 8.14.40. On the horse Bucephalus, similarly given human traits by some ancient writers, see A. R. Anderson, "Bucephalas and His Legend," *American Journal of Philology* 51 (1930): 1–21.

33. Consult J. S. Romm, "Aristotle's Elephant and the Myth of Alexander's Scientific Patronage," *American Journal of Philology* 110 (1989): 566–75; J. M. Bigwood, "Aristotle and the Elephant Again," ibid. 114 (1993): 537–55; and Roger French, *Ancient Natural History* (London: Routledge, 1994), pp. 103–9. For an interesting fictional treatment, see L. Sprague de Camp, *An Elephant for Aristotle* (New York: Doubleday, 1958).

famously, the Carthaginians under Hannibal. Rome's legions, however, never relied much on these expensive monsters.

By late antiquity, elephants were again exotic and rarely seen in Greece or Rome.[34] Later, in medieval Europe, people who read accounts of elephants in ancient warfare could scarcely imagine the creatures. Illuminated manuscripts and murals portraying these battles betray the inability of artists to conjure up the true appearance of elephants (see fig. 4). Even though King Louis IX of France sent King Henry III of England an (African) elephant in 1255, which drew large crowds to observe the beast at the Tower of London, an illuminated manuscript presented in 1463 to Charles the Bold shows how unfamiliar elephants still were in the West.[35] One panel illustrates Curtius's narrative of the battle of the Hydaspes.[36] In it, the elephants look ridiculously like large, peg-legged horses with awkward trunks and tusks. The extent to which elephants can easily be misunderstood and misrepresented in art reminds us how valuable the medallions are as a firsthand record of these animals in battle. As another example, many medieval and modern depictions of the battle of the Hydaspes River show wooden towers on the elephants' backs.[37] Such towers, strapped to elephants as fighting platforms protecting three or more soldiers each, were introduced later in antiquity, but they are

34. Stanley Burstein, *Graeco-Africana: Studies in the History of Greek Relations with Egypt and Nubia* (Athens: Aristide Caratzas, 1995), pp. 215–19.

35. See G. C. Druce, "The Elephant in Medieval Legend and Art," *Archaeological Journal* 76 (1919): 1; see also Julio Berzunza, "A Digression in the *Libro de Alexandre:* The Story of the Elephant," *Romantic Review* 18 (1927): 238–45.

36. The manuscript panel may be studied in C. A. Robinson, Jr., "The Two Worlds of Alexander," *Horizon* 1 (1959): 46.

37. Some examples of towers inaccurately placed on Porus's elephants: the French manuscript panel cited in the previous note; a fifteenth-century Serbian manuscript in Sophia's *Ethnike Bibliotheke ton Agion Kyrillou kai Methodiou;* Bernard Picart's 1704 engraving of Charles Le Brun's painting of the battle; and Tom Lovell's painting in *National Geographic* 133 (1968): 58–59. See also Hans Delbrück, *History of the Art of War,* vol. 1: *Warfare in Antiquity* (1920; reprint, Lincoln: University of Nebraska Press, 1990), p. 221.

Figure 4.   Two medieval representations of the elphant.

anachronisms in all depictions of the fight between Alexander and Porus. This the medallions verify.[38]

Had there been more of these medallions made, and had subsequent artists been more likely to encounter and copy the design, errant representations of the beasts and the battle might not have become so common. Even so, some investigators have suggested that the medallions were known far and wide in the ancient world. In 1968, for instance, the prominent scholar Salvatore Settis directed everyone's attention to a possible reference to the elephant "coins" in an early Latin play, Plautus's *Curculio* ("The Weevil"), written in the second century B.C.E.[39] This famous Roman playwright adapted Greek comedies—often involving comic twists built around the eventual recognition of a person or a prop—for the Italian stage, the plots of which were later borrowed by writers such as Shakespeare and Molière. In *Curculio*, a stolen signet ring provides this key to the resolution of the play. Plautus describes the seal

38. Paul Goukowsky, "Le roi Pôros, son éléphant et quelques autres," *Bulletin de correspondance héllenique* 96 (1972): 473–502.

39. Salvatore Settis, "Alessandro e Poro in *Campis Curculionis*," *La parola del passato* 23 (1968): 55–75.

on this ring as "A warrior with shield, splitting apart an elephant with his sword" (line 424). Settis took one of the characters in the play, Therapontigonus, a bragging conqueror recently returned from India, to be a parody of Alexander the Great. Recalling the extraordinary nature of the elephant medallions as memorials of that campaign, Settis proposed that these very artifacts inspired the plot device of the signet ring. He furthermore recalled the anecdote about Aristobulus's exaggerated history—the one that so annoyed Alexander—in which the king was said to have killed an elephant with a single blow.[40] In both instances, Aristobulus's history and Plautus's play, we encounter the same fantasy of Alexander felling an enemy elephant in one superhuman stroke.

The parallels suggested by Settis are certainly interesting. He postulates a series of steps that leads from the actual medallion to a stage-prop ring in faraway Italy. But certain facts erode our confidence in this alleged path. First, of course, the scene on the medallion bears no real resemblance to the ring. One has a *cavalryman* without a *shield* driving his *spear* at the *riders* of a retreating elephant; the other depicts a soldier *slicing* an elephant in two with his *sword*. Beyond the presence of an elephant, one whole and one halved, these are not the same image at all. To force a link requires us to introduce the Aristobulus anecdote, in which, at least, Alexander does kill an elephant. Here we must split the difference: the king uses a spear (as on the "coin" but not the ring) to kill the beast (as on the ring but not the "coin"). The remaining associations are wholly nonexistent.

To be fair, however, scholars other than Settis have postulated a direct connection between such stories and the medallions. Some believe that Aristobulus's anecdote directly inspired the design of the "coins," while others argue conversely that the medallion shaped part of the literary tradition reflected in Aristobulus.[41] We have no reason to imagine the en-

40. Lucian *Quomodo historia conscribenda sit* 12 (discussed in chapter 3 above).
41. On the priority of the medallion: N. G. L. Hammond, *Sources for Alexander the Great: An Analysis of Plutarch's "Life" and Arrian's "Anabasis Alexandrou"* (Cambridge: Cambridge University Press, 1993), p. 110 n. 23 (relating to the Bu-

graver of the medallions working under the particular influence of Aristobulus's text, especially since Alexander disavowed the feat and destroyed the manuscript that described it. Why would a die engraver therefore design a medallion based on this infuriating and discredited version of events? On the other hand, why would Alexander so despise Aristobulus's account if it truly copied a medallion the king himself had commissioned? In actuality, the text and medallion really have nothing much in common. At most, we might consider whether (if the anecdote is true) Aristobulus took the idea of a royal duel from the medallion and tried to improve upon it with the slaying of the elephant. This extra element may well have annoyed Alexander because it exceeded his own official version and, given the Greeks' sympathy for Porus's pachyderm, attributed an unlikely (and unlikable) act to Alexander.

Any further ligature connecting the anecdote to the unknown Greek play that lent its plot to Plautus's *Curculio* cannot be detected. The only alternative is that one of these playwrights actually saw an elephant medallion in Greece or Italy and himself concocted the signet ring as a plot device. Of course, this still does not explain why the ring bears no credible resemblance to the medallion. Furthermore, we have absolutely no other evidence to suggest that the elephant medallions were known anywhere in the Mediterranean world. To the best of our knowledge, they were neither produced in large numbers nor circulated in territories west of modern-day Iraq.

Throughout the middle decades of the twentieth century, various theories were offered about the medallic coins, ranging from the suggestion that they depicted the battle with Darius at Gaugamela to linking them with the ring in Plautus's play. Unfortunately, none of these solutions to the mystery could settle the debate begun by the first appearance of the Franks medallion at the British Museum. The discov-

---

cephalus legend); on the priority of the anecdote: Paul Goukowsky, *Essai sur les origines du mythe d'Alexandre*, vol. 1 (Nancy: Université de Nancy, 1978), p. 283 n. 76.

eries of two more specimens had added fresh fuel to the fire, but sometimes it was the scientists themselves who got burned. This proved especially true in the context of contaminated evidence. Nothing hurts science and history more than deliberate misinformation. In evolutionary biology, Darwin's work received a ringing endorsement when, on December 22, 1912, a *New York Times* headline declared: "Darwin Theory Is Proved True." Unfortunately, the bones of "Piltdown Man" were just the sort of evidence that experts did not need; the whole affair was an elaborate and damaging hoax.[42] In numismatics, counterfeit coins likewise taint our data and falsify the results of the hardest labors. Forgeries deceive us with designs and denominations that never existed; they give the false impression that certain issues were greater in number than was actually the case; and if poorly copied, they distort the features of authentic mintages.

These numismatic deceptions can arise at any time, either contemporaneously with legitimate issues (to fool the handlers of circulating currency in the marketplace) or much later (to fool the collectors of valuable vintage coins). An example of the first kind that resulted in the exile of Diogenes of Sinope, the founder of Cynicism, was allegedly known to Alexander the Great.[43] Ancient laws against adulterating or counterfeiting coins were quite severe.[44] Even so, ample literary and material evidence attests to those in Greece and Rome willing to run these risks.

42. On the Piltdown hoax, see, e.g., John Walsh, *Unraveling Piltdown: The Science Fraud of the Century and Its Solution* (New York: Random House, 1996); and Frank Spencer, *The Piltdown Papers, 1908–1955* (London: Oxford University Press, 1990).

43. The crime is recounted by Diogenes Laertius 6.20–21 and 6.49. Alexander reportedly met with Diogenes and referred to his illegal mintages in a metaphor for the export of Greek culture: Plutarch *Mor.* 332C.

44. See, e.g., George Boon, "Counterfeit Coins in Roman Britain," in *Coins and the Archaeologist*, ed. John Casey and Richard Reece, 2d ed. (London: Seaby, 1988), pp. 102–88. Also useful is Erwin Dietrich, "Fälscher und Fälschungen," *Helvetische Münzen-Zeitung* 22, 10 (1987): 423–31.

More dangerous for us, however, is the latter crime, involving modern forgeries of ancient coins and medals. Working skillfully in out-of-the-way places, forgers use many techniques to produce passable fakes of desirable specimens. Some pieces are cast from the molds of genuine coins, while others may be hand-struck from counterfeit dies. If the cheat has real talent, the latter can be especially difficult to detect. Constantine Christodoulos, a notorious Greek forger in the early twentieth century, amazed the keenest of numismatists when authorities finally confiscated his masterful counterfeit dies.[45]

Every student of ancient history knows the desirability of Alexander's famous coinage, and thus of the lucrative market that inspires the fraudulent to help meet that demand among collectors. During his travels in the nineteenth century, the historian David George Hogarth encountered the work of an expert forger in Tarsus who "used to fabricate by the score the common *drachmas* of Alexander the Great to sell to tourists."[46] In very poor countries, such as Afghanistan, the practice of counterfeiting ancient coins has been particularly widespread.[47] We know that the Oxus Treasure suffered inevitable contamination from forged material as it passed through the region on its way to avid European collectors.[48]

Numismatic detectives would not, therefore, be surprised to learn that fake elephant medallions might exist, with some of them still counted as genuine by unsuspecting scholars and collectors. Legitimate concerns have been raised about two specimens in India: one in the collection of the Banaras Hindu University, and the other in the Indian Museum of

45. Joannes Svoronos, *Christodoulos the Counterfeiter* (Athens, 1922; reprint, Chicago: Ares, 1975).

46. D. G. Hogarth, *A Wandering Scholar in the Levant*, 2d ed. (London: Murray, 1896); cf. pp. 25–26 for the story of how an "ignorant" peasant tricked him on the purchase of some ancient coins.

47. See, e.g., A. N. Lahiri, *Corpus of Indo-Greek Coins* (Calcutta: Poddar Publications, 1965), pp. 62–65.

48. G. K. Jenkins, "A Group of Bactrian Forgeries," *Revue numismatique* 7 (1965): 56.

Calcutta. The Banaras specimen (Appendix B, F 1) appeared in an un-published catalogue compiled in 1965 by T. P. Verma for BHU's Department of Ancient Indian History, Culture, and Archaeology; this is undoubtedly the same medallion published in that year by A. K. Narain, a member of that very department, to illustrate his influential article on "Alexander and India."[49] This medallion was surely copied from a mold taken of the first known example that Sir Augustus Franks donated to the British Museum. To confirm this hypothesis, the numismatist need only examine photographs of the medallion held in the Calcutta Museum (Appendix B, F 2). Published as genuine in 1977, it plainly has all of the damning characteristics of the Banaras fake.[50] In fact, these pieces appear to be duplicates from the same surreptitious mold.[51]

The problem does not end there. For instance, another copy by the same forger (Appendix B, F 3) also found its way into a private collection.[52] At about the same time, yet another (Appendix B, F 5) passed through the antiquities market in Kabul, Afghanistan.[53] One of these forgeries can be traced back at least as far as 1926. In that year, a fake elephant medallion (Appendix B, F 4) was known in Paris and may, for a time, have been in the Bibliothèque nationale.[54] At least five identical imposter medallions can therefore be recognized, all of them modeled on the 1887

49. A. K. Narain, "Alexander and India," *Greece and Rome* 12 (1965): 155–65 and pl. 1. This article has been reprinted many times in collections of Alexander studies, but usually without the illustrations.

50. S. P. Basu, *The Second Supplementary Catalogue of Coins to Volume I* (Calcutta: Indian Museum, 1977), p. 35. This specimen was apparently accessioned after 1932, the date of the *First Supplement*.

51. Both medallions were accepted as genuine by Pandey, "Commemorative Medal," pp. 1–7.

52. A photograph of this medallion from the H. L. Haughton collection was examined in the archives of the American Numismatic Society in New York.

53. A plaster cast of this example was examined in the Bibliothèque nationale in Paris.

54. Accessioned as Y6431, now appropriately in the forgery trays of the museum.

Franks specimen. The great French archaeologist Paul Bernard has suggested that our counterfeiter was at work very early, surely before the second genuine specimen came to light in 1926.[55] As Bernard concluded, the casting and copying must have been done when the first medallion reached the bazaars of Rawalpindi at the time of the Oxus Treasure. Then, after selling the genuine piece to a knowledgeable buyer (Franks) at the highest possible price, the dealers kept the molds in order to increase their profits by producing a series of fakes for the less wary.

No doubt, the con men meant to make some money and little else; they did not actually conspire to deceive historians with false witnesses to the past. We cannot be so sure about other cases of counterfeiting the elephant medallions. When forgers boldly go beyond the exact duplication of genuine types, the danger to truth increases exponentially. A number of invented (rather than imitated) coins have mystified historians over the years. This kind of problem originated quite early in the development of numismatic studies. Anxious to complete the historical record through coins, some people simply fabricated the necessary evidence—not unlike biology's Piltdown Man fiasco.[56] Thus, several die-struck forgeries of the elephant medallion show an intentionally modified design (as opposed to one that merely poorly copies the originals). These specimens are kept in the so-called black cabinets of reputable numismatic dealers to keep them off the market and provide material for research into suspicious types. Two such black cabinet specimens (Appendix B, F 7 and F 8), both from crude dies, try to improve the battle scene

55. Paul Bernard, "Le monnayage d'Eudamos, satrape grec du Punjab et 'maître des éléphants,' " in *Orientalia Iosephi Tucci Memoriae Dicata*, ed. G. Gnoli and L. Lanciotti (Rome: Istituto italiano per il Medio ed Estremo Oriente, 1985), 1: 65–94, esp. pp. 68–69 n. 11.

56. An interesting case is provided by G. Rouille, *Promptuaire des médailles des plus renommées personnes qui ont esté depuis le commencement du monde, avec brève description de leurs vies et faicts, recueillie des bons auteurs*, 2 vols. (Lyon, 1553), which illustrates "coins" of Agamemnon, Noah, and even Adam.

by extending the ground line (or exergue) all the way across the design, from the elephant's front feet back to the hind legs of Alexander's horse. On the genuine specimens, this line never reaches beyond the elephant, thus stopping short of the cavalryman and leaving his horse as if floating in air. The natural inclination of the eye to *want* the longer ground line may explain why the forger chose to improve the design by filling it in for us.

In fact, there is another example of this very phenomenon in a different medium. When Percy Gardner published the first known elephant medallion in 1887, a drawing illustrating the piece inaccurately showed the ground line extending all the way across the battle scene.[57] Our forger may, of course, have been influenced by this published drawing; however, this seems a less likely probability. The illustration does not include the Greek letter *xi* (Ξ) in the field, as do these forgeries. Also, the reverse of the fake medallions shows the full helmet and flying Nike, not shown on the Franks medallion. The counterfeiter clearly knew the later specimens, which reveal the full designs of the obverse and reverse, but chose to improve the composition by adding a longer ground line.

The next step in the forger's progress may be seen on a medallion made from the same obverse die as Appendix B, F 8.[58] Not content with the Alexander reverses already engraved on the basis of published genuine examples and used for F 7 and F 8, the forger decided upon more improvements by the time F 9 was produced (see plate 13). On this bogus medallion from Beirut, a notorious center of the forgery trade, Alexander's cape falls all the way to his feet instead of stopping short at his knees. The engraver has replaced the AB monogram with a new, more elabo-

57. Percy Gardner, "New Greek Coins of Bactria and India," *Numismatic Chronicle* 7 (1887): 177.

58. I am very grateful to Harlan Berk of Chicago and Frank Kovacs of San Mateo for bringing these unpublished specimens to my attention (see App. B, F 7–9).

rate one that has no exact match among the more than one thousand such markings known on Alexander's genuine coinage.[59] Most notably, the forger decided to remove all historical doubt about Alexander's responsibility for this medallion by adding the king's name in the genitive (possessive) case: ΑΛΕΞΑΝΔΡΟΥ, meaning "coin of Alexander."[60] This convenient inscription, like the ground line on the other side, fills in what we might otherwise expect to see on the dies. Experts have often noted that all of Alexander's regular coinage bears his name in the genitive case; this is, in fact, the opening pronouncement of Alfred Bellinger's standard reference on the subject.[61] The conspicuous absence of the king's name prompted many numismatists, including Bellinger, to identify the elephant medallions as commemorative artifacts rather than actual coins intended for circulation.[62] This set them apart from Alexander's currency and no doubt troubled some collectors. By doctoring his dies and thereby lending the design a reassuring imprimatur, the Beirut forger hoped to appease potential buyers. In doing so, he unfortunately corrupted the numismatic record.

The existence of numerous cast and die-struck forgeries patently complicated the worldwide investigation into the mystery of the elephant medallions (see Appendix B). By 1972, with only three genuine specimens available for study, consensus seemed impossible on every point except one—the standing figure crowned by Nike was surely

---

59. All of these Greek markings have been compiled by Martin Price, *The Coinage in the Name of Alexander the Great and Philip Arrhidaeus* (London: British Museum Press, 1991), 2: 571–630.

60. Note, however, that the Greek letter *xi* (Ξ) in Alexander's name has a different form than the same letter on the obverse die.

61. Alfred Bellinger, *Essays on the Coinage of Alexander the Great* (New York: American Numismatic Society, 1963), p. 1.

62. Ibid., p. 27. Martin Price's catalogue of the British Museum coins, *Coinage in the Name of Alexander the Great* (1991), does not illustrate the British Museum elephant medallions, since they do not bear the king's name, even though Price did consider them to be local issues of Alexander's.

Alexander the Great. But scholars had wrangled incessantly about everything else: the meaning of this image (history or allegory?), what the king wore (a Persian/Greek/Homeric headdress?), who rode the horse (Eucratides? Alexander? Taxiles?), who sat on the pachyderm (Porus? Darius?), why the object (a coin or a medal?) was created (to glorify the Hydaspes, Gaugamela, or some other battle?), who commissioned it (Eucratides? Alexander? Taxiles?), when it was made (328 B.C.E.? 324 B.C.E.? 150 B.C.E.?), where it was struck (Bactria? India? Babylon?), and how many were produced (a few or many thousands?). What everyone needed desperately was more material evidence, which suddenly appeared in an extraordinary discovery that no one could have predicted.

FIVE

Another Treasure

In September 1973, Martin Price and Nancy Waggoner, curators at the British Museum and the American Numismatic Society respectively, attended the prestigious International Congress of Numismatics held in New York and Washington, D.C. During a lunch break, they suddenly heard from Nicholas Duerr the astonishing news of a major find in Iraq.[1] Duerr, a numismatist based in Geneva, related to his colleagues that during the winter of 1972/73, a hoard of some 1,800 silver coins had been unearthed near Babylon.[2] The cache had apparently been buried in two deposits, giving one portion a reddish patina distinct from the other. Duerr photographed all of the contents brought to him in Geneva; he then gave the pictures of the Alexander types to Price for detailed study, and the pictures of the many Athenian-style coins found in the hoard to Hélène Nicolet-Pierre in Paris.[3] Price, a leading authority on Alexander's

1. Details may be found in Martin Price, "Circulation at Babylon in 323 B.C.," in *Mnemata: Papers in Memory of Nancy M. Waggoner,* ed. William Metcalf, pp. 63–72 (New York: American Numismatic Society, 1991), esp. p. 63.

2. Personal communication from Michel Duerr, the son of Nicholas, to whom I owe a debt of gratitude for the following information.

3. Before the appearance of Alexander's very fine coinage, the dominant Greek currency had been the tetradrachms of Athens. Many imitations of the

coins, wisely collaborated with Nancy Waggoner because of her particular expertise on Alexander's mint at Babylon, where many of the coins in the hoard had apparently been struck.

Duerr himself was able to publish only two brief notices of the hoard before his untimely death in 1982.[4] In those publications, he announced that among the coins in the 1973 Iraq hoard, there were at least three more genuine specimens of the elephant medallion (see, e.g., plate 5). Even more startling, Duerr revealed the existence of a smaller, related variety of elephant "coin," of which there were no fewer than six specimens in the hoard. At least one additional example had been in a private Swiss collection for some years, its connection to the large medallions being unrecognized until the discovery of the Iraq hoard.[5] Duerr described these new types as tetradrachms, ranging in weight from 15.8 to 16.7 grams, with varying die axes. He surmised that at least three examples had been overstruck on Babylonian lion staters, coins that had been produced by local satraps. The designs depicted a striding Indian elephant without riders on one side and a standing bowman (clearly Indian, so tentatively identified by Duerr as Porus) loosing an arrow (see plates 6–10) on the other. These "coins" carried precisely the same Greek markings

---

Athenian "owls" were struck in the East and circulated widely until finally replaced by Alexander types. The Iraq hoard contained large numbers of both currencies, plus other regional issues. See a recent study by P. G. van Alfen, "The 'Owls' from the 1973 Iraq Hoard," *American Journal of Numismatics* 12 (2000): 9–58.

4. Duerr published a paper on the new elephant/bowman type in the proceedings of the 1973 Congress: "Ein 'Elephantenstater' für Porus," in *Actes du 8ème Congrès international de numismatique, New York–Washington, septembre 1973*, ed. Herbert A. Cahn and Georges Le Rider (Paris: Association internationale des numismates professionnels, 1976), 1: 43; and a somewhat more detailed report appeared in print earlier: Duerr, "Neues aus Babylonien," *Schweizer Münzblätter* 24 (1974): 33–36. An English translation by A. Ilsch with updated notes was published by the editor of *Numismatic Digest* 2 (1978): 4–7.

5. At the 1973 numismatic congress, Duerr reported five of these coins, adding the other specimens in his later report (see n. 4 above).

(AB and Ξ) found on the large medallions. Duerr felt certain that all of these elephant designs were engraved by the same artist and were intended to honor Porus as an equal in Alexander's universal empire.

Suddenly, the long-lived mystery of the elephant medallions seemed to involve twice as many large specimens (the so-called decadrachms showing the elephant battle and victorious Alexander) plus a whole new set of smaller "coins" (the so-called tetradrachms featuring the standing Indian bowman) that no one had ever anticipated. Through the agency of numismatic dealers at Bank Leu in Zurich, the British Museum and the American Numismatic Society rapidly acquired their own specimens of the elephant/bowman tetradrachms and wrestled with what this new evidence meant.[6] Presciently, Duerr remarked that the Iraq hoard might yet reveal other elephant types previously unknown to numismatists. Indeed, it soon did.

In April 1975, Bank Leu sold at public auction some of the contents of the 1973 Iraq hoard.[7] A poor example of the large elephant medallion (Appendix A, E/A 10) brought over $20,000; one of the new bowman types (Appendix A, E/B 2) realized more than $14,000 when the hammer finally fell. Then there appeared in the auction another new type (Appendix A, E/C 1), featuring an Indian elephant with two riders on one side and a chariot scene including four horses, the driver, and an archer on the other (see plate 11). This third elephant type, purchased by the Bibliothèque nationale in Paris for over $11,000, lacked the Greek markings (AB and Ξ) found on the other varieties, but seemed nonetheless to belong to the same series because of its style and subject matter.

As with the earlier Oxus Treasure, this new discovery dispersed rapidly through various intriguing channels. For example, one large ele-

6. Accessions: BM 1973–12–4–1; ANS 1974–145–4. The National Museum in Copenhagen also acquired a very nice specimen of the large medallion (decadrachm): Otto Mørkholm, "Athen og Alexander den Store, Fra bystat til guddommeligt kongedømme," *Nationalmuseets Arbeidsmark* (1974): 89–95. See App. A.

7. *Antike Munzen* 13 (April 1975), lots 130–32.

phant medallion (Appendix A, E/A 6) was purchased in the Middle East
by an American expert, who then sold it to another prominent collector
in California. This second man then sold it to a third connoisseur,
bought the same piece back later, and eventually sold it once again into
the famous Nelson Bunker Hunt Collection in Texas. This medallion
was displayed in various museums around the United States, first as part
of the Search for Alexander exhibit (Boston) and then in the Hunts' own
Wealth of the Ancient World exhibit (Fort Worth, Richmond, Detroit,
Dallas). In June 1990, Sotheby's in New York auctioned the Hunt Collection, offering the medallion at an estimated price of $35–45,000; the
winning bid was actually $57,750.[8] Similarly, the smaller medallic coin
with the elephant/bowman designs sold by Bank Leu in 1975 (Appendix
A, E/B 2) went to the Viscount Wimborne Collection and subsequently
appeared in two auctions by Sotheby's and one by Numismatic Fine
Arts.[9] In this protracted process, some of the hoard's contents entered
museum collections in New York, Paris, Copenhagen, and London,
while most of the new material fell into private hands in Europe, Asia, the
Middle East, and the United States. Some of these medallions have since
been condemned as modern forgeries, signaling another round of counterfeiting to capitalize on the marketability of the new material (see Appendix B).

In the face of such feverish activity, numismatic scholars struggled to
keep track of these medallions in order to study the original composition
of the hoard as completely and confidently as possible (see Appendix C).
After the brief notices published by Duerr, the Royal Numismatic Soci-

8. The peregrinations of this specimen have been reconstructed from inter-
views of some of the owners. See also Sotheby's Catalogue 6043 with superlative
text by C. Lorber: *The Nelson Bunker Hunt Collection, Highly Important Greek and
Roman Coins*, lot 103; and *Wealth of the Ancient World: The Nelson Bunker Hunt and
William Herbert Hunt Collections* (Forth Worth, Tex.: Kimbell Art Museum,
1983), pp. 209–10.

9. Sotheby's, April 1991, lot 43; Numismatic Fine Arts 27, December 1991,
lot 51; and Sotheby's, October 1993, lot 36.

ety and the International Numismatic Commission took up the chase in successive volumes of the publication *Coin Hoards*, and the plan was for Price and Waggoner eventually to produce a definitive study.[10] Unfortunately, this important project never could be completed: Waggoner died in 1989, leaving the task to Price, who himself passed away in 1995. As a result, our best information on the hoard comes from Price's interim commemorative paper honoring his deceased colleague, which lists over 300 specific items believed to have been in the original find. As with the Oxus Treasure, however, we can never hope to reconstruct a complete record of this remarkable cache. The original listing of coins is very vague, and we have at our disposal no close accounting of some major categories, such as the Alexander tetradrachms and the imitation Athenian owls. What follows in the literature is an increasingly precise tally, with periodic additions based upon numismatic material that came on the market later, *presumably* from the original find in Iraq. To be sure, this is not an unusual pattern; most large hoards are broken up into lots and shopped around the major auction houses over a period of years. Astute scholars and dealers anticipate this and keep their eyes open for coins on the market most likely from the dispersed hoard. Over time, they piece together a picture of the original find based upon scattered information, experience, and intuition. This can be seen in Appendix C.

Coins coming on the market as late as 1989 were attributed by Price to the 1973 Iraq hoard. It is, after all, a reasonable bet that the elephant medallions showing up in this period were indeed part of the Babylon hoard and not random new discoveries or specimens from some other, unannounced find. Yet this cannot be proven and must be treated by careful investigators with prudent caution. A mystery this large should not depend for its solution on the *exact* reconstruction of a hoard like that from Iraq in 1973. It is simply too easy for important material to be

10. *Coin Hoards* 1 (1975), no. 38; *Coin Hoards* 2 (1976), no. 49; *Coin Hoards* 3 (1977), no. 22; *Coin Hoards* 8 (1994), no. 188. See also Price, "Circulation at Babylon," pp. 63 and 69–72.

culled early and sold privately, without a trace, or for extraneous coins to be pitched into the lots being offered for sale in order to boost prices with inventory otherwise less marketable.

Under such circumstances, those on the case should be grateful for the attentive detective work done by Duerr, Price, Waggoner, and others. First, what is known of the Iraq hoard points very strongly, if not conclusively, to a burial date of ca. 323–322 B.C.E.[11] This would prove the old theory that the elephant medallions were indeed struck during Alexander's lifetime, since some of the specimens in this hoard show signs of considerable wear. Second, the hoard provides as many as seven additional published examples of the large medallion for study—a dramatic and welcome increase over the three genuine specimens that had come to light over the previous ninety-three years. Third, the mystery takes on an exciting new dimension with the discovery of two smaller (tetradrachm) varieties of elephant medallion, one the elephant/bowman type and the other the elephant/chariot type. These designs might help experts to understand the meaning of the large elephant/Alexander medallions; conversely, any theories about the large decadrachms must now account for the smaller tetradrachms as well (see Appendix A).

This surprising new evidence reinvigorated the case and brought forth a spate of published theories. In 1978, Hélène Nicolet-Pierre discussed the three types of medallion acquired from the hoard by the Bibliothèque nationale in Paris. She again noted the possibility that the large medallions were overstruck on older decadrachms, and that on the Paris

11. Price, "Circulation at Babylon," p. 65: "On the evidence of the Alexander coinage, this hoard found at Babylon was buried almost certainly in 323/2 B.C., before the coinage in the name of Philip [III, Alexander's half-brother and immediate successor] had gained currency." Georges Le Rider is now willing to lower the date a few years, but apparently not as late as 317 B.C.E.: "Antimène de Rhodes à Babylone," *Bulletin of the Asia Institute* 12 (1998): 137; similarly, Hélène Nicolet-Pierre, "Argent et or frappés en Babylone entre 331 et 311 ou de Mazdai à Séleucos," in *Travaux de numismatique grecque offerts à Georges Le Rider,* ed. Michel Amandry and Silvia Hurter, pp. 285–305 (London: Spink, 1999).

specimen (Appendix A, E/A 5), an *ancus,* or hooked elephant goad, could plainly be seen along with the spear in the left hand of the elephant driver (mahout). Nicolet-Pierre particularly stressed the unity and coherence of this entire ensemble of "coins" both on technical and artistic grounds. These three issues "à l'éléphant" clearly had a common purpose, but what was it? The complete lack of an inscription, she argued, placed these coins in the Persian (rather than Greek) tradition of coinage. She judged them to be limited, local, "anecdotal" emissions of uncertain meaning, which did not circulate in Greece with the regular currencies of Alexander and his successors.[12] This deduction won some followers, but others preferred to believe that these medallions constituted a very extensive imperial currency that spread throughout Alexander's realm.

In the same year, Paul Goukowsky reconsidered these medallions in a long discussion of Alexander's apotheosis.[13] These were, he concluded, extraordinary commemorative issues almost certainly struck by Alexander in early 323 B.C.E. at Babylon; they were intended to show the world his superhuman deeds as *Theos Aniketos* ("the invincible god"). Goukowsky identified Alexander's headgear as a Thracian helmet, not a Persian kyrbasia; the king's appearance was therefore deemed purely Macedonian rather than ethnically mixed. Even so, said Goukowsky, Alexander took away from his Macedonian troops all credit for the victory in India, the king laying claim in the medallion's images to a personal "Herculean" exploit that validated his own divinity.

Three years later, Alcibiades N. Oikonomides unfairly criticized Goukowsky's limited knowledge of the elephant medallions.[14] For his part, Oikonomides paid special attention to the reverse design of the standing Alexander, describing in great detail each element of the king's

12. Hélène Nicolet-Pierre, "Monnaies 'à l'éléphant,' " *Bulletin de la Société française de numismatique* 33 (1978): 401–3.

13. Paul Goukowsky, *Essai sur les origines du mythe d'Alexandre,* vol. 1 (Nancy: Université de Nancy, 1978), pp. 61–63.

14. Alcibiades N. Oikonomides, "Decadrachm Aids in Identification of Alexander," *Coin World International,* November 25, 1981: 31–32.

military equipment, although he unfortunately mistook the drapery behind Alexander's left arm for a small cavalry shield *(pelte)*.[15] He concluded
that the purpose of the large medallions was to honor the "last stand" of
Alexander's warhorse Bucephalus. These "coins," he argued, served the
practical function of financing the construction of the city Bucephala,
founded on the banks of the Hydaspes in 326 B.C.E. This solution tried
to fix the decadrachms rather precisely in time and place, but it offered
no explanation whatsoever for the related tetradrachm issues. Nicholas
Hammond, a great pioneer in Macedonian studies, met this particular
problem by assigning altogether different interpretations to the large and
small medallions.[16] Hammond argued that the silver decadrachms must
commemorate Alexander's victory over Porus, saying: "No other battle
is likely." As for the smaller tetradrachms with the bowman and elephant,
Hammond avoided any direct association of these with the battle; he
guessed instead that they recalled an elephant hunt of the type mentioned by Arrian (4.30.8). The other medallions with elephant and chariot, plainly depicting a battle rather than a hunt, do not figure in Hammond's analysis at all. Thus, we have in Hammond's view a miscellany of
artifacts relating to different aspects of the Greek experience in India, the
purposes of none of which are clear or consistent in nature.

The first numismatist really to deal with the problem of reconciling
the apparently contradictory messages on the various medallions was
Martin Price himself. For years, the general idea had been that the large
medallions celebrated a Macedonian victory, and most agreed that this
meant the defeat of Porus at the Hydaspes. But the new smaller types do
not seem to convey this same message. They feature Indian military
units (elephants, archers, chariots) with no trace of defeat anywhere in

---

15. Because the Bunker Hunt decadrachm (App. A, E/A 6) shows plainly that
the *pelte* is really just the folded fabric of Alexander's cloak, Oikonomides condemned it as a forgery: "Scholarship, Research, and The Search for Alexander,"
Ancient World 4 (1981): 68 n. 1.

16. N. G. L. Hammond, *Alexander the Great: King, Commander and Statesman*
(Park Ridge, N.J.: Noyes Press, 1980), p. 284.

their designs; indeed, the victorious Macedonians are nowhere to be seen. The smaller tetradrachms thus seem to hail the power of Porus's army, while the large decadrachms discordantly proclaim its ineffectiveness and total rout.

So while some experts (e.g., Oikonomides) merely sidestepped this issue, and others settled for multiple messages (Hammond), Price came up with a clever—although ultimately unconvincing—solution. First, he theorized that the elephant medallions were not minted to *commemorate* the battle with Porus, but rather to *anticipate* it. The large type depicting Alexander in pursuit of the retreating rajah, with Alexander crowned victorious on the reverse, had to predate the battle, because following the engagement, the two were friends and allies; it would then have been quite inappropriate to taunt Porus with these images, according to Price. This hypothesis would place the mintage in early 326 B.C.E., perhaps as the Macedonians prepared for the campaign. It was in this period, Price notes, that Indian forces under Taxiles joined up with Alexander. The smaller medallions would thus represent these *allied* forces of Indian elephants, archers, and chariots rather than units in the enemy's camp. As such, this pre-battle "coinage" was, Price thought, a bold expression of Alexander's supposed policy of concord and community within his empire and constituted "one of the most powerful statements in the history of numismatics."[17]

It would be a strange and hubristic phenomenon, even for a leader as unique as Alexander, to celebrate a victory *in advance* of the actual battle. One might hope for success, but a pre-victory celebration runs counter to the very nature of Greek culture. Furthermore, Price locates the mintage itself not at Taxila, but far away in Babylon, Susa, Persepolis, or Ecbatana, where this peculiarly "Indian" message might have had little

17. Martin Price, "The 'Porus' Coinage of Alexander the Great: A Symbol of Concord and Community," in *Studia Paulo Naster Oblata*, vol. 1: *Numismatica Antiqua*, ed. S. Scheers, pp. 75–85 (Leuven: Peeters, 1982), quotation at p. 85.

meaning.[18] How would it be possible in, say, Babylon to sort out the images of enemies from allies on these medallions?

Paul Bernard attempted to explain the contradictory messages on the medallions by setting them in a *later* historical context.[19] He agreed on a mint in the area of Babylon, but placed the mintage there some years after Alexander's death, when various Greek and Macedonian generals were battling for supremacy. In these struggles, Bernard argued, Alexander's former satrap of the Punjab, Eudamos, commanded an Indian force that might have occasioned the issuance of the elephant medallions to showcase their power and to recall Alexander's glory. There is an inconsistency here, however: depicting the failure of Porus and his elephants at the Hydaspes surely undermines the alleged message of the smaller medallic coins. Just as important, everything known about the 1973 Iraq hoard stands against Bernard's chronology. This solution to the mystery has therefore gained little support among other investigators.

While Price and Bernard could not effectively overcome the inconsistency in the new evidence, they did contribute a great deal to our understanding of the individual images on the medallions. Both men proved that these artifacts portray the appearance and equipment of Indian soldiers in the fourth century B.C.E. with incredible accuracy. The die engraver must actually have seen these troops, whose hairstyles, for example, match the descriptions in ancient texts. According to Strabo 15.1.71 and Arrian *Indika* 16.4, these Indians wore long beards and tied their hair atop their heads in braided buns, held fast with cords.[20] Their

18. Ibid., pp. 83–84.

19. Paul Bernard, "Le monnayage d'Eudamos, satrape grec du Pandjab et 'maître des éléphants,'" in *Orientalia Iosephi Tucci Memoriae Dicata*, ed. G. Gnoli and L. Lanciotti (Rome: Istituto italiano per il Medio ed Estremo Oriente, 1985), 1: 65–94.

20. Percy Gardner believed the figures to be wholly un-Indian in appearance and identified them as Yueh-chi nomads: "New Greek Coins of Bactria and India," *Numismatic Chronicle* 7 (1887): 179–80; see also chapter 2 above.

archers used bows as tall as a man, which had to be anchored on the ground with the left foot (Arrian *Indika* 16.6), precisely as depicted on the elephant/bowman medallions. Bernard pointed out the accuracy of the clothing, the *ancus*, the banner carried by a rider on the elephant/ chariot variety, and the correctness of the elephant's anatomy (once called into question by earlier commentators).[21] He agreed with Price that Alexander wears no "mixed" Graeco-Persian headgear, but rather a fine plumed and crested helmet of the Thraco-Phrygian type.[22]

Most important, Bernard demonstrated a central fact about ancient elephants and their royal riders. Based upon compelling ethnographic evidence, we must now assume that, as customary with Indian rajahs, Porus managed his own elephant, sitting at its neck. In all previous studies, which placed Porus on the back of the bull elephant, the presumption was that he must be the rearmost rider, seated behind the mahout, fending off Alexander's attack. Bernard reversed these figures, with an Indian attendant grabbing the enemy's spear as his rajah rises up, weapons and goad in hand, to attack Alexander. This changes the entire dynamic of the engagement in ways that may prove critical to understanding the message on these medallions.[23]

Gradually, the floodgates closed against the flow of fresh evidence from the 1973 Iraq hoard. Working with a published total of twenty-four

21. For example, B. V. Head and G. F. Hill had insisted the rear legs of the elephant were rendered inaccurately: Head, *Historia Numorum*, 2d ed. (Oxford: Clarendon Press, 1911; reprint, London: Spink & Son, 1963), p. 833; Hill, "Decadrachm Commemorating Alexander's Indian Campaign," *British Museum Quarterly* 1 (1926/27): 37.

22. A helmet like that shown on the medallions has been discovered in the famous Macedonian tomb at Vergina (northern Greece) associated with Alexander's family: see, e.g., E. N. Borza, "The Royal Macedonian Tombs and the Paraphernalia of Alexander the Great," *Phoenix* 41 (1987): 113–14.

23. Some writers, still following closely the earlier work of Price, have missed Bernard's analysis of the figures on the elephant; see, e.g., the recent study of Federica Smith, *L'immagine di Alessandro il Grande sulle monete del regno (336–323 a.C.)* (Milan: Ennerre, 2000), pp. 15–18.

genuine medallic coins of three types and two denominations, with much die linkage in each group (see Appendix A), Price and Bernard wrapped up the first century of scholarly publication about the medallions (1887–1987). In the second century of study, many experts have merely fallen back upon old interpretations. Before his death, for example, N. G. L. Hammond restated the odd proposition that the small bowman/elephant type commemorated a hunt in India.[24] Although Alexander did enlist the aid of Indians experienced in elephant hunting (Arrian 4.30.8), there is no reason to associate an archer with this endeavor. We are quite well informed about the methods used in India at this time to hunt and trap elephants, thanks largely to Arrian, in a long passage not cited in this context by Hammond.[25] Even wild elephants were lured into hidden enclosures, baited, and herded by trained animals; elephants that were already tame were simply rounded up like cattle.[26] The use of archers was wholly superfluous. A medallion alleged to commemorate one of Alexander's elephant hunts should, it would seem, portray the king himself rather than a type of soldier not known to have played any role in capturing the beasts.

The notion that the large medallion honored the warhorse Bucephalus has also returned to print. In 1994, M. C. J. Miller repeated exactly the same arguments advanced by his teacher A. N. Oikonomides thirteen years earlier.[27] Like Oikonomides (to whom I personally made

24. N. G. L. Hammond, *The Genius of Alexander the Great* (Chapel Hill: University of North Carolina Press, 1997), p. 206.

25. Arrian *Indika* 13–14. For a good discussion of related sources, see A. B. Bosworth, *From Arrian to Alexander: Studies in Historical Interpretation* (Oxford: Clarendon Press, 1988), pp. 41–45. Also helpful is the summary by H. H. Scullard, *The Elephant in the Greek and Roman World* (Ithaca, N.Y.: Cornell University Press, 1974), pp. 56–59.

26. A. B. Bosworth believes that Alexander hunted the latter, domesticated variety: see his *A Historical Commentary on Arrian's "History of Alexander,"* vol. 2 (Oxford: Clarendon Press, 1995), p. 196.

27. M. C. J. Miller, "The 'Porus' Decadrachm and the Founding of Bucephala," *Ancient World* 8 (1994): 109–20. Miller makes no acknowledgment of

this point prior to his death in 1991), Miller failed to strengthen the argument in a rather obvious way. The claim that the elephant-battle obverse was struck to commemorate Bucephalus and to finance the construction of the honorific city Bucephala could be matched by the reverse design, featuring Alexander crowned by Nike (Victory), for the honorific city Nicaea, founded near Bucephala at the same time. While this would make greater sense of the decadrachm, it cannot overcome the remaining problem of the related tetradrachms, which bear no detectable reference to this theme of celebratory cities.

In 1989, Wilhelm Hollstein once again attributed the presentation coins to the Indian ruler Taxiles.[28] Hollstein revisited the report in Curtius (8.12.15) that Alexander received eighty talents, or 2.28 tons, of coined silver from Taxiles. In linking this reference specifically to the elephant medallions, Hollstein was following up a suggestion raised and then dismissed by Martin Price as "highly speculative."[29] Meanwhile, Carmen Arnold-Biucchi (Waggoner's successor at the American Numismatic Society) placed the medallions back in Babylonia as the work of some local satrap, analogous to the lion staters produced there by the Persian Mazaeus.[30] Thus, in recent decades, experts have again assigned these medallic coins to the usual suspects: Taxiles, Alexander, or one of the latter's satraps.

The search among Alexander's satraps has seemed the most promis-

---

the earlier work by Oikonomides. On the foundation of these cities, see P. M. Fraser, *Cities of Alexander the Great* (Oxford: Clarendon Press, 1996), pp. 161–62.

28. Wilhelm Hollstein, "Taxiles' Prägung für Alexander den Grossen," *Schweizerische Numismatische Gesellschaft* 68 (1989): 5–17.

29. Price, "Concord and Community," p. 84. It is to be noted, too, that the medallions do not in any way correspond to the Indian tradition of coinage from Taxila, where punch-marked bars prevailed before (and even after) the arrival of the Macedonians. On these issues, see Michael Mitchiner, *The Origins of Indian Coinage* (London: Hawkins, 1973).

30. Carmen Arnold-Biucchi, "I decadrammi nel mondo greco: Monete o medaglie?" *Rivista italiana di numismatica e scienze affini* 95 (1993): 243–50.

ing approach in the very latest investigations. Here, once more, a possibility mentioned in passing by Martin Price has gained new life. In 1982,
Price wrote of the Greek letters found on most of the medallions: "One
might toy with the idea that the monogram [AB] represents Abulites and
the *xi* [Ξ] Xenophilos, satrap and commander of the garrison respectively
at Susa."[31] The prominent Berkeley archaeologist and art historian Andrew Stewart found this possible connection worth reconsidering in his
classic book *Faces of Power: Alexander's Image and Hellenistic Politics* (1993).
In a detailed evaluation of the medallions (excluding the elephant/char-
iot type as a related but separate issue), Stewart drew attention to an unusual incident involving Abulites, Alexander, and a specific group of
coins. According to Plutarch (*Alex.* 68.7), Alexander ordered Abulites to
bring badly needed provisions to the army after its disastrous march
through Gedrosia. Abulites, however, brought 3,000 talents (about 86
tons) of coinage instead, which Alexander angrily threw to his horses.
Naturally, the animals could not eat the silver, and the king drove home
his rebuke of the satrap by saying: "What good have you done by bringing us *this*?" Alexander then jailed Abulites for his lapse of judgment.[32]

In light of this incident, Stewart asked whether these 3,000 talents
might have included the elephant medallions, produced with the initials
of Abulites and Xenophilos as a special (but under the circumstances un-
welcome) mintage for Alexander. This tentative suggestion found additional support in Robin Lane Fox's long and insightful article on the
problem of the medallions. Lane Fox first considered and then rejected
a number of recent solutions. He criticized attempts to couple the
"coins" with specific texts or incidents, such as Taxiles' monetary gift to
Alexander (Hollstein), Alexander's policy of world brotherhood (Price),
the commemoration of Bucephalus (Miller), or the command of Indian
troops by Eudamos (Bernard). The attribution of the medallions to Ab-

31. Price, "Concord and Community," pp. 83–84.
32. Andrew Stewart, *Faces of Power: Alexander's Image and Hellenistic Politics*
(Berkeley: University of California Press, 1993), pp. 201–6.

ulites and Xenophilos, however, appeared to Lane Fox a promising theory, even though an "overlap between a text and a coin-issue is a rare coincidence." Joking that "future examples should also be tested for hoof-
prints," Lane Fox settled upon the lettering (AB and Ξ) on these "coins"
(excluding, of course, the elephant/chariot types) as a key factor linking
them to Abulites and Xenophilos, and thereby to the anecdote in
Plutarch.[33]

There exist, however, a few possible flaws in this increasingly popular
resolution of the case. First, some textual specialists doubt the whole
story about Alexander and Abulites' coins. J. R. Hamilton, for example,
deems it "highly unlikely" that the king would have ordered the satrap of
distant Susa to bring such aid; Plutarch perhaps made a mistake here,
meaning instead Phrataphernes and Stasanor from the satrapies of Aria
and Drangiana.[34] Second, Arrian (7.4.1) records the arrest and execution
of Abulites under different circumstances at Susa. Third, if Xenophilos
did join Abulites in the manufacture and dispatch of the medallions, he
somehow avoided his partner's fate: Xenophilos was still a commander
and treasurer at Susa after Alexander's death.[35] Fourth, the AB monogram might in fact be read in other ways, such as BA or perhaps BAB,
which would not correspond in any fashion to the name Abulites. Fifth,
while Abulites certainly knew something about elephants, there is no evidence that he (much less Xenophilos) had a detailed knowledge of Indian weapons and warfare.[36] It remains to be seen in a subsequent dis-

33. Robin Lane Fox, "Text and Image: Alexander the Great, Coins and Elephants," *Bulletin of the Institute of Classical Studies* 41 (1996): 87–108; quotations
from p. 108.

34. J. R. Hamilton, *Plutarch, "Alexander": A Commentary* (Oxford: Clarendon
Press, 1969), pp. 184, 191.

35. Attested there in 317/16 B.C.E. by Diodorus 19.17.3, 19.18.1, and
19.48.6.

36. The acquaintance with elephants is attested by Curtius 5.2.10, which
records that Abulites surrendered a dozen of these animals to Alexander when
Susa was captured.

cussion whether the "coins" themselves support a connection with Abulites and Xenophilos, even if we doubt the anecdote in Plutarch about Alexander throwing money to the hungry horses.

Whatever its merits, the recent interest in Alexander's satraps still does nothing to explain the various designs on the medallions. Only one important effort has lately been made to explore this part of the mystery, and it takes us to the opposite extreme from Martin Price's theory of "unity and concord" in Alexander's empire. In 1996, A. B. Bosworth proposed a particularly cynical view of Alexander and the elephant "coins," reflecting Bosworth's dreary picture of Alexander's career as a whole:

> my theme is the underside of victory, the huge unjustifiable cost in human life of a war of imperial annexation and the horror of killing which it entailed. The concomitant squandering of resources is another story again. It imposes the reflection that the history of Alexander is the history of waste—of money, of forests stripped for siege works and navies, and above all of lives. That perspective cannot be lost. The price of Alexander's sovereignty was killing on a gigantic scale, and killing is unfortunately the perpetual backcloth of his regime.[37]

In just five sentences, Bosworth makes five references to killing and loss of life in order to drive home his particular view of Alexander's place in history. He reinforces that approach through his own interpretation of the medallions. On the larger decadrachms, Bosworth sees the dramatic commemoration of Alexander's victory over Porus and, on the reverse, the king's obvious claim to divinity: "The royal mint could not have made it clearer that the king was not only son of Zeus Ammon but Zeus incarnate and as such invincible."[38] The two series of smaller tetradrachms deliver the same message by depicting units of the defeated Indian army.

37. A. B. Bosworth, *Alexander and the East: The Tragedy of Triumph* (Oxford: Oxford University Press, 1996), p. 30.
    38. Ibid., p. 169.

Far from expressing a simple victory or a policy of world brotherhood, these medallions had a particularly sinister purpose:

> In a manner unique in ancient coinage [Alexander] was sending a message to people who could never hope to witness an Indian army in the flesh. These were the outlandish and formidable forces which he had faced in battle and crushed. . . . In the context of the troubles in Greece which followed the Exiles' Decree it would constitute a blunt warning. Beware the consequences of revolt. The army which crushed Porus will easily crush you.[39]

One might agree in every respect to Bosworth's interpretation of the images on these "coins" and still be baffled by this final assessment of their intended message.[40] This facet of Bosworth's bold theory falls asunder on two key points: the unlikely audience for whom Alexander allegedly minted them, and the ambiguous means by which the king's alleged warning was delivered.

According to Bosworth, the elephant medallions were meant neither for Alexander's own troops nor for the eastern provinces, but rather for a distant population that had never seen—and never would see—an Indian army "in the flesh." The idea was apparently to show the uninitiated what an Indian army looked like: its "outlandish and formidable" elephants, archers, and chariots. This would ostensibly serve as a "blunt warning" to those stirred up by the unrest in Greece, troublemakers who needed reminding that what Alexander's army had done to these Indians might just as easily be done to them. To have *any* effect as propaganda, however, the medallions would actually have had to reach that intended audience in Greece and other territories far from the East.[41] Unfortu-

---

39. Ibid., p. 8.

40. As I have noted in Holt, "Alexander the Great Today: In the Interests of Historical Accuracy?" *Ancient History Bulletin* 13, 3 (1999): 111–17, esp. pp. 115–17.

41. It has been argued that Bosworth merely suggests a "general" propaganda warning that would have been "particularly appropriate" (but not aimed directly) at Greece: Ian Worthington, "Alexander and 'the Interests of Historical Accu-

nately, we have absolutely no evidence to suggest that these "coins" ever circulated outside the areas directly controlled by Alexander's main army from 326 to 323 B.C.E. None of the medallions has ever been found in Greece, or indeed anywhere west of Babylonia. So far, the medallions seem to have been localized with—and most probably within—the very army that had defeated Porus. Bosworth has therefore imagined a very unlikely audience for the elephant medallions.

Furthermore, it makes no sense that these artifacts *could* have delivered the message imagined by Bosworth, even if they had reached the hands of potential troublemakers in Greece and elsewhere. If we begin with the premise that Alexander wished to warn his empire against rebellion, particularly in areas that would never see the kinds of forces his army had bested in India, how would the king or his agents most likely have set about this task? The designers of the medallions would, above all else, have had to do three things: (1) issue the "coins" in a denomination that would naturally maximize the impact of the mintage; (2) leave no doubt that Alexander lay behind the warning; (3) make it clear that the Macedonian army had soundly defeated all of the Indian forces being displayed. Reasoning in this way, we find that the elephant medallions actually do none of these things. If they had, there would be no long-standing mystery about who minted them, and why.

How would a population that knew nothing firsthand of Indian military units make any more sense of the medallions than have we? The first modern Europeans to handle the large decadrachm were able to persuade themselves that Central Asian nomads were depicted on the elephant. We have also seen that scholars have variously identified the horseman and manufacturer as Taxiles rather than Alexander. Had Alexander wished to deliver a clear message in the manner suggested by

racy': A Reply," *Ancient History Bulletin* 13, 4 (1999): 140. Even if true, that would not answer my criticism, for there is still no numismatic evidence to suggest *any* westward circulation of the medallions, and it is clear Bosworth means western territories far from the army in the East.

Bosworth, then surely the king would have been less ambiguous by at least including—as he did on all of his other coinages—his own name as the issuing authority. Nor would Alexander have chosen such an inappropriate denomination for his main message. Very large "coins" of this kind do not circulate among the general population, and they would thus have had a notably limited reach as propaganda. The smaller denominations might have been more suited to the task, but they have inexplicably poor designs for such a purpose. That is why an example of the elephant/bowman type in a Swiss collection was never associated with Alexander at all until the discovery of others in the 1973 Iraq hoard; unless seen alongside the large medallions, these "coins" could not be identified and thus, singly, could convey no warning whatsoever. No propaganda to be broadcast far and wide could depend on the medallions traveling everywhere together as a package. How would anyone far from Alexander's army know that these small medallions depict enemy forces rather than (as some modern experts interpret them) friends and allies? What suggests that these forces were ever defeated and, if so, were nonetheless formidable in battle? Simply imagine an Athenian or Milesian examining, say, the bowman/elephant type. No matter how well informed about Alexander's campaigns, the Greek would be hard-pressed to guess that the figures depicted were being defeated by the Macedonian army in India, and that Alexander wished him to understand that he might be next. He might have a better chance of comprehending the victory message on the large decadrachm, but he had virtually no chance of ever seeing one. Bosworth's theory does not seem plausible.

Truth, like beauty, seems to lie in the eye of the beholder. Looking at the very same medallic coins, Price perceived a message of concord and community, while Bosworth read from them an imperial directive of ruthless intimidation. How could the careful and expert scrutiny of this numismatic evidence produce such opposite, incompatible theories? We are accustomed to such problems in our analyses of the written sources for Alexander's life, but generally we expect material evidence to be guileless and therefore more honest and reliable. As Ernst Badian once said

of Alexander studies, "Coins will one day be the most important source, since independent of literary conventions and prejudices."[42] As *corroborative* evidence that is true, but clearly coins can be products of corrupting and confusing conventions all their own.[43] The design—or interpretation—of a coin is subject to prejudice no less than a page from Arrian or Plutarch. So, when others like Bosworth rightly complain that scholars frequently take literary passages out of context in order to manipulate them ("All too often, the concern is to brush aside unpalatable facts, and argue from what the sources should have said"),[44] we ought to beware the same mistreatment of the material evidence. As Percy Gardner noted about numismatics: "If a fact inconvenient to one's theories be discovered, it must not be set aside or neglected but viewed from every side until it is thoroughly assimilated."[45]

It has been shown, for example, that Bosworth himself brushed aside some inconvenient facts about the elephant medallions in order to make them say—out of context—what he thought they *should* have said given his particular views on Alexander. Arguing a priori where a preexisting theory or opinion tightly governs a line of reasoning amounts to what is called special pleading. Scholars predisposed to certain ideas about Alexander will, if not careful, turn every source to that purpose. This remains one of the classic problems in historiography, especially in cases involving controversial figures such as Alexander. We naturally judge the past based upon our own experiences and the values of the age in which we live, so that one generation's hero may become another's monster. In this way, major historical interpretations of Alexander the Great have

42. Ernst Badian, "Alexander the Great, 1948–67," *Classical World* 65 (1971): 53.

43. Something Badian patently understood and considered unnecessary to state, as demonstrated in his various studies of Roman coins, e.g.: "Two Numismatic Phantoms: The False Priest and the Spurious Son," *Arctos* 32 (1998): 45–60.

44. Bosworth, *Alexander and the East*, p. 167.

45. Percy Gardner, *Autobiographica* (Oxford: Basil Blackwell, 1933), p. 29.

changed radically in response to factors that have little to do with the ancient evidence and much to do with modern attitudes toward war, imperialism, justice, human rights, and so forth.

In the Victorian world of Darwin, Franks, and Kipling, Alexander's reputation enjoyed all the advantages of unabashed British imperialism and the so-called White Man's Burden. In 1852, Sir Edward Creasy commended Alexander's career because "[i]t broke the monotony of the Eastern world by the impression of Western energy and superior civilization; even as England's present mission is to break up the mental and moral stagnation of India and Cathay by pouring upon and through them the impulsive current of Anglo-Saxon commerce and conquest."[46]

Not surprisingly, beginning in 1943, everything after the semi-colon in Creasy's jingoistic prose was quietly stricken from subsequent editions of his book. Times change. Even so, the basic image of benevolent conquest (whether Anglo-Saxon or Macedonian) lingered on, famously in the works of Sir William Woodthorpe Tarn (1869–1957), who infused Alexander with the values of a Victorian gentleman.[47] Tarn's Alexander was idealistic, modest, kind, generous, just, chivalrous, and brave; he sought deification only as "a limited *political* measure for a purely political purpose, and nothing else."[48] There could be nothing religious (!) about making himself a god, for that would be a distasteful act; Alexander merely sought divine status to legalize his necessary intervention in the politics of "free" Greek cities. Tarn did not like, and so dismissed, the famous remark attributed to Demosthenes about Alexander's demand for deification: "Let him be the son of Zeus, and of Poseidon, too, if he wants."[49] Zeus, as we shall see, was quite sufficient for Alexander's ego,

---

46. Sir Edward Creasy, *Decisive Battles of the World* (1852; reprint, New York: D. Appleton, 1898), p. 66.

47. Sir William Woodthorpe Tarn, *Alexander the Great*, 2 vols. (Cambridge: Cambridge University Press, 1948).

48. Tarn, *Alexander*, 2: 371.

49. Hyperides *Against Demosthenes* 31, discussed by Tarn in *Alexander*, 2: 363, 373.

yet Tarn downplayed even that ambition. Tarn's Alexander could have no serious faults, and so the sources that alleged them were not to be trusted. For example, the Vulgate tradition (Tarn used the term derisively) allegedly rested upon slanders and lies, and so Tarn deftly argued away all reports therein of Alexander's drunkenness, savagery, paranoia, and perversion. When Tarn (trained as a lawyer) had finished his special pleading, all that remained in the historical record was a compassionate Boy Scout who had (gently) conquered the world to make it a better place. It was a pretty picture, and the public naturally adored it so long as conquering heroes were still fashionable.

But times change, and the past with it. After the horrors of a Second World War, the superiority of European civilization and the blessings of its imperialism seemed less self-evident. So, too, the youthful innocence of Alexander in the eyes of many historians. In 1958, Ernst Badian began publishing a series of articles that skillfully exposed the prejudice and error in Tarn's conception of Alexander.[50] Badian proved time and again that Tarn's methods deliberately distorted the sources wherever necessary to protect his a priori vision of a blameless Alexander. For example, Tarn's lofty portrayal of his hero could not tolerate the reported escapades of the eunuch Bagoas, a scandalous minion attested in Curtius and Plutarch. In a process aptly condemned by Badian as "only the rationalization of prejudice," Tarn tried to discredit these Vulgate sources in order to deny the very existence of the unwanted eunuch.[51] Painstakingly, Badian demonstrated "in paradeigmatic fashion the havoc wrought by prejudice in source criticism."[52] As this and other studies took effect, Badian made it possible (indeed, necessary) to replace Tarn's Victorian Alexander with another more fitting for this postimperial, postheroic

50. Ernst Badian, "Alexander the Great and the Unity of Mankind," *Historia* 7 (1958): 425–44; and id., "The Eunuch Bagoas: A Study in Method," *Classical Quarterly* 8 (1958): 144–57.

51. Tarn, *Alexander the Great*, 2: 319–23; Badian, "Bagoas," p. 156.

52. Badian, "Bagoas," p. 145.

age. Thus, Badian has given us an Alexander more scheming than dreaming, an insecure genius who rid himself of all constraints whether moral, political, or paternal: "an almost embarrassingly perfect illustration of the man who conquered the world, only to lose his soul."[53]

Many studies of Alexander's campaigns reflect the salutary influence of Badian's methodology, and of his more sober assessment of the king's career.[54] Unlike Creasy and Tarn, I have—along with many of my peers—tried to see these wars from the losing side; to assess the damages done to places such as Bactria and Sogdiana; to consider whether Alexander's glory brought more bitterness than brotherhood to the peoples caught in his path. Above all, I have shown that Tarn's magnum opus on Alexander's eastern legacy, *The Greeks in Bactria and India*, must be thoroughly reassessed, because its undisciplined use of numismatic evidence greatly distorted the truth.[55] Tarn's romanticized version of that story, with Greeks and natives living out Alexander's enlightened promise of universal love, hides a less uplifting history of incessant war, intrigue, and exploitation. It should not be counted a coincidence that my generation no longer sees in the world Alexander made the best hopes of Western imperialism, but rather the familiar hazards of failed colonialism: a large, impoverished, exploited Third World; not a reassuring melting pot, but a boiling cauldron of resentment and resistance.

Alexander's early demise left others to shape the future free of the king's personal vision. We must be careful, therefore, to limit Alexander's responsibility for everything that went wrong in the empire he cre-

53. Ernst Badian, "Alexander the Great and the Loneliness of Power," *Journal of the Australasian Universities Language and Literature Association* 17 (1962): 91.

54. Frank Holt, *Alexander the Great and Bactria: The Formation of a Greek Frontier in Central Asia* (Leiden: Brill, 1988); id., "Alexander's Settlements in Central Asia," *Ancient Macedonia* 4 (1986): 315–23; id., "Spitamenes against Alexander," *Historikogeographika* 4 (1994): 51–58; id., "Alexander the Great and the Spoils of War," *Ancient Macedonia* 6 (1999): 499–506.

55. Frank Holt, *Thundering Zeus: The Making of Hellenistic Bactria* (Berkeley: University of California Press, 1999).

ated but barely lived to consolidate or control. Mine may be called a moderate view: Alexander was not as noble and wholesome as Tarn believed, but also not as vile and deranged as some scholars have lately suggested. Bosworth's perception of Alexander the cruel conquistador has gained credence among a growing crowd of scholars and writers, from Michael Wood in his popular book and BBC documentary to Ian Worthington in his latest articles. This image of Alexander has replaced Tarn's Eagle Scout with a cunning serial killer. Worthington now describes Alexander in ways that would have baffled the Victorians: bipolar (p. 49), sacrilegious (pp. 46–47), foolish (pp. 47 and 51–52), a failure as king (pp. 44, 51), and a questionable general (pp. 45–47).[56] This is the new orthodoxy about Alexander, a scholarly consensus that has captured the cynical spirit of our times so completely that it blinds us to less extreme interpretations.

So, at the other end of the pendulum swing, we meet again the danger of an Alexander contrived from current events and a priori arguments.[57] Like vampires, historians seldom see themselves in the mirrors they hold up to history. We idealize objectivity, and thus we like to believe that we have polished the mirror free of all distortions and extraneous images. But the study of the past is, of course, woefully human and subjective—one might as easily say personal and biased. History always to one degree or another betrays in its mirror the presence and preoccupations of the historian and the times. Admitting this is the first step toward good methodology, because only then can we *look* for ourselves in

56. Michael Wood, *In the Footsteps of Alexander the Great* (Berkeley: University of California Press, 1997); Ian Worthington, "How 'Great' Was Alexander?" *Ancient History Bulletin* 13, 2 (1999): 39–55.

57. See on this point the debate concluded in the pages (and at the web site) of the *Ancient History Bulletin (AHB)*: Frank Holt, "Alexander the Great Today: In the Interests of Historical Accuracy?" *AHB* 13, 3 (1999): 111–17; answered by Ian Worthington, "Alexander and 'the Interests of Historical Accuracy': A Reply," *AHB* 13, 4 (1999): 136–40; answered by Holt, "The Death of Coenus: Another Study in Method," *AHB* 14, 1–2 (2000): 49–55.

the mirror and account for the distortions of history made in our own image. When the past unselfconsciously wears our face and mimes our intentions, it usually reflects an extreme vantage point unrecognized as flawed and fatal to the facts. Such was the hero created by Tarn, and such now is the anti-hero fashioned by some scholars of my generation.

SIX

A Closer Look

The elephant medallions must be more than another Rorschach test in which to see, with equal claims of propriety, Alexander the Beatified or Alexander the Beast. How, then, should we handle these mysterious artifacts in order to reach reliable conclusions about Alexander's reign? The key is to avoid, as far as possible, any forms of special pleading based upon preconceived notions about Alexander. Our views of the king must conform to the evidence of the medallions and not vice versa. So let us begin with the physical objects, allowing them first to speak for themselves rather than for one modern camp or another. The procedure should be logical and rigorous: (a) determine what are the precise images on each of the denominations, drawing upon corroborative evidence whenever possible; (b) establish as reasonably as we can where the medallions were made, how many were produced, and under whose authority; and (c) interpret the function of this entire mintage *as a group* in terms of its intended audience and message, learning from this what we can about the king and his contemporaries. There can be no question, of course, that the elephant/Alexander and elephant/bowman types must be treated as a group, since they are united by style, subject matter, and markings (AB and Ξ). The placement of the elephant/chariot type in this same group seems assured in terms of style and subject, although present ex-

amples lack the Greek markings. Even the exclusion of the chariot variety, because it has no markings, would still leave us the fundamental problem of mixed messages on the other two types. Ideally, a solution must be found that makes sense of the indisputable elements in this group and accommodates the likely inclusion of the elephant/chariot type as a reassuring bonus.

We shall proceed, therefore, with a closer look at the actual images on these medallic coins, beginning with the least controversial: the reverse of the large so-called decadrachms. By creating a composite picture based upon all of the genuine specimens, no one of which preserves every detail because of the irregular strikings and wear, we discern a warrior standing in regal splendor from head to toe (see fig. 5). He is literally dressed to kill. He wears a gorget (neck guard) and helmet with forward-sweeping peak adorned with a bristled (horsehair?) crest and tall, feathered plumes. Much discussed as possibly Homeric or a hybrid Graeco-Persian design, this helmet can now be positively identified as the Phrygian type (sometimes also called Thracian) used in Alexander's army. A bronze example in the Ioannina Museum (no. 6419), found at Vitsa in Epirus, even preserves the sockets for the attachment of crest and plumes.[1] Less elaborate versions, lacking the plumes and crest, appear in contemporary fourth-century B.C.E. paintings and sculpture.[2] We know that the accoutrements, by size/shape/color, were designed to distinguish various personages in battle.[3] According to Plutarch *(Alex.* 16.7), Alexander was easily rec-

1. The helmet is illustrated in René Ginouvès, ed., *Macedonia from Philip II to the Roman Conquest* (Princeton: Princeton University Press, 1994), p. 78.

2. For examples, on the so-called Alexander Sarcophagus and a fresco from the "Kinch" tomb in Macedonia: Andrew Stewart, *Faces of Power: Alexander's Image and Hellenistic Politics* (Berkeley: University of California Press, 1993), items 100 and 101–2.

3. See, e.g., the account of King Pyrrhus's distinctive helmet in Plutarch *Pyrrhus* 11. The extent to which a ruler might go to sport a uniquely identifiable helmet may be seen on various Hellenistic coins, particularly those of King

Figure 5.   The reverse of the
large medallion.

ognizable (even to his enemies) by the conspicuous crest of his helmet,
which had a dramatically tall white plume on each side.[4] At the battle
of the Granicus River, where the Persians were drawn to the singular
headgear of the enemy king, Alexander came under concentrated attack: a Persian nobleman managed to get close enough to strike
Alexander's helmet with a battle-ax, breaking off the crest and one of
the white plumes.[5] At Gaugamela, Alexander wore a helmet made of
iron, polished to a gleaming silver luster, the handiwork of one
Theophilos; a gorget decorated with precious stones was fitted to it.[6]
Just such a unique iron helmet of the Phrygian type has been discovered in the royal Macedonian cemetery at Vergina (ancient Aegae), in

Tryphon ("the Magnificent"): Norman Davis and Colin Kraay, *The Hellenistic
Kingdoms: Portrait Coins and History* (London: Thames & Hudson, 1973), no. 102.

   4. J. R. Hamilton, *Plutarch, "Alexander": A Commentary* (Oxford: Clarendon
Press, 1969), p. 40.

   5. Plutarch *Alex.* 16.10; Arrian 1.15.8; Diodorus 17.20.6.

   6. Plutarch *Alex.* 32.9.

a tomb identified as that of either Alexander's father or his half-brother. One expert has attributed this helmet to Alexander himself, based in part on the evidence of the elephant medallions.[7] Whether indeed archaeologists have recovered one of Alexander's actual helmets buried as an extraordinary family heirloom, we can see that the image on the medallions matches what we know of the royal Macedonian headgear worn at that time.[8]

The remaining armor and weaponry of our standing warrior is equally Macedonian, rather than "mixed" or Persian, and has its parallels (or actual pieces) in the tomb at Vergina. Below the neck-guard, he wears a round-tipped scabbard hung from a shoulder strap, as shown on the so-called Alexander Mosaic from Pompeii (plate 1). The precise type appears to be a *xiphos*, a straight, double-edged sword, rather than a *makhaira*, the curved, single-edged cavalry saber, the handle of which was shaped like the head of a beast or bird of prey (lion, eagle, etc.).[9] The xiphos on the medallions, comparable also to the one found on the floor of the royal Macedonian tomb at Vergina, has a spindle-shaped handle. The length of this sheathed weapon, from the scabbard's bouterolle (the metal tip) to the sword's hilt (plainly visible on the Franks specimen, plate 2), may be judged by the length of the warrior's arm from elbow to fingertip (a cubit) as measurable on the 1926 example in the British Mu-

7. Eugene Borza, "The Royal Macedonian Tombs and the Paraphernalia of Alexander the Great," *Phoenix* 41 (1987): 112–14.

8. N. G. L. Hammond, "Arms and the King: The Insignia of Alexander the Great," *Phoenix* 43 (1989): 217–24, esp. p. 221. There is no evidence to associate a Persian tiara with this headgear: see Ernst Fredricksmeyer, "Alexander and the Kingship of Asia," in *Alexander the Great in Fact and Fiction*, ed. A. B. Bosworth and E. J. Baynham, pp. 136–66 (Oxford: Oxford University Press, 2000), pp. 153–54.

9. Ironically, our best physical evidence for ancient weaponry of these types comes from the excavated temple at Takht-i Sangin, the probable "home" of the Franks medallion. On the swords found there, see Boris Litvinsky and Igor Pichikyan, "Handles and Ceremonial Scabbards of Greek Swords from the Temple of the Oxus in Northern Bactria," *East and West* 49 (1999): 47–104.

seum (see plate 3). This rough calculation gives us an ensemble appropriately thirty-two inches (81 cm) long. This weapon may seem suspiciously out of place, but as one archaeologist reminds us: "It is interesting to note that when fighting on horseback Alexander the Great used a *xiphos*," rather than a cavalryman's makhaira.[10] This idiosyncrasy accords with the images on the medallic coins.

Our soldier also, it seems, wears a cuirass (breastplate), as found in the Vergina tomb and depicted on the Alexander Mosaic; the belt and overlapping fringes from the warrior's waist to his thighs can be seen on the medallions. As in the mosaic and other artworks, a cavalry cloak *(chlamys)* drapes over the man's left shoulder and falls behind him.[11] On the medallions, the deep folds are quite noticeable, *over* the biceps—those who have seen in this shape a cavalry shield *(pelte)* hanging *behind* the shoulder have clearly been mistaken. The warrior's shins and feet are not easily examined on the available specimens, but they were probably protected by a tight *kothornos* of light leather, with exposed toes.[12]

Held upright in the grip of the man's left hand is a tall shaft, variously identified as a scepter or a spear *(sarissa)*. The length falls considerably short of a Macedonian cavalry sarissa, which would at 4.5 to 5.5 meters (about 15 to 18 feet) stand more than twice the height shown on the medallion; on the other hand, it corresponds nicely to the length of a scepter (two meters) reportedly from the royal tomb at Vergina.[13] Naturally, we must consider the limitations faced by the die engraver, who could not have represented a Macedonian sarissa accurately on the flan of the medallion, except by truncating its length severely. No decision

10. Ibid., p. 103.

11. A good example of the helmet (without plumes), cuirass, and cloak may be found on a fourth-century B.C.E. stele from Pelinna: see Ginouvès, ed., *Macedonia from Philip II to the Roman Conquest*, p. 51.

12. As illusory as the shield are the greaves (metal leg-guards) some have seen on the medallions: M. C. J. Miller, "The 'Porus' Decadrachm and the Founding of Bucephala," *Ancient World* 25 (1994): 111–12.

13. Borza, "Paraphernalia," p. 116.

between a scepter and a spear can therefore be made solely on the basis of observable length. If a sarissa were intended, then we should expect to see both a large spear point and a counterbalancing blade at the other end.[14] On the medallion, the upright shaft has a leaf-shaped point, but no visible counterpoint at the ground line. As an alternate possibility, could a scepter take this form? On Alexander's voluminous regular silver currency, scepters of many varieties appear in the left hand of the seated figure of Zeus.[15] Some have smooth shafts, others "dotted"; some have finials at both ends. Almost any long rod, even one looking quite like a spear, could pass for a scepter in the artwork of these dies. Thus, it would be safe on present evidence to declare this object a scepter without much fear of direct contradiction; but it might actually be a cropped sarissa nonetheless. We have no basis for absolute certainty on this point.

The object grasped by the warrior in his other hand presents no such problem: it is clearly and quite dramatically a bolt of lightning. Rendered as a barbed shaft in a fashion often encountered on ancient coins and other artworks, this divine instrument could only be wielded by Zeus, or some hero-god especially endowed by (or as) the god himself. As the leading divinity of the Greek pantheon, Zeus controlled the sky and, most significantly, the weather. He gathered clouds, shook the earth with thunder, unleashed rain, and struck fiercely with his lightning. In this aspect, Zeus appeared awesome and invincible.[16] This Olympian god, however, is not known to have dressed in Macedonian military gear. We

14. Minor Markle, "The Macedonian Sarissa, Spear, and Related Armor," *American Journal of Archaeology* 81 (1977): 323–39; Peter Manti, "The Macedonian Sarissa, Again," *Ancient World* 25 (1994): 77–91.

15. Martin Price, *The Coinage in the Name of Alexander the Great and Philip Arrhidaeus*, 2 vols. (London: British Museum Press, 1991).

16. Lightning and thunder were not easily explained in the ancient world except as spectacular divine forces; even so, Lucretius, Seneca, and others tried later to "naturalize" these phenomena (with limited success). See Roger French, *Ancient Natural History* (London: Routledge, 1994), pp. 158–59, 173–75.

do not see Zeus as a cavalry commander on the medallion, but rather a cavalryman with the attribute of Zeus being crowned by a flying Nike, winged goddess of victory.[17] Although she sometimes appears on Greek coins and pottery crowning a victorious athlete (or even the winning horses in a race), here she clearly celebrates a military triumph by the extraordinary uniformed warrior. Who is he?

Our god-like hero, boldly associated with Zeus the Thunderer, wears the equipment of a Macedonian cavalryman of the highest rank. His helmet is marked by distinctive plumage, and he perhaps even bears a royal scepter, but he favors an infantry sword. He is undoubtedly clean-shaven and youthful in appearance. This description tallies in every respect with Alexander the Great; indeed, no alternative seems possible. It is well known that Alexander received recognition as the son of Zeus and, with soaring pretensions, allowed the painter Apelles to portray him clutching a thunderbolt in his hand.[18] The actual appearance of this "Alexander Keraunophoros" ("Alexander Carrying a Thunderbolt"), considered "one of the most renowned portraits in the history of Greek art," remains somewhat conjectural.[19] Some art experts surmise that in this painting, the king sits on the throne of Zeus, a scepter in his right hand and the bolt of lightning cradled in his left arm (as copied, perhaps, in a painting from the House of the Vettii at Pompeii).[20] Others prefer the so-called Neisos gem, now in the Hermitage Museum, as a possible copy.[21] It depicts Alexander standing, nude, with the thunderbolt in his right hand

17. One scholar seems to think that the winged figure is a bearded male: Federica Smith, *L'immagine di Alessandro il Grande sulle monete del regno (336–323 a.C.)* (Milan: Ennerre, 2000), p. 16.

18. Plutarch *Alex.* 4.3; *Moralia* 335A and 360D; cf. Pliny *Natural History* 35.92.

19. Stewart, *Faces of Power,* p. 191.

20. J. J. Pollitt, *Art in the Hellenistic Age* (Cambridge: Cambridge University Press, 1986), pp. 22–23 with illustration.

21. Stewart, *Faces of Power,* pp. 199–200 and figs. 66–67.

and an aegis on his left arm; a sword, shield, and large eagle are also shown with the king.

All of this, but especially the thunderbolt, strongly associates Alexander with the god of the sky and announces that the king commands some of Zeus's divine power and therefore demands some of the same respect. It is a bold step in the exaltation of a ruler, making Alexander the equal of a god (but not replacing that god). There can be little doubt that Alexander himself sponsored this whole transformation, and that he commissioned its representation both in the painting by Apelles and on the elephant medallion.[22] Which artwork came first, we have no means of knowing; they cannot be compared except for the fact that both place a bolt of lightning in Alexander's hand. That similarity points only to an official iconography of the king's emerging status (another example of this is considered below). So far, we have a clear identification of Alexander on the large medallions that is universally accepted. R. R. R. Smith calls it "our only certainly contemporary image of Alexander."[23] This alone makes the portrayal fundamentally important for the history of art and religion.[24]

On the obverse of the large medallic coin we find the equally unprecedented battle scene that has for so long defied scholarly consensus

22. Ibid., pp. 192–96 makes a good case that only Alexander could have commissioned and borne the costs of the Apelles painting. Stewart believes, however, that the medallions were "minted on private initiative" and inspired by Apelles' work (p. 196).

23. R. R. R. Smith, *Hellenistic Royal Portraits* (Oxford: Clarendon Press, 1988), p. 40.

24. "It would, indeed, be very tempting to draw the straight-forward conclusion that Alexander was the first 'god in uniform' and that he, general and god at the same time—as depicted also in a decadrachme of the mint of Babylon—started the Egyptian-Alexandrian tradition of representing not only the native gods in military attire but also the Graeco-Roman gods who in classical times were preferably represented in the nude or loosely draped," Ernst Kantorowicz writes in "Gods in Uniform," *Proceedings of the American Philosophical Society* 105 (1961): 373.

Figure 6.   The obverse of the large medallion.

(see fig. 6). It is absolutely a bolt from the blue, a numismatic tour de force that has no direct antecedent. Indeed, the closest the Greeks had ever come before to producing such a medallion were the beautiful celebratory issues of fifth-century B.C.E. Sicily.[25] Those stunning coinages, some of them quite large and some of them signed by their die cutters, glorified the achievements of various tyrants and cities. We find victorious racing chariots being crowned by flying Nikes and cavalrymen spearing fallen infantrymen; but, even there, we encounter nothing quite so extraordinary as the designs on the elephant medallions and the unusual absence of any inscribed reference to the issuing authority.

On the elephant medallions, the Macedonian cavalryman wears precisely the outfit already noted on the medallion's reverse (plumed helmet, cloak, cuirass); the sword, which would hang on the rider's left side opposite our vantage point, cannot be detected on this side of the medallion. This must, then, be a Macedonian cavalryman and not (say) an Indian soldier such as Taxiles or his brother. We cannot escape the obvious con-

25. See, e.g., G. K. Jenkins, *Ancient Greek Coins,* 2d ed. (London: Seaby, 1990), pp. 84–108.

clusion that the cavalryman on both sides of the medallion must be the same victor, and hence Alexander the Great. He clearly holds the Macedonian sarissa and is attacking the retreating elephant (as opposed to the old theory that the spear has been jabbed back *at* the horseman). This is plainly visible on the medallions and only makes sense when we further recognize that the cavalryman is the crowned victor from the other side of the medallic coin and so hardly a victim of the elephant rider.

The horse (a stallion, by all appearances) rears upward in the most familiar equestrian pose of Greek battle art, a normal convention of ancient copybooks. We find the same composition in the so-called Alexander Mosaic, Apulian vase-paintings of Alexander in battle, the so-called Alexander Sarcophagus from Sidon, and various statues.[26] On the elephant medallion, the horse's position appears especially natural given the upward aim of Alexander's spear. The lines of the bridle can be discerned, and also the outline of an animal skin or blanket upon which the king rides. There were, of course, no stirrups in that period; the rider depended upon great skill and strong legs to stay mounted during the vicissitudes of battle.

Is this animal on the medallions the famous warhorse Bucephalus, Alexander's favorite charger? According to legend, this high-strung (and high-priced) horse could not be handled by King Philip's staff until the young Alexander rode the animal.[27] Bucephalus (meaning "Ox-head" in Greek) became Alexander's constant companion and was implausibly rumored by Onesicritus to be the same age as Alexander. The horse died at or soon after the battle of the Hydaspes, either of wounds or old age, and was honored there with a city founded in his name. Obviously, we

26. All illustrated and discussed in Stewart, *Faces of Power*, figs. 21, 26, 27, and 103, with comparative material; cf. Margarete Bieber, *Alexander the Great in Greek and Roman Art* (Chicago: Argonaut, 1964).

27. For sources and discussion, see A. R. Anderson, "Bucephalus and His Legend," *American Journal of Philology* 51 (1930): 1–21.

cannot see the distinctive markings (an ox-like brand or white blaze) of Bucephalus on this medallic coin, so no one can be certain of this identification.[28] Alexander did use other horses at times, not surprising given the rate of attrition for cavalry mounts during the arduous campaign. The Macedonians, for example, lost over a thousand horses to injuries or exhaustion at Gaugamela.[29] In Bactria and Sogdiana, Alexander's cavalry had to requisition fresh mounts on several occasions because their own had been ruined by unremitting service.[30] The slaughter of horses in battle can be witnessed in such art works as the Alexander Mosaic and the Alexander Sarcophagus. Naturally, given the Macedonian kings' obligation to lead by example, royal mounts suffered no less than others: the blow that lamed Philip also killed his horse, and Alexander allegedly lost horses from under him at the battles of Granicus and the Hydaspes.[31] The latter case may or may not refer to Bucephalus.

In any event, of the thousands of horses killed during Alexander's campaigns, only Bucephalus received the exceptional honors of a city-foundation and a prominent place in Alexander mythology; his appearance on the medallion would therefore make much sense unless we insist that the scene captures an actual historical moment known to have occurred after the collapse of this particular horse. We cannot go that far. If we take the horse to be Bucephalus, there is still no reason to make this

28. In later numismatic iconography, during the reign of Seleucus I, Bucephalus takes on distinctive horns (as does Alexander's helmet): see Arthur Houghton and Andrew Stewart, "The Equestrian Portrait of Alexander the Great on a New Tetradrachm of Seleucus I," *Schweizerische Numismatische Rundschau* 78 (1999): 27–35.

29. Arrian 3.15.6. Alexander himself wore out several mounts in this battle: Curtius 4.15.31.

30. Arrian 3.30.6; cf. 4.5.5. As N. G. L. Hammond pointed out in his study of "Cavalry Recruited in Macedonia down to 322 B.C.," *Historia* 47 (1998): 425, the main limitation of cavalry in Alexander's reign was not manpower but the availability of good horses.

31. Justin 9.3.2; Plutarch *Alex.* 16.14; Curtius 8.14.34.

animal the star of the large medallion and much less the commemorative purpose for the whole mintage. He was famous and played his last role in this battle, and his legend evoked—like the Gordian Knot and other prodigies—a divine prophecy of world conquest.[32] This seems quite enough to account for the animal's depiction on the medallion. In any event, Bucephalus or not, it simply would not do to have the king chasing down the elephant on foot.

That bull elephant moves to the right, its feet solidly upon the ground line, which does not reach back as far as the rearing horse. The convex back and the shape of the head and ears distinguish this as an Indian elephant. Some have worried that the die engraver misrepresented the hind legs by "reversing" the knees, but this is not the case, as the left rear leg plainly shows. The physiology is correct and leaves no doubt that the artist or his source had a reasonable knowledge of these beasts (see chapter 4 above). Beginning with this engraving, the Greeks created a long line of numismatic pachyderms for the Hellenistic rulers of the East, who kept large, well-advertised herds for military purposes; none of these images is any more naturalistic than the one on our medallions.[33]

The two riders on the elephant appear unusually large compared both to their mount and to the attacking cavalryman. The driver, seated at the elephant's neck, would stand taller than the pachyderm, if I am correct in thinking that the protrusion visible at the elephant's front leg is this man's foot. He brandishes a spear (shorter than the attacker's sarissa) in his upraised right hand and holds another—along with the hooked goad—in his left hand. His hair has been tied up in a bun, and he seems bearded. His compatriot appears likewise, though unarmed and desperately engaged with the cavalryman's sarissa. Certainly, this man's right hand grasps the weapon, which seems to have penetrated his side; his other hand reaches down and may convulsively grip the extruded point

32. Anderson, "Bucephalus," pp. 3, 17–18.
33. H. H. Scullard, *The Elephant in the Greek and Roman World* (Ithaca, N.Y.: Cornell University Press, 1974). If anything, the medallions do a far better job than many other coins—especially those of such western rulers as Juba and Caesar.

of the sarissa. Alexander has dealt this figure a mortal wound, and the driver reacts too late to save him.

It has been shown (chapter 5) that the very large elephant driver must be the rajah Porus if this scene illustrates, either symbolically or faithfully, Alexander's battle against him at the Hydaspes River. Indeed, no other interpretation makes as much sense of the image. This cannot be Gaugamela, and the enemy cannot be Darius. These warriors are patently Indian, rendered with amazing accuracy. At most, we might argue that these are anonymous foes—two generic Indians in desperate and dangerous retreat, representing the Macedonian victory so dramatically celebrated on the medallion's other side. But, that being the case, a portrayal of the defeated enemy king himself (no matter how much admired by Alexander) best conveys that triumph here, just as the so-called Alexander Mosaic prominently includes Darius. The extraordinary size and warlike demeanor of the Indian warrior in the regal position at the elephant's neck reinforces that notion. All ancient accounts agree that Porus was a broad-chested giant of a man, standing from 6 to 7.5 feet tall (about 1.8 to 2.3 m).[34] His remarkable size, "nearly exceeding the limits of human stature" (Curtius 8.14.13), allowed him to sit upon his large elephant like other men upon a horse (Plutarch *Alex.* 60.12); this is not a bad description of the relative proportions shown on the medallion. Porus's size may account for the odd reports in the Vulgate tradition that Alexander ordered his men to leave behind oversized camps and armor at the Hyphasis River as a deceptive measure. The exaggerated beds, five cubits (about 7.5 feet) long, would have suited Porus; why should the victorious Macedonians seem any less impressive to the unconquered peoples beyond the Hyphasis River?[35]

34. Plutarch *Alex.* 60.12; Arrian 5.19.1; Diodorus 17.88.4; Curtius 8.14.13. Alexander, by contrast, stood probably only about 5'7": see Stewart, *Faces of Power*, p. 72.

35. Plutarch *Alex.* 62.7; Diodorus 17.95.1–2; Justin 12.8.16; Curtius 9.3.19. Porus's stature became the legendary standard for Indians: Pliny *Natural History* 7.22.

The large medallions, then, depict Alexander on horseback attacking a fleeing elephant on which two Indians ride, one of them probably Porus rising up and twisting back to fend off his enemy, but too late to save his faithful attendant, who has taken the thrust of Alexander's sarissa. There exists a fascinating but heretofore unrecognized parallel between this commemorative image and the so-called Alexander Mosaic (plate 1).[36] The latter came to light on October 24, 1831, during excavations in the House of the Faun at Pompeii.[37] Thousands of times larger than the silver medallion, the mosaic blends together millions of colored tesserae to form a massive battle scene. Though busy with weapons and warriors from end to end, the unmistakable "heart of the picture" (as Andrew Stewart calls it)[38] is the interplay of three key figures: Alexander, Darius, and the dying Persian between them. This, of course, mirrors the three men on the medallion: Alexander, Porus, and the dying Indian between them. In both cases, Alexander rides in from the left on his rearing horse and spears an enemy. The impaled victim twists around and grabs the sarissa with his right hand, whether as an involuntary reflex or a determined effort to sacrifice himself for his king. High on the right, the monarch thereby saved from Alexander's attack twists backward in a desperate response to the loss of his comrade. The parallels in theme and composition are all the more remarkable when we consider that two very different battles against quite dissimilar foes have been rendered so alike in different media, each engagement reduced to the same shorthand dynamic between opposing kings and a sacrificed intermediary. Of all the ways to depict these battles, and there *are* quite different renditions of the

36. Some experts such as Federica Smith, *L'immagine*, p. 15, have noted only the iconographic assimilation of Alexander the mounted sovereign in battle; the parallels far exceed this common theme, embracing (as will be shown) other combatants as well.

37. Andrew Stewart, *Faces of Power*, pp. 130–50; Ada Cohen, *The Alexander Mosaic: Stories of Victory and Defeat* (Cambridge: Cambridge University Press, 1997), with earlier bibliography.

38. Stewart, *Faces of Power*, p. 144.

same moment in the Darius battle to be found in contemporary paintings, it seems extraordinary that the mosaic and medallion capture (or concoct) the same poses from the same angle.[39]

The minor discrepancies between mosaic and medallion are easily understood: naturally, Darius retreats in a chariot, whereas Porus does so on an elephant; Porus holds a spear and *ancus* in his left hand rather than a small Persian bow, and raises another spear in his right—as opposed to Darius's empty hand—too late to save his companion; Alexander wears his helmet on the medallion, the same one that allows us to identify him from the reverse, whereas in the mosaic—probably to better show his expression—his helmet has been dislodged. The large and colorful mosaic can naturally enhance the picture with secondary figures and greater facial detail in ways no medallion ever could, but in essence we confront in this interaction of the three key characters the same synopsis of Alexander's victories in Persia and India.

These comparable depictions of Alexander in battle against his two royal foes might well represent an emerging, "official" iconography for his wars not unlike the thunderbolt marking his personal authority. This possibility has important ramifications. For example, the latest interpretations of the Alexander Mosaic have taken a predictable turn in light of current historiography and the new orthodoxy. A century or more ago, most commentators viewed the mosaic as entirely complimentary to Alexander and his invincible Macedonian army. The Persians appeared weak and helpless, reeling from the shock of the young king's attack. In time, of course, modern sympathies changed, and the Persians gradually came to appear more heroic and the Macedonians less so. Some of this revisionism makes a lot of sense and explores new insights from art history. Thus, experts such as Andrew Stewart and Ada Cohen have recently written about the "visual rhymes" in the piece and the possibilities of understanding the composition as a narrative or dramatic text, a "photograph," or a complex mixture of *realia*, fantasy, and philosophy. But now

39. Ibid., pp. 150–57; Cohen, *Alexander Mosaic*, pp. 64–68.

historians have turned this work into another way to challenge Alexander's heroism and alleged greatness. Today, we read that the intention of this piece was to denigrate the Macedonian king as a demonic monster soon after his death. Ernst Badian writes of Alexander's "ruthless ugliness" and Darius's "compassionate horror" as reflections of a tradition openly hostile to the Macedonian king, one perhaps sponsored by Cassander "as part of his vengeance against Alexander."[40] Because of the manner in which the mosaicist has rendered the stark, dead tree, and because everything (including Alexander and his "recalcitrant horse") allegedly leans to the left away from the momentum of the *Persian* charge, Badian perceives a calculated slap at Alexander: "The representation as a whole may justly be called not merely not heroic, but deliberately unheroic."[41]

This may, of course, be correct; however, we must consider the possibility that this interpretation follows the pendulum swing of professional opinion about Alexander the Less-than-Great too far. After all, the argument that "in fact *no* Persian except for the charioteer clearly leans away from the enemy" (Badian's emphasis) brushes aside the inconvenient fact that the Persian tending the riderless horse beside Darius's chariot emphatically does so.[42] Nor is Alexander unable to handle his horse, so that both recoil unheroically from the Persians; in truth, horse and rider have just accomplished a notable feat—driving a spear completely through an enemy soldier without benefit of stirrups. In these instances, the horseman must always quickly pull back at impact or release the sarissa altogether and draw his sword.[43] Horse and rider are not here shown as clumsy or cowardly, but rather as capable and commanding.

That very pose we have already studied on the large elephant medal-

40. Ernst Badian, "A Note on the 'Alexander Mosaic,' " in *The Eye Expanded: Life and the Arts in Graeco-Roman Antiquity*, ed. Frances B. Titchener and Richard F. Moorton, Jr., pp. 75–92 (Berkeley: University of California Press, 1999), p. 84.

41. Ibid., p. 82.

42. Ibid., p. 79.

43. Minor Markle, "Macedonian Sarissa," p. 334; cf. Stewart, *Faces of Power*, pp. 144–45.

lions, where the message of Alexander's enviable invincibility could not be more certain, just as it is on the so-called Alexander Sarcophagus from Sidon and other artworks. More important, the aforementioned parallels between the medallion (which *cannot* be considered critical of Alexander) and the mosaic make it difficult to accept Badian's anti-heroic reading of the latter, which ought likewise to be seen as a laudatory portrayal of the Macedonian king. This does not mean, of course, that the Persians are rendered as unmanly or unworthy. In fact, Andrew Stewart's cogent remarks about the center figure in the mosaic, the warrior skewered by Alexander's sarissa, highlights the Persians' heroism. Stewart argues that this man grasping the spear "must have actually thrown himself on it. No womanish Oriental, he is a man of high courage, one who belies the racist stereotype of the craven barbarian."[44]

Darius, though doomed in the end, has been saved at this perilous moment by Fortune—and a self-sacrificing compatriot as brave as any Greek or Macedonian on the field that day. Alexander thus has his glory, but not without some respect also being accorded his worthy adversaries. This same balanced attitude seems, then, to find expression on the obverse of the large medallic coin as a sponsored motif. Alexander is not presented in either artistic medium as a villain, but as a warrior king putting his enemies to flight. But for a courageous act of sacrifice, the opposing ruler would be killed by Alexander's own hand. This spares everyone's honor, while still driving home the essential fact of a complete Macedonian victory.

These observations indicate that the battle between Alexander and Porus has been shown symbolically. There is no reason to worry whether we can find some ancient text that exactly describes this very scene. As a metaphor for Alexander's victory, rendered beautifully on metal dies, the composition does not concern itself with whether Bucephalus was then still alive or whether the two kings ever came this close in the course of the actual battle. All of the figures and their equipment have been faith-

44. Stewart, *Faces of Power,* p. 145.

fully rendered, but the pose has been dictated by an emerging artistic motif for Alexander at war. That Alexander is obviously heroic, intense, deadly, and frightening; he exemplifies the Macedonian ideal, not ours. His *arete* (martial prowess) does not thrive on the weakness of his enemies, but on their worthiness as opponents. This was essential to the Homeric code by which he lived and conquered. Whether this sort of man suits us today is not the issue; he was a product of his times, proud of it, and duly portrayed as such on the medallion and in the mosaic.

The reverse of the medallic coin shows Nike crowning the victorious Alexander, who wears Macedonian battle dress and wields Zeus's lightning bolt, as no ordinary mortal can. To call this artifact a victory medallion seems appropriate in every respect, but what of the related specimens that turn the numismatic spotlight on the Indian army? What do we see there, and how can it be reconciled with Alexander's bold declaration of divine invincibility?

On the obverse of one set of the so-called tetradrachms, we observe a riderless male Indian elephant walking to the right. There is no ground line, and a circle of small dots encloses the design. On some specimens, this pachyderm appears sturdy and bulky like the one on the large medallions, but most of the animals have long legs, small heads, and thin trunks (e.g., Appendix A, E/B 2; plate 7). The toes are unusually pronounced and the ears deeply scalloped. The legs and trunks are all positioned as on the larger design. The reverse also has a dotted border, but this feature is not visible on most examples. The main feature here is a bearded standing archer, wearing his hair tied up high atop his head and his long tunic tightly belted at the waist. This figure can be confidently identified as Indian, as can his distinctive weapon, which has to be anchored against his left foot.[45] His arrows, drawn from a quiver slung across his back, and

45. The ancient sources include Strabo 15.1.71 and Arrian *Indika* 16.1–7 (based upon the eyewitness accounts of Nearchus and Megasthenes). These authorities could not agree whether the linen (or cotton) tunics were white or brightly colored. For the commemoratives and Indian ethnography, see Paul

the very long draw of the bowstring, remind us of Arrian's description (*Indika* 16.6): "Indian infantry use a bow as tall as the archer, which they rest on the ground and hold steady with the left foot while shooting; they draw the string a very long distance, since their arrows are just a little short of three cubits [ca. 1.2 m = 4 ft] long."

These missiles were aimed with frightening accuracy and struck with enough force to pierce shields and breastplates. The best Indian bowman, according to legend, preferred to die rather than risk failure when challenged by Alexander to shoot an arrow through a finger-ring.[46] At the Hydaspes, these archers were much dreaded by the Macedonians until muddy conditions threw off their aim.[47] Early attempts to identify this standing archer as Porus have not found much support, and rightly so.[48] No sources suggest that the rajah ever fought in this fashion, especially given the royal imperative to wage war from the back of an elephant. Other theories associate this Indian bowman with the hero Perseus, or with the Achaemenid archer-king found on Persian coinages.[49] These interesting suggestions have no compelling merit, given the specifically Indian context and iconography of these medallions. Where the corroborative evidence is overwhelming, as for the recognition of Alexander and Porus on the larger "coins," we must accept the outcome; however, the smaller medallic coins allow no such identifications of the warriors dis-

---

Bernard, "Le monnayage d'Eudamos, satrape grec du Pandjab et 'maître des éléphants,' " in *Orientalia Iosephi Tucci Memoriae Dicata*, ed. G. Gnoli and L. Lanciotti (Rome: Istituto italiano per il Medio ed Estremo Oriente, 1985), 1: 65–94, pp. 72–79.

46. Plutarch *Moralia* 181B; Alexander admired the captive's pride and so released him with rich rewards.

47. Curtius 8.14.19.

48. Suggested by Duerr, but countered by Martin Price, "The 'Porus' Coinage of Alexander the Great: A Symbol of Concord and Community," in *Studia Paulo Naster Oblata*, vol. 1: *Numismatica Antiqua*, ed. S. Scheers, pp. 75–85 (Leuven: Peeters, 1982), p. 81.

49. Ibid., pp. 81 and 84.

played there. To insist nonetheless that every figure has a name drawn from the textual tradition recalls the naïveté of early archaeology, when everything discovered by Schliemann received its Homeric sobriquet.

Porus's chariots were just as feared as the Indian archers and similarly hampered by the mud.[50] On the other set of smaller medallions, a chariot pulled by four bounding horses travels to the right. There is no ground line, but a circle encloses the design. The horses have their hair braided into tufts rising between their ears, and their reins sweep back to the two fists of a charioteer. The vehicle's eight-spoked wheels crowd the horses and do not roll at the level of the animals' rear hooves, obviously because the engraver was hard-pressed to fit the group onto the small die. The body of the chariot is compact, with looped handholds at the back. An archer stands at the front of the car, shooting his arrow straight ahead. He, like the driver, wears his hair in a style already noted as Indian on the other specimens. Unlike the infantry archer, however, he has a long-sleeved garment. His weapon cannot be the same as that used by the infantry, since it must be drawn and the arrow released without anchoring it on the ground; it is therefore shorter, and lacks the complex curvatures of the infantry bow. The arrows are likewise shorter, with large points.

We know, of course, that chariots played an important role in Porus's battle plans. Aristobulus reports that Porus's son commanded a squadron of 60 chariots that intercepted the Macedonians at the river crossing; others add that he wounded Alexander and killed Bucephalus. Ptolemy's version puts the chariots at 120, with an escort of 2,000 cavalry, and records a battle in which Porus's son died with about 400 of his cavalrymen, whereupon all of the chariots were captured.[51] Ptolemy, of course, took part in this particular engagement. Another tradition identifies

---

50. Curtius 8.14.4–5; Arrian 5.15.2.

51. Arrian 5.14.3–5.15.2; cf. Plutarch *Alex.* 60.8. On Plutarch's account, alleged to be drawn from Alexander's actual letters, see the analysis in J. R. Hamilton, "The Letters in Plutarch's *Alexander*," *Proceedings of the African Classical Association* 4 (1961): 9–20, esp. pp. 16–18.

Porus's brother as the commander of this force, composed of 100 chariots and 4,000 cavalry.[52] Curtius remarks here that each chariot was drawn by four horses (a quadriga), as seen on the medallions. His description of the personnel assigned to each chariot does not, however, tally with the medallic coins: he lists two archers, two men with shields, and two armed drivers, for an improbable total of six soldiers per vehicle. This may be an exaggeration, for it would require a huge chariot indeed to provide a fighting platform for so many men; otherwise, we must imagine these vehicles in part as transports to convey squads of infantry to disembark and fight on foot in conjunction with the charioteers. It may be argued, on the other hand, that the medallions, already "crowded" in design, could only represent part of a chariot's full complement of soldiers. In any event, on this one point, we find a discrepancy between a text and these small commemoratives.

The other face of this artifact shows within a circle border another Indian elephant striding to the right, carrying two riders. Compared to the others, this pachyderm moves with obvious speed, its tail and legs indicating a rapid gait, matched by the outstretched banner held aloft by the rear rider, who twists and looks back, while the mahout—goad in hand—faces forward. Both men wear their hair in Indian fashion, and the driver seems to have a long beard. The banner-bearer sits upon a large blanket or covering, which is held by straps across the elephant's lower body. Relative to their mount, these Indians are smaller than the men depicted on the large medallion; the driver is especially diminutive by comparison. Neither man on the tetradrachm appears armed in any way. On the other hand, the pose of the rear rider and the movement of the elephant suggest a retreat—indeed, a more urgent one than on the decadrachms, except that the flag bearer does not seem to be wounded by a sarissa. Still, he appears to be watching a pursuer, and there may be a spear shaft

---

52. Curtius 8.14.2–3. Diodorus 17.88.1 gives a cursory account that sets the chariots in the main battle; Justin 12.8.1–8 gives no details. Polyaenus, *Strategems* 4.3.21 mentions a grandson of Porus's as leader of this advance guard.

etched at the elephant's rump. This scene, while very much like that on the large medallion, obviously does not portray the same beast or riders. We do not see Porus and his attendant here, but either another pair, who have expended their javelins and must flee, or part of a ceremonial (signal?) corps that has been routed. Given the fluttering banner and the elephant's caparison, the latter—a memorable sight during the battle and one worth recording on the small medallions— seems more likely.

All five of the battle scenes on these three types of medallion move in the same direction, from left to right. Only the post-battle figure, that of Alexander being crowned, lacks this motion. He is, however, still conspicuously dressed in his fighting gear. Each medallic coin couples an Asian elephant on the obverse with a warrior or warriors on the reverse. On the smaller medallions, the soldiers are demonstrably Indian and still battling—obviously neither yet victorious nor vanquished. They offer no telltale signs of being either the allies or foes of the unseen Macedonians. All of the elephants, however, convey the idea of loss and retreat: two have their riders harried by pursuers, and the other has lost its riders altogether. These medallions display an obvious unity and symmetry, but the precise message remains to be discerned. No one can deny that these objects constitute a truly extraordinary step in the development of numismatic art. The images, individually and as a group, are unique and occur quite remarkably without an inscription to identify the issuing authority. Something exceptional is going on here, but what, when, where, and why?

SEVEN

A Dark and Stormy Night

The impressive artwork on the elephant medallions provides us a fine series of images straight from the scrapbook of Alexander's campaign against Porus. No other great victory in his career so strikingly involved these elements of Indian archers, chariots, and elephants. Most of the details known from ancient texts and art about the military dress and equipment of the Indians can be seen with unexpected fidelity on these medallic coins, just as they capture in miniature the descriptions that have come down to us of the rival kings Alexander and Porus. The extraordinary nature of this numismatic art program also matches the peculiar characteristics of this mintage in other, more technical terms. Compared to contemporary coinages in the era of Alexander and his early successors, these artifacts deviate in many ways from the expected norms of the royal mints. In these anomalies lurk some important clues.

The first technical peculiarity to consider is just how few elephant medallions were actually manufactured. On present evidence, those scholars who have argued that this was a huge mintage must be mistaken.[1] Their error diminishes the likelihood that these monetary medals

1. See, e.g., Robin Lane Fox, "Text and Image: Alexander the Great, Coins and Elephants," *Bulletin of the Institute of Classical Studies* 41 (1996): 104; A. B. Bosworth, *Alexander and the East: The Tragedy of Triumph* (Oxford: Oxford University Press, 1996), pp. 6–8 (as discussed in chapter 6 above).

enjoyed a widespread distribution for propaganda purposes. The small number of extant specimens and their extensive die-linkage denote a very limited issue that did not disperse widely. As shown in Appendix A, one obverse die accounts for nine of the large medallions (90%); one obverse die produced seven of the elephant/bowman specimens (64%); and all three of the elephant/chariot types were struck from the same obverse die (100%). Altogether, we have only two obverse dies for the published decadrachms and four total for the two tetradrachm issues: just six dies account for three coin-types in two denominations. This seems very meager indeed compared to other mintages at the time. For example, in Alexander's regular coinage just one issue (Wreath ΔI) of just one denomination (tetradrachm) from just one mint (Side) found in just one hoard (Demanhur) represents at least thirty-six obverse dies.[2] This example underscores another important point. The output of Alexander's mints, plus those of his first successors, was staggering by any measure available to us; without question, millions of coins from thousands of dies poured into circulation. François de Callataÿ has calculated that 28,000,000 Alexander drachms were produced in Asia Minor down to 300 B.C.E.; Martin Price more than doubled that estimate for this single denomination in one region of the empire.[3] The elephant medallions, even if originally numbering in the tens of thousands, therefore constitute a tiny—almost negligible in terms of numbers—fraction of the mint activity for this period. As currency or propaganda, they would be a mere drop in this vast sea of silver and gold spreading across Alexander's realm.

Even within the small region from which most of the specimens have come (Babylonia, in modern Iraq), the elephant commemoratives represent a small proportion of the precious metal available for hoarding. In

2. Margaret Thompson, "Paying the Mercenaries," in *Studies in Honor of Leo Mildenberg*, ed. Arthur Houghton et al., pp. 241–47 (Wetteren, Belgium: NR Editions, 1984), pp. 242–44.

3. Martin Price, *The Coinage in the Name of Alexander the Great and Philip Arrhidaeus* (London: British Museum Press, 1991), 1: 66.

the 1973 hoard, the material drawn from circulation there included hundreds of regular Alexander tetradrachms, hundreds of imitation Athenian owls, and hundreds of local lion staters (see Appendix C); in this context, the number of elephant medallions is quite small, only about 1 or 2 percent of the number buried by the unknown owner. In nine other Babylonian hoards from the time of Alexander and his first successors, we find no elephant medallions among the 250 or more coins buried there; yet, these caches included four of Alexander's regular (though rare) Hercules/Zeus decadrachms and at least forty-two of the local lion staters.[4] Thus, even in Babylonia where twenty-one of the twenty-four published elephant medallions have been found, these medallic coins appear quantitatively to have been quite rare emissions—a very small production all but invisible in the local currency, much less abroad in other territories such as Syria, Asia Minor, or Greece.[5] This was a very special and reserved series of commemoratives.

Another noteworthy feature of these medallions, beyond the designs and limited edition, involves their erratic weights and uncertain denominations. Many of the imperial coinages of this period are known for their careful adherence to established weight standards.[6] Pre-weighed planchets were prepared in order to maintain quality control in this crucial matter of circulating money. If struck on the Attic standard, a decadrachm at that time should theoretically weigh 42.0 grams, and a tetradrachm 16.8 grams; it has been argued by Martin Price that these

4. Margaret Thompson et al., eds., *An Inventory of Greek Coin Hoards* (New York: American Numismatic Society, 1973), pp. 248–49 (nos. 1749–53, 1757, 1759–61).

5. For example, none of the huge hoards of this period—some of them containing thousands of coins—include the elephant medallions: ibid., nos. 1664 (over 8,000 coins at Demanhur, Egypt), 1508 (over 7,000 coins at Saida, Phoenicia); *Coin Hoards* 8 (1994), no. 189 (ca. 1,300 coins at an unknown find spot).

6. Otto Mørkholm, *Early Hellenistic Coinage* (Cambridge: Cambridge University Press, 1991), pp. 7–11.

same weights correspond to five shekels (42.0) and two shekels (16.8) on a specifically Babylonian standard.[7] The elephant medallions might thus be considered products of one weight system or the other. Numismatists naturally expect some aberrations in the weights of actual currency due to wear and other factors. For example, the standard Alexander decadrachms found in the 1973 Iraq hoard (i.e., those with the regular coin-type of Hercules/Zeus) should weigh 42.0 grams. The five specimens for which weights have been recorded show a range from 41.72 to 43.23 grams, with a mean of 42.32 and a median of 41.89 grams. By contrast, the large elephant medallions (which on either proposed standard should weigh the same as the normal decadrachms, 42.0 grams) have a broader and lower range of 38.71 to 42.20 grams, with a mean of only 39.98 and a median of just 39.88 grams.[8] This deficiency stems in part from the worn condition of the medallions, but these wide-ranging weights also suggest a lack of quality control in a group that so dramatically falls below the requisite standard. The smaller medallic coins (whether as tetradrachms or two shekels) likewise demonstrate poor quality in terms of a broad range from 14.72 to 16.71 grams, with a low mean (15.81) and median (15.89). Not one of the smaller medallions meets either standard's established weight (16.8), although in fairness one specimen (Appendix A, E/C 3; plate 12) has been deeply cut and thereby reduced in weight after manufacture.

These figures reflect, of course, necessarily small samples. Even so, the evidence presents an unusual character: like medals, these objects were produced in small numbers from finely detailed dies, without an identifying inscription; but, like a poorly supervised currency, they ex-

7. Martin Price, "The 'Porus' Coinage of Alexander the Great: A Symbol of Concord and Community," in *Studia Paulo Naster Oblata*, vol. 1: *Numismatica Antiqua*, ed. S. Scheers, pp. 75–85 (Leuven: Peeters, 1982), p. 76. One Babylonian shekel represented one-sixtieth of a mina.

8. Excluding, of course, the cut specimen (E/A 8) from the computations.

hibit notable variations in weight. Even if, as suggested here, these medallions functioned both as medals and coins, we might be surprised that so little care was taken to keep them to a more consistent standard, given their special nature. This last anomaly has its parallel in the lamentable level of skill shown in the striking of nearly every specimen. Such marvelous dies were carelessly positioned on the planchets and unevenly hammered, producing medallions that sometimes appear crude (e.g., Appendix A, E/A 10) and far below the technical criteria of the time. Part of the problem may have been the planchets themselves. They surely were not carefully prepared in terms of weight, and perhaps also not in size and shape. Beginning with G. F. Hill in 1927, many experts have suggested that the medallions were overstruck on some other never-identified coinage, resulting in the bad strikings with low relief and occasional blemishes.[9] Upon closer examination, however, those specimens struck considerably off-center (e.g., Appendix A, E/A 1 and E/C 3; plates 2 and 12) show no traces whatsoever of an under-type on the unhammered portions of the flan.[10] Unless better evidence surfaces in the future, it seems more probable that the flans were roughly made and somewhat spherical; if not hammered skillfully, the dies were unable to impress themselves evenly and flatly across the flan's globular surface.[11] The result was a thick, dumpy medallic coin with irregular edges and imperfect relief to go along with the erratic weights. These are the telltale signs of hurried, poorly supervised minting.

The rather haphazard hammering on inconsistent planchets must be coupled with unadjusted die axes (see Appendix A). For the large medal-

9. Sir George F. Hill, "Greek Coins Acquired by the British Museum," *Numismatic Chronicle*, 5th ser., 7 (1927): 205.

10. Price, "The 'Porus' Coinage of Alexander the Great," pp. 78–79.

11. Paul Bernard, "Le monnayage d'Eudamos, satrape grec du Pandjab et 'maître des éléphants,'" in *Orientalia Iosephi Tucci Memoriae Dicata*, ed. G. Gnoli and L. Lanciotti (Rome: Istituto italiano per il Medio ed Estremo Oriente, 1985), 1: 65–94, pp. 81–82.

lions, the alignments of eight have been recorded and published: four (50%) at 5:00, three (38%) at 12:00, and one (12%) at 11:00. All three axes have die links to one another. These facts do not suggest hinged or notched dies, which would produce either one consistent die axis or two opposite ones (i.e., 11:00 and 5:00). The observable pattern is erratic. On the published elephant/bowman types, the alignments of six specimens are known: four (67%) at 9:00, one (17%) at 3:00, and one (17%) at 5:00. Here we observe slightly better consistency, and almost a pattern indicative of notched dies with opposing axes (9:00 and 3:00); however, even this arrangement has at least one exception. Only the two examples of elephant/chariot medallions with recorded alignments have consistent die axes (12:00), though this extremely small sample may be misleading. We can only determine that, overall, the manufacturers of these large and small medallions took no pains to produce a uniform mintage in regard to weight, shape, centering, or die axis.

There is inconsistency, too, in the use of borders and control marks on these medallions. An engraved border on the large medallions is very rarely visible, but part of a circle of dots can be detected on the obverse of the Franks specimen (see plate 2). On the smaller types, a border is almost always present; however, the elephant/bowman examples use dots, whereas the elephant/chariot types have a solid line. The elephant/chariot type has no control marks that are visible, whereas many of the other large and small types have the Greek *xi* (Ξ) on the obverse (elephant) side and the AB monogram on the reverse. On some of the latter types, the markings on one or both sides are missing. We cannot always be sure whether this is simply the result of wear and/or poor striking, or if some dies actually did not carry the control mark (e.g., the reverse of E/B 6 in Appendix A). In recent studies, much attention has been devoted to these markings in an effort to attribute them to specific people or places. For instance, some experts associate these medallions with the Susa mint, where these markings sometimes appear on regular coin issues; some identify these letters as the "initials" of Abulites and Xenophilos; and still

others have seen in the (B)AB monogram an abbreviation for Babylon or Alexander Basileus ("King Alexander").[12]

None of these interesting suggestions has enough corroborative evidence to support it. Nearly everyone now dismisses the "King Alexander" and "Babylon" readings for (B)AB. At Susa, the two control marks AB and Ξ never actually appear together on the same imperial issues, and the connection to Abulites and Xenophilos was judiciously dropped by the numismatic expert who first suggested it.[13] The AB monogram appears at several mints, and other members of Alexander's administration had names beginning either with AB or BA.[14] It is true, of course, that only Susa brings together both markings in some way, but this may be no more than a coincidence. Nothing else about these medallions indicates that they were designed or distributed as regular currency at some established mint under the authority of particular satraps and treasury guards, and the appearance of "signatures" on both obverse and reverse lies beyond the norm of fourth-century Greek coinages. The nearest analogy might be the so-called lion staters from Babylon that have a Greek letter (M) on the obverse and two more letters (ΛY) on the reverse. These issues, however, appear to be later and much better manufactured than the elephant medallions. Indeed, the sloppy striking of the latter does not measure up to Babylon's standards, as though these medallions were the earlier, unusual products of a traveling or makeshift mint. The dies, however, show considerable attention to the details of Indian dress and weaponry. This does not square with the incident often

12. For examples, see M. C. J. Miller, "The 'Porus' Decadrachm and the Founding of Bucephala," *Ancient World* 25 (1994): 114–17; Lane Fox, "Text and Image," pp. 105–6; Bernard, "Le monnayage d'Eudamos," p. 91; Price, "The 'Porus' Coinage of Alexander the Great," pp. 83–84.

13. Price, "The 'Porus' Coinage of Alexander the Great," pp. 83–84; cf. Price, *Coinage in the Name of Alexander the Great and Philip Arrhidaeus*, p. 452.

14. See Helmut Berve, *Das Alexanderreich auf prosopographischer Grundlage* (Munich, 1926; reprint, Salem, N.H.: Ayer, 1988), vol. 2.

cited in support of a mintage by Abulites and Xenophilos at Susa, namely, the money tossed by Alexander to his horses.[15] Quite the contrary, these men presumably had the *technical* ability, facilities, and experience to produce fine coinages, but hardly the intimate knowledge of Indian warfare so confidently displayed in the *artwork* of the dies. And this anecdote, even if true (see chapter 5), still does nothing to explain the actual designs on the medallions.

The medallions themselves strongly suggest a different context. They must be the work of a good set of artists familiar with the military forces who waged the Punjab campaign in India.[16] Their dies were utilized in a less-than-ideal minting operation, small but hurried, sometime and somewhere between the battle of the Hydaspes and the return to Babylon (326–324 B.C.E.). In 1887, Percy Gardner had tried hard to connect the Franks medallion with something other than Alexander's battle with Porus. Later, Deena Pandey and others labored to hoist Darius of Persia onto the elephant, fending off Alexander in the heat and dust of Gaugamela and thereby leaving Porus unbowed and unbeaten in the annals of Indian history. But the weight of evidence and dispassionate analysis have fallen squarely on the side of the battle of the Hydaspes River, and that conviction has only grown stronger with the new Indian types found in the 1973 Iraq hoard. The battle of the Hydaspes River, then, provides a reliable terminus post quem and the estimated burial date of the Iraq hoard, around 323 B.C.E., establishes a terminus ante quem.[17] To be more precise, we should expect a mintage sometime be-

15. See Lane Fox, "Text and Image," pp. 106–7.

16. It is just possible that these artists "signed" their work, the die cutter Ξ . . . specializing in the elephant designs while AB . . . (or BA . . .) engraved the standing warriors. The elephant/chariot types may have afforded no room to initial the designs, or they were the work of other artists.

17. There has not been much dispute about the burial date of the 1973 Iraq hoard, discussed most recently by Peter van Alfen, "The 'Owls' from the 1973 Iraq Hoard," *American Journal of Numismatics* 12 (2000): 10; Lane Fox, "Text and Image," pp. 90–97; Hyla Troxell, *Studies in the Macedonian Coinage of Alexander*

tween the summer of 326 B.C.E. and perhaps the departure from India in late 325 B.C.E. After that time, the army was either struggling through the Gedrosian desert or safely back in territories near enough to have used established mints. The concentration of finds at Babylon is, of course, the result of a single hoard. This need not in any way locate the manufacture of these medallions at Babylon or other established mints in Mesopotamia. In fact, the medallions probably traveled with the army and thus show up where troops were later concentrated.

This means that the medallions were a special issue for veterans of the Indian campaign, no doubt authorized by Alexander and produced as best as could be managed on the road in the East, then carried back to Mesopotamia. They were simply not intended to be circulating coins of the usual imperial varieties, but rather as rare commemorative medallions, or *aristeia*—valuable rewards for distinguished military service.[18] Such honors and prizes were a feature of ancient warfare and naturally had intrinsic value, allowing them to function as money whenever needed.[19] This would easily account for their accumulation and burial as valuables in, say, the 1973 Iraq hoard. As rewards designed specifically for Macedonian troops, it seems likely that they were regarded as decadrachms and tetradrachms rather than as "foreign" five- and two-shekel pieces. Besides, Persian coinage had never played a strong role in the economy of

the Great (New York: American Numismatic Society, 1997), pp. 74, 85; and Georges Le Rider, "Antimène de Rhodes à Babylone," *Bulletin of the Asia Institute* 12 (1998): 137.

18. Barclay V. Head may have been thinking along these lines nearly a century ago when he suggested that the Franks medallion "was probably intended for a medal for presentation to Macedonian officers rather than for use as current money." See Head, "The Earliest Graeco-Bactrian and Graeco-Indian Coins," *Numismatic Chronicle* 6 (1906): 9.

19. Such prizes might consist of coins, crowns, tokens, ceremonial armor, booty, and other objects. "The monetary value counted for much; but the Greek soldier was also very susceptible to the sentimental charms of distinction," H. W. Parke remarks in *Greek Mercenary Soldiers* (1933; reprint, Chicago: Ares, 1981), p. 234.

the eastern empire, making it wholly unnecessary for Alexander to strike this patriotic Greek mintage on a Babylonian standard.[20]

We do know that Alexander periodically awarded service prizes of various types to his soldiers. At Susa in 324 B.C.E., for example, the king "conferred gifts to his men in accordance with their rank or their acts of courage in moments of danger. He distributed gold crowns as decorations for exemplary bravery."[21] It would be tempting to associate the elephant medallions with this very ceremony, especially given the possible connection to the Susa mint that some scholars have posited. But if we look closer, Arrian's list of those honored with gold crowns may stand against this.[22] He cites Peucestas for shielding Alexander at the Malli town; Leonnatus for his service in India and the victory at Ora; Nearchus for his sea voyage from India; Onesicritus for his skill as helmsman of the royal ship; and Hephaestion plus the bodyguards for (unspecified) service. It is noteworthy that all of *these* special awards commemorate actions that occurred *after* the campaign against Porus; not one of these men played a significant role in the battle of the Hydaspes River.[23] Thus, it appears that at Susa, the king was rewarding valor and service for the period since the last great battle, that is, from the time of the voyage down the Indus to the return back west. In fact, we know that awards specifically for bravery in the fight against Porus had already been given, as was customary, soon after the battle.[24] It makes sense that the medallions, if indeed distributed to commemorate the battle of the Hydaspes and to reward the troops, formed part of the special ceremony for that campaign held in 326 rather than the observance for later operations in 324. Manufactured in haste during a monsoon, using Greek die cutters

20. See Georges Le Rider, *La naissance de la monnaie: Pratiques monétaires de l'Orient ancien* (Paris: Presses universitaires de France, 2001), pp. 165–205.

21. Arrian 7.5.4.

22. Arrian 7.5.4–6; cf. *Indika* 42.9.

23. See their biographies in Waldemar Heckel, *The Marshals of Alexander's Empire* (London: Routledge, 1992).

24. Curtius 9.1.6; Diodorus 17.89.3.

but probably the labor of Indian mint workers unfamiliar with the striking of round, high-relief medallions from a totally different numismatic tradition, we might easily understand the lapses in quality so evident on these monetary medals.[25] In the Punjab, with a war still to wage, a monsoon to endure, and cities and a fleet to build, Alexander could not do the obvious and simply order this important but technically subpar mintage to be melted down and restruck. At Susa or Babylon, this erratic (but clearly significant) production could easily have been fixed. It never was, unless some of the worst pieces were quickly hammered again in India, giving the appearance of overstrikes noted by several experts. The king was clearly in too great a rush to do much else.

As *aristeia* designed in that specific context, the medallions certainly needed no inscription identifying Alexander as the issuing authority. Just as important, this interpretation allows us to see that our modern quandaries about the inconsistent messages apparent on this series of artifacts stem from our expectations of a universal coinage from a central mint. The problem melts away when we understand that the recipients were Macedonian veterans in the field who knew all the particulars firsthand and needed no inscriptions or iconographic explanations, as would have been the case for civilian populations far away and unfamiliar with the battle. All we need do is revisit that battle and find in the medallions the special memory of it that Alexander wished to preserve for the men who had recently fought there.

The archers and chariots cannot, of course, be Alexander's allies; they must be counted among Porus's forces. Martin Price's theory of "concord and community" requires us to believe not only in that controversial construct embraced by Tarn and others, but also in the notion that these medallions were struck in Mesopotamia *before* the battle as medallic har-

25. Taxiles, for example (as indicated in previous chapters), operated a mint that produced Indian silver bars bearing various simple stamps. The possible requisition of this facility obviously does not mean that Taxiles was the authority behind the elephant medallions.

bingers of victory. Furthermore, if these artifacts were really meant to promote Taxiles' allied role in the Macedonian army of invasion, then Alexander had a fundamental change of heart before the battle. Price cites Arrian 5.8.5 for the fact that 5,000 Indians marched with Alexander to the Hydaspes River; but he does not notice that these forces were then left behind at the base camp when Alexander led his main army across the river to engage Porus.[26] Only when Alexander had won the battle did these Indian allies, as part of Craterus's command, cross the Hydaspes and join in the slaughter of Porus's fleeing troops.[27] It was at this point that Taxiles himself, and other Indian allies such as Meroes, finally played their part by trying to assist Alexander in the arrangement of Porus's surrender.

If Alexander had imagined that his Indian allies would be so important to his cause that a special mintage was in order to honor them as "symbols of Indian power" (to quote Price, p. 82), it is strange that he used these troops only as reserves. Other Asian forces with his army (Bactrians, Sogdians, Scythians, Dahae) were not commemorated in any way as allies and yet were included in the critical turning force that won the battle.[28] Alexander made no effort to let his Indian allies live up to the hype on these medallions. Nor do the elephants shown on the smaller medallions convey this idea of powerful and important allies. Although Alexander had gathered more than one hundred elephants of his own before the battle, he had no intention at all of using them against Porus.[29] On the smaller medallions, one of the Indian elephants is clearly re-

26. Price, "The 'Porus' Coinage of Alexander the Great," p. 82.

27. Arrian 5.11.3–4 and 5.18.1.

28. A. M. Devine, "The Battle of the Hydaspes: A Tactical and Source-Critical Study," *Ancient World* 16 (1987): 91–113.

29. H. H. Scullard, *The Elephant in the Greek and Roman World* (Ithaca, N.Y.: Cornell University Press, 1974), p. 66. Alexander never relied upon elephants, but images of war elephants (ridden by Macedonians in armor) appeared on the king's elaborate funeral cart: Diodorus 18.26–27.

treating with its riders—hardly a symbol of allied power. The other elephant is riderless and, given the unity and symmetry of the whole series, seems to be retreating to the right as well. These images all represent the enemy units arrayed by Porus against Alexander as described in the written sources. With that fact in mind, let us look again at the medallions in relation to this battle.

For scholars today, the least controversial aspect of the medallions is the identification of Alexander crowned by Nike on the large examples. It was a crushing victory, and although Alexander may have admired and pardoned Porus, he patently took pride in this battle and had no qualms about celebrating his success. The defeated rajah retained his kingdom as Alexander's gift, but the Macedonian ruler left (without apologies) a city named Nicaea in honor of his triumph over Porus's army. The large victory medallion suits this context well, including the symbolic image on the obverse of Porus retreating before the lance of Alexander. There the rajah still struggles, spears in hand, but his fate is inescapable. We must not, like Price, think this inappropriate and thereby unlikely: "The ignominious portrayal of the defenceless [sic] king running away pursued by Alexander can hardly be described as complimentary to Alexander's new ally."[30] Alexander never hid his light under a bushel, for Porus or anyone else. Perhaps a gentlemanly Alexander, Tarn's original standard-bearer for community and concord, would not have risked injury to Porus's pride in this way, but long before the medallions were discovered, we knew that Alexander celebrated Porus's defeat lavishly. There is no reason to ignore these sources or to argue away the obvious and corroborative message on the large medallions: Alexander has driven Porus and his army from the field and been duly crowned victorious.

The only thing "shocking" about the images of triumph on the large medallion is the lightning bolt of Zeus. While not unique, as the painting by Apelles makes clear, it is noteworthy that Alexander holds *this* di-

30. Price, "The 'Porus' Coinage of Alexander the Great," p. 80.

vine attribute on *this* occasion. Alexander, in full battle dress, stands here not as the god in general, but as the general who is god. He has won the battle with the special aid of Zeus, as the son of Zeus, and as the equivalent of Zeus—a kind of triumphal trinity into which, intentionally, a host of extraordinary things could be read by different viewers. Allegedly from the time of Alexander's conception, Zeus's thunder and lightning had announced the god's support of his "son."[31] This continued throughout Alexander's life; one thinks of his prophetic success with the Gordian Knot (Arrian 2.3.8).[32] Such associations prompted the popular anecdote that once, following a terrifying clap of thunder, the philosopher Anaxarchus queried Alexander, "Can you, the son of Zeus, thunder like that?" The king replied with a laugh that he would not wish thus to frighten his friends.[33] But what about his enemies? What is the connection between Alexander's victory over his enemies and the thunderbolt held in his hand?

One of the most memorable features of the battle of the Hydaspes River was the violent weather. No Greeks had ever waged war in the midst of a monsoon before. These incredible storms were obviously the handiwork of Zeus, and, while Porus hoped that they would hinder Alexander, the tempests quite significantly helped the cause of the Macedonians, to such an extent that they are credited on several counts by the written sources. Although wet and miserable, not to mention vulnerable to lightning strikes, Alexander's turning force was able to conceal its movements under the cloak of a particularly violent thunderstorm on the

31. Plutarch *Alex.* 2.3 tells the story that on the eve of her marriage to Philip, Olympias dreamed she heard a clap of thunder and that a lightning bolt struck her womb.

32. Discussed by Ernest Fredricksmeyer, "Alexander, Midas, and the Oracle of Gordium," *Classical Philology* 56 (1961): 160–68.

33. Plutarch *Alex.* 28.4; Athenaeus 6.250–51. On the explication of this joking anecdote, see Paul Bernard, "Le philosophe Anaxarque et le roi Nicocréon de Salamine," *Journal des Savants*, January–June (1984): 3–49.

fateful eve of the battle: "A deluge from heaven fell during the night and helped to mask Alexander's preparations and then his crossing of the river. The rattling of weapons and the clamor of orders were countervailed by the pounding rain and thunder."[34] To this account by Arrian, Curtius (8.13.23–26) adds that although the tempest terrified Alexander's soldiers, the king braved the dangers in order to use the storm to his advantage. Its noise defended his army from detection, and then—when the rains suddenly stopped—the thick clouds blanketed the area in a deep, protective darkness. According to Plutarch *(Alex.* 60.4), "on a dark and stormy night" Alexander crossed the Hydaspes River even though torrential rains, winds, and lightning tormented his men. As Peter Green remarks in his biography of Alexander, these travails turned out to be a "godsend."[35]

This should at last be appreciated as the central meaning of the large medallion. Literally stealing Zeus's thunder, Alexander takes credit for the remarkable, frightening, but fortuitous weather that helped to win the battle. Any veteran of the campaign would immediately understand the significance of this image, and presumably appreciate Alexander's extraordinary powers, personality, and leadership all the more. In addition, according to ancient accounts, these storms brought two more miraculous advantages to the Macedonian army. The heavy rains that covered the embarkation the night before also protected Alexander's troops from two of Porus's most dangerous military units on the day of battle itself. First, when Alexander's turning force had finally made it across the Hydaspes, they were intercepted by a wave of four-horse chariots sent by Porus to stop or delay them. At this critical juncture, according to Aristobulus, these chariots could have prevented the crossing altogether had the Indians halted, disembarked, and fought on foot to guard the river-

34. Arrian 5.12.3.

35. Peter Green, *Alexander of Macedon, 356–323 B.C.* (Berkeley: University of California Press, 1991), p. 394.

bank.[36] Ptolemy, who participated in this engagement, describes how the Macedonians attacked and overwhelmed the Indian force.[37] He includes a very important observation, also confirmed in the Vulgate tradition, that the chariots proved to be useless to the enemy because they became mired in the rain-soaked ground and could neither maneuver in battle nor make an escape.[38] Thanks to the storms of the previous night, every one of these Indian chariots was captured with unexpected ease by Alexander's grateful troops. This, too, was the work of the benevolent man-god who brandished the lightning bolt on their numismatic *aristeia*.

Next, when these same Macedonians faced the "wall" of Porus's main army, they dreaded not only the war elephants but also the deadly accuracy and unusual power of the large Indian bows.[39] Here, as already with the chariots, the rain-soaked field quite miraculously rendered the archers impotent. The bowmen could not anchor their weapons securely on the muddy ground, making it impossible to fire with effective aim, force, or rapidity.[40] They, too, were overcome by the divine intervention of Alexander's storms. Here, at last, we discover the consistent theme of the elephant medallions that solves our mystery. The two Indian military units put out of commission by the stormy weather turn out to be the very ones depicted on the smaller medallions. Other enemy forces, such as the formidable Indian cavalry, have no place on these artifacts. In fact, unless we understand the message of divine interdiction that unifies all of these designs, the conspicuous selection of archers and chariots might

36. Arrian 5.14.3. On this and the following variants, see A. B. Bosworth, *A Historical Commentary on Arrian's History of Alexander*, vol. 2 (Oxford: Clarendon Press, 1995), pp. 287–93.

37. Arrian 5.14.4–15.2.

38. Corroborated in Curtius 8.14.4–8 as part of the main battle.

39. The comparison of the deployed Indian army to a city wall, with elephants as towers spaced among the infantry, became a literary commonplace: Curtius 8.14.13; Diodorus 17.87.5; Polyaenus 4.3.22.

40. Curtius 8.14.19; cf. Arrian 5.15.5 for Porus's (justifiable) concerns about the muddy conditions.

otherwise seem strange for what has been called "one of antiquity's greatest cavalry battles."[41] Taken together in sequence, the medallions capture the course of a memorable battle in which rainstorms unexpectedly defeated the chariots and then the archers. This led to the rout of the entire Indian army, whose signature arm, the elephants, first turned in flight and then lost their riders and fled. In Curtius's highly charged account, we read: "The elephants, at length burdened by wounds, stormed upon and trampled their own men; the drivers themselves were tossed to the ground and crushed to death. Like cattle, now more terrified than hostile, they were driven from the battlefield."[42] That is precisely what we observe on the small medallions.

This numismatic narrative ends, of course, with the large-scale depiction of Porus retreating on his own elephant, relentlessly pursued by Alexander himself. As a result, the Macedonian god-king receives the crown of victory from Nike while holding the divine weapon of his army's deliverance. The different medallic coins, therefore, do not contradict one another at all; they complement and complete a single story with breathtaking numismatic bravado. This message makes sense even without the chariot type, but of course its inclusion only increases our confidence in this interpretation. To his troops, Alexander retells the stages of the battle in simple pictures that highlight his supernatural leadership; he reminds men who have grown weary and worried that he has special powers to exercise on their behalf. This was a particularly important time to make such a case, for our sources tell us that the battle against Porus blunted the Macedonians' courage and may have contributed to the so-called mutiny at the Hyphasis River a few months later.[43] Another factor in the soldiers' displeasure was the monsoon itself,

41. Arther Ferrill, "Alexander in India," *Military History Quarterly* 1 (1988): 82.

42. Curtius 8.14.30; cf. Arrian 5.17.5–7.

43. Plutarch *Alex.* 62.1. After the battle, Alexander rested his army and entertained the men with athletic and equestrian games: Arrian 5.20.1. Curtius 9.1.1–2 recounts a great harangue to bring the army back to its fighting spirit.

which complicated every operation (city-founding, marching, river crossings) and compounded everyone's daily misery.[44] These were the same great rains that Alexander had supposedly commanded against their enemies in the battle of the Hydaspes, and it now behooved him to make a virtue of necessity and formally claim credit for having employed the weather as the ultimate weapon of war. As military awards, the medallions were thus intended simultaneously to answer the army's complaints and concerns and reassert Alexander's deified status as "Stirrer of the Storm."[45]

Wars must, of course, be waged in all kinds of weather, and except for the foot soldiers' perennial complaints of cold and damp, most conditions pass unheralded. But in the thick of battle, any unexpected—and decisive—meteorological phenomenon takes on special significance. In the ancient world, grateful warriors often credited their deliverance to miraculous tempests, tides, and tsunamis; commanders encouraged such notions, not only to reassure their troops, but also to reflect and reinforce their own charismatic authority. The more dramatic and unexpected the circumstances of storm or flood, the more certainly some god or gods had intervened on behalf of one side against the other.

In the Old Testament, for example, when the Canaanite commander Sisera led his "chariots of iron" against the Israelites on the frontier at Megiddo, he could never have imagined that a thunderstorm would lead to his demise. Yet, by obvious divine intervention, a deluge roiled the waters of the river Kishon and stung the faces of his Canaanites. Torrents swamped the heavy squadrons and swept them away, leaving Sisera at the

44. On the sources for this crucial period, see Frank Holt, "The Hyphasis 'Mutiny': A Source Study," *Ancient World* 5 (1982): 33–59. See also Green, *Alexander*, pp. 401–2.

45. I take the phrase from Lord Byron's *Manfred* 1.1.100–104:

> I am the rider of the wind,
> The stirrer of the storm;
> The hurricane I left behind
> Is yet with lightning warm.

mercy of Heber's wife, who merrily hammered a tent spike through his head.[46] The biblical Song of Deborah celebrates this miraculous defeat of the Canaanites and the murder of their leader with gruesome monotony.[47] Similarly, the Old Testament reports that when David called upon God for deliverance, "The Lord thundered from heaven" and sent lightning against his enemies.[48] Weather was yet again the weapon of choice when God promised Ezekiel an intervention of flooding rain and hail, just as Isaiah had earlier proclaimed that the Lord of Israel would pummel the Assyrians with hailstones.[49] It was just such a storm that allegedly destroyed an Amorite army as it fled from Joshua's troops: "the Lord cast down great stones from heaven upon them . . . and they died; they were more which died with hailstones than they whom the children of Israel slew with the sword."[50]

In the midst of their own wars, the Greeks and Romans also looked upon such events as evidence of divine favor for the eventual victor. In the second century B.C.E., for example, Tryphon of Apamea routed a force commanded by Sarpedon, but the triumphant army was then suddenly smashed by a tsunami along the Phoenician coast. This dramatic reversal of fortune left piles of once-victorious men dead among the fishes flung on shore. Sarpedon's grateful troops gloated at the sight and thanked the sea-god Poseidon for their deliverance from Tryphon.[51] Two hundred years earlier, in the lifetime of Alexander the Great, the Greek general Timoleon faced certain defeat at the Krimisos River in Sicily, where a Carthaginian army vastly outnumbered his forces. At the last moment, however, the gods sent a thunderstorm that saved the desperate Greeks.[52] In this downpour, the heavier armament of the Carthagini-

---

46. Judges 4 and Josephus *Jewish Antiquities* 5.5.4: the campaign to seize control of the Valley of Jezreel against King Jabin of Hazor.

47. Judges 5.

48. 2 Sam. 22.7–18.

49. Ezek. 38:22; Isa. 30:30.

50. Josh. 10:11.

51. Strabo 16.2.26; Athenaeus *Deipnosophistai* 8.333b–d (citing Poseidonius).

52. Plutarch *Tim.* 28; Diodorus 16.79.3–80.6.

ans quickly became a deadly liability: they could not hold their ground, and those who slipped in the mud could not rise again before the Greeks were upon them. Timoleon's troops, inspired by this miracle, slaughtered the enemy without mercy and even managed to destroy the Carthaginian chariots, which, as with the Canaanites at Kishon and the Indians at the Hydaspes, could not maneuver in the flood and mire. Finally, the surging waters of the Krimisos drowned many of the fleeing Carthaginians, whose heavy armor dragged them under; those who did escape allegedly feared to sail home, believing stormy seas would only complete their destruction.[53] Alexander surely knew all about this celebrated battle in Sicily; significantly, his companion Demaratos of Corinth had actually fought there as one of Timoleon's lieutenants.[54]

That the gods favored Timoleon in his great struggle was said to be manifest by his interpretation of omens and his extraordinary battlefield demeanor.[55] Historians later reported that when Timoleon ordered his men to attack, his voice thundered as if some god were speaking.[56] Charismatic leadership thrived on such traditions, and we are reminded of the anecdote about Alexander's ability to thunder. Sometimes these stories arose spontaneously among grateful troops, as Plutarch claims was the case at the Krimisos River, while some ancient leaders found ways to inculcate the useful idea that the gods were on their side. According to Polybius 10.8–14, the Roman general Scipio used his knowledge of local tides to calculate when his troops could cross the lagoon protecting New Carthage in Spain. Scipio then foretold that Neptune

53. Diodorus 16.81.2.

54. On Demaratos in Sicily, see Plutarch *Tim.* 21, 24, 27. He procured Bucephalus for Alexander, fought for the king at the Granicus, and was given a lavish funeral when he later died in the East (Berve, no. 253). Alexander took a particular interest in early Sicilian history: Plutarch *Alex.* 8 (listing the works of Philistus).

55. Plutarch *Tim.* 26; Diodorus 16.79.3–5.

56. Plutarch *Tim.* 27.

would intervene with conspicuous aid during the assault, so that his men credited Scipio and the god when ebb tide exposed a passage to the city. Polybius himself marveled that historians aware of Scipo's immaculate deception nevertheless believed that Neptune truly interceded on the general's behalf to win the battle.[57]

Centuries later, it was said that the emperor Marcus Aurelius (or his Egyptian friend Anuphis) called upon the god Mercury to rescue a Roman army beleaguered by barbarians. Magically, a violent thunderstorm quenched the thirst of the desperate legions and then, as if calling in a modern air strike, the emperor directed lightning bolts against the enemy's position.[58] This wondrous occurrence was later commemorated in art on the so-called Antonine Column in Rome.[59] In time, of course, this meteorological miracle was credited instead to the prayers of Christian troops who appealed to the same God who had saved the Israelites from the chariots of Sisera.[60] There was never any question of divine intervention, only rival claims of whose god should get the credit.

Spontaneous or sponsored, the deep conviction that supernatural forces serve and protect certain special commanders can be found throughout history. In Genghis Khan's battle against his blood brother Jamugha, a storm conjured by one army was allegedly turned against it

57. See Gerhard Wirth, "Alexander und Rom," in *Alexandre le Grand: Image et réalité*, ed. Ernst Badian, pp. 181–221 (Geneva: Fondation Hardt, 1976), pp. 185–86 and Badian's remarks on pp. 215–16.

58. Scriptores Historiae Augustae *Aurel.* 24.4; Dio 72.8–10. Rain also came to the relief of Alexander's men as they crossed the desert to Siwah: "The desolate route is piled with sand and waterless. Alexander nonetheless had plenty of rain from the heavens, and this was attributed to the god." This judgment by Arrian (3.3.3–4) derives from a popular account going back to Alexander's court historian Callisthenes and presumably encouraged by Alexander himself. See, e.g., Plutarch *Alex.* 27.1–4.

59. On the Antonine Column, see C. Caprino et al., *La colonna di Marco Aurelio* (Rome: "L'Erma" di Bretschneider, 1955), pp. 88–89 (segment 16).

60. Eusebius 5.5.1–7.

by Heaven's favor for the other.[61] This victory was believed to have made possible the unification of the Mongols as the necessary prelude to Genghis's Alexander-like conquests. The Ming dynasty of China, having ended Mongol rule, reached back into its own mythic past to craft a novel *(Three Kingdoms)* in which, too, a leader used his powers to summon a thunderstorm to assail his enemies. With greater power, however, the other side tamed the tempest and crushed its astonished summoners.[62] Tales such as these embody an age-old reverence for storms and those who claim to control them; that same awe and military aspiration remain quite alive in the modern world. During the Vietnam War, American leaders attempted to manipulate the forces of nature in order to achieve specific military aims. A rainmaking program overseen by the Defense Department used cloud seeding in an attempt "to extend the effects of the monsoon season" in such a way as to hinder the enemy and help U.S. troops.[63] While apparently less effective than the results claimed by Alexander in the monsoon of 326 B.C.E., these modern programs have seemed alarming enough to necessitate a Convention on the Prohibition of Military or Any Other Hostile Use of Environmental Modification Techniques (adopted by the United Nations and later ratified by the United States in 1979).[64]

What now is science was once religion. As one scholar has noted: "Of all

61. See Paul Kahn, ed., *The Secret History of the Mongols* (Boston: Cheng & Tsui, 1998), pp. 54–56. I owe this and the following reference to James Millward.

62. Moss Roberts, ed., *Three Kingdoms: A Historical Novel* (Berkeley: University of California Press, 1999), pp. 15–16.

63. United States Senate, *Hearing before the Committee on Foreign Relations: Environmental Modification Techniques* (Washington, D.C.: Government Printing Office, 1979), p. 18.

64. For background, see Arthur Westing, ed., *Environmental Warfare: A Technical, Legal, and Policy Appraisal* (London: Taylor & Francis, 1984). A curious case of reverse "EnMod," war influencing weather rather than weather influencing war, may be found in the theories of Edward Powers, *War and Weather*, 2d ed. (Delavan, Wisc.: E. Powers, 1890). Powers believed that the noisy concussions of big battles caused storms to form.

the factors which steeled the Macedonians to battle by far the most prominent in our [written] sources is religion. The most meticulous measures
were taken to generate the conviction that the gods were on their side."[65]

On the elephant medallions, Alexander claimed personal powers of
environmental modification for military purposes. Marcus Aurelius later
did precisely the same, not only on monuments, but also on money
minted to commemorate his supernatural victory.[66] On some of these issues, the inscription reads "RELIG AVG" referring to the emperor's own
religio, or god-like power and sanctity, as manifest in his miraculous
storm. More impressively, other specimens (in both gold and silver)
replicate on their reverses many of the very features found on the reverse
of the large elephant medallion: Marcus Aurelius stands to the right in
military dress, holding a spear or scepter upright in his left hand (see
plate 14). In his right hand, he wields the lightning bolt, while the goddess Victory crowns him.[67] These close similarities do not mean that
Marcus Aurelius copied the actual design from one of Alexander's medallions; on the Roman coin, Nike stands rather than flies, and she also
holds a palm branch. The resemblance derives instead from the corre-
sponding messages of divine power used to marshal storms against one's
enemies. The Roman case, amply documented and undisputed, confirms
in numismatic terms that this image can indeed be connected with a
storm-won battle and not taken simply as an expression of vaguely divine
authority.

As with Darwin's worms, we have discovered in these humble art-

65. Alan Lloyd, "Philip II and Alexander the Great: The Moulding of Macedon's Army," in *Battle in Antiquity*, ed. id., pp. 169–98 (London: Duckworth,
1996), p. 184.

66. See, e.g., Clive Foss, *Roman Historical Coins* (London: Seaby, 1990), p.
139; R. A. G. Carson, *Coins of the Roman Empire* (London: Routledge, 1990), p.
51; and Harold Mattingly et al., eds., *Coins of the Roman Empire in the British Museum*, 2d ed. (London: British Museum Press, 1968); vol. 4, pt. 2, nos. 601–3.

67. For background, see Alfred Bellinger and Marjorie Barlincourt, *Victory as
a Coin Type* (1962; reprint, Rockville Center, N.Y.: Durst, 2001).

works a truly grand design. Poorly struck metal weighing altogether not much more than half a kilogram (about 1.2 pounds) has revealed to us a theology of war during a turning point in world history, art, and numismatics. These medallic coins, produced at a decisive moment in Alexander's reign, opened a new chapter in the use of numismatic materials to narrate a particular view of a contemporary event. In doing so, they bridged two great traditions: "In the fifth century, battles were commemorated with strong mythological overtones. By the end of the fourth century, battles seem to have been depicted as real historical events."[68]

Unlike the Alexander Mosaic, with which the large medallions share so much, the latter reflect a claim to divinity, whose singular purpose was to reassure a specific audience of Alexander's special powers. Seen in this light, after so many decades of debate, the elephant medallions finally make sense, *both singly and as a group*. With this new knowledge, it becomes apparent that the king who distributed these rewards to his troops is not to be confused with the altogether saintly or sinister stereotypes met in chapter 5. This man had a massive ego, an army of exceptional ability, and a military mind second to none; that combination carried him to India in the pursuit of fame and glory exceeding even the homage paid to his Homeric heroes. Through unmatched deeds, he fought to break clear of the Macedonian traditions that had kept even Philip in thrall. Alexander differed from other military leaders in the degree—not the direction—of his ambitions. Others aspired to greatness, Alexander to greatestness. The closest he ever came to achieving that goal was in his last major battle (no other measure, political or economic, would do). On the banks of the Hydaspes River, he faced a worthy opponent under exceptional circumstances. Alexander and his army could never have imag-

---

68. Ellen Rice, "The Glorious Dead: Commemoration of the Fallen and Portrayal of Victory in the Late Classical and Hellenistic World," in *War and Society in the Greek World*, ed. John Rich and Graham Shipley, pp. 224–57 (London: Routledge, 1993), p. 229.

ined a night and a day like this when they set out from Greece eight years earlier. The battles of Granicus, Issus, and Gaugamela had been hard-fought, with dire consequences for the history of Western civilization, but those campaigns were waged on ground known to the Greeks, against familiar enemies, whose weapons and tactics had long been tested. India, lying at the world's edge, brought astonishing new trials, including monsoons and elephants.

Alexander met these obstacles brilliantly and triumphed with his ego and genius unscathed. The third element of his troika, however, began to totter; after its defeat of Porus, the Macedonian army lost its indefatigable capacity to keep up with Alexander's driving ambition. Even Alexander understood that he could not go it alone. The bond between veterans and king somehow had to be reinforced, but as always on his terms. Therefore, sometime shortly before or just after the hiatus at the Hyphasis, Alexander met an extraordinary problem with extraordinary measures. With cunning, he congratulated his men on their bravery in the recent battle but at the same time urged them to see in that victory the invincible power of their god-loved and god-like king. He put before them reminders of what *he* had done with them and for them: enemy chariots neutralized, deadly archers incapacitated, and elephants thereby rendered powerless and frightened away like cattle. In camps sodden by storms, soldiers could compare their various medallions and easily make of them the story we have finally traced at this great distance from those dramatic events.

Charismatic leadership requires a certain amount of megalomania and self-promotion, and these medallions show Alexander to have been unrestrained in his eagerness to enhance his image as *isotheos*, an equal of the gods. He had been edging toward divinity for some time, perhaps from the very beginning, if the stories are true that his mother Olympias actually planted the possibility of Zeus's paternity in his mind.[69] Validations

69. Plutarch *Alex.* 2.5–6 and 3.2–4.

came—or were invented—at various points in his reign: Gordium, Mt. Climax, Siwah, and, of course, at the Hydaspes River. After this victory, he encouraged his troops to see him still as their Macedonian king and commander, familiar in every respect but for that thunderbolt and what it implied about the defeated archers, chariots, and elephants. To accept the *aristeia* was to accept the message stamped upon them. With that message, Alexander also hoped to inspire and reassure his men about what lay ahead.

Cleverly, Alexander exalts himself without belittling his enemies; after all, where is the shame in yielding to a supernatural power? The disgrace would be to abandon this god-like king and his ambitious dreams, to slacken in devotion to his unique personality, to doubt his ability to overcome every obstacle. It was his army—not his enemies or allies—that Alexander meant to influence with these extraordinary medallions. The Macedonians apparently lost heart nonetheless, and the grand experiment failed. In their packs, the worn-out warriors carried their *aristeia* back to Babylon, where the god-king again did the unthinkable—he suddenly died. This belied Alexander's invincibility, but not the fact that the leadership of which he had boasted on the medallions was indeed unsurpassable and irreplaceable. Beginning in battles waged around his body at Babylon, others struggled in vain to take his place but succeeded only in fragmenting the empire. Many in Bactria and India fell victim to these new trials of strength, including Porus. Five years after Alexander's demise, a Macedonian officer assassinated Porus and confiscated his elephants in order to use them in the ongoing wars of imperial succession.[70]

Meanwhile, here and there, worried souls hid their wealth—coins, medallions, bullion, bowls—until it was safe to recover their valuables again. For some, that day never came. Their treasures stayed in the deepening underworld of Darwin's worms until retrieved by those like us two thousand years or more away. For many decades, a mere blink perhaps in biological time, modern experts have struggled to understand this

70. Diodorus 19.14.8.

mysterious evidence of the elephant medallions. If in some degree we finally comprehend their extraordinary purpose, then the work begun by Franks, Gardner, and Head has served us well. These elephant medallions have taken us as deep as we may ever get into the mind of Alexander the Great.

THE PUBLISHED ELEPHANT MEDALLIONS

No.	Marks	Weight	Axis	Obverse	Reverse	Disposition
E/A = Elephant/Alexander						
E/A 1	?[1]/AB[2]	42.20[3]	↘	1	A	BM1887-6-9-1[4]
E/A 2	Ξ/?	39.66	↑	1	B	BM1926-4-2-1[5]
E/A 3	?/?	38.71	↖	1	B	ANS1959-254-86[6]
E/A 4	Ξ/?	40.74	↘	1	B	Copenhagen[7]
E/A 5	?/AB	39.88	↘	1	C	BN1978-21[8]
E/A 6	Ξ/AB	40.94	↘	1	C	uncertain[9]
E/A 7	?/AB	40.04	?	1	D	uncertain[10]
E/A 8	Ξ/?	40.39	?	1	D	uncertain[11]
E/A 9	Ξ/AB	38.96	↑	1	E	uncertain[12]
E/A 10	Ξ/AB	38.73	↑	2	F	uncertain[13]
E/B = Elephant/Bowman[14]						
E/B 1	Ξ/AB	16.71	←	1	A	ANS1995-51-68[15]
E/B 2	Ξ/AB	14.72	←	1	A	uncertain[16]
E/B 3	Ξ/AB	15.38	←	1	A	BM1973-12-4-1[17]
E/B 4	Ξ/AB	15.49	←	1	B	BN1978-22[18]
E/B 5	Ξ/AB	15.36	→	1	C	uncertain[19]
E/B 6	?/?	?	?	1	D	uncertain[20]
E/B 7	Ξ/AB	15.99	?	1	E	uncertain[21]
E/B 8	?/?	15.80	?	2	F	uncertain[22]
E/B 9	Ξ/AB	16.30	↘	2	G	ANS1974-145-4[23]

No.	Marks	Weight	Axis	Obverse	Reverse	Disposition
E/B 10	Ξ/AB	?	?	3	H	uncertain[24]
E/B 11	Ξ/AB	16.14	?	3	I	uncertain[25]
		E/C = Elephant/Chariot				
E/C 1	none	15.97	↑	1	A	BN1975-194[26]
E/C 2	none	15.74	?	1	A	uncertain[27]
E/C 3	none	16.20	↑	1	B	ANS 1990-1-1[28]

1. Not visible on this specimen, as also on other examples indicated below with a question mark.

2. Alternatively, this monogram may be read as BA in retrograde or, less likely, BAB.

3. All weights are reported in grams.

4. Donated in 1887 by Sir Augustus W. Franks; first published by P. Gardner, "New Greek Coins of 'Bactria and India," *Numismatic Chronicle* 7 (1887): 177–81, and anonymously in *American Journal of Numismatics* (October 1887): 40. Provenience: "Khullum Bokhara."

5. Published by Sir George F. Hill, "Decadrachm Commemorating Alexander's Indian Campaign," *British Museum Quarterly* 1 (1926–27): 36–37; "Greek Coins Acquired by the British Museum," *Numismatic Chronicle*, 5th ser., 7 (1927): 204–6. Provenience: Perhaps Iran, as reported by R. B. Whitehead, "The Eastern Satrap Sophytes," *Numismatic Chronicle*, 6th ser., 3 (1943): 70 n. 1.

6. Donated by Burton Y. Berry; published in *Sylloge Nummorum Graecorum: The Burton Y. Berry Collection* (New York: American Numismatic Society, 1961), no. 295, which there lists the weight as 37.78 gr. No provenience on record.

7. Acquired by the Copenhagen National Museum from Bank Leu in 1974. Published by Otto Mørkholm, "Athen og Alexander den Store, Fra bystat til guddommeligt kongedømme," *Nationalmuseets Arbeidsmark* (1974): 89–95. To be published by Jan Zahle and Sabine Schultz in *SNG Copenhagen Supplement*, item 1269. Provenience, as presumed for all of the remaining medallions recorded here: the 1973 Iraq hoard.

8. Purchased from a private collector and published in *Coin Hoards* 1 (1975), no. 38 photo 4, and later by H. Nicolet-Pierre, "Monnaies 'à l'éléphant,'" *Bulletin de la Société française de numismatique* 33, 7 (1978): 401–3.

9. *Coin World*, November 19, 1980, p. 3. Purchased by an American collector in the Middle East and passed through the hands of several owners; later publicly exhibited, e.g., in *Wealth of the Ancient World: The Nelson Bunker Hunt and William Herbert Hunt Collections* (Forth Worth, Tex.: Kimbell Art Museum, 1983), pp. 209–10. Appeared in Sotheby's Auction 6043 (June 19, 1990), lot 103.

10. Reported in commerce by Martin J. Price, "Circulation at Babylon in 323 B.C.," in *Mnemata: Papers in Memory of Nancy M. Waggoner*, ed. William Metcalf, pp. 63–72 (New York: American Numismatic Society, 1991), p. 70 (no. 12) and pl. 15.

11. Reported in a private U.S. collection; published in Busso Peus Nachf. Auction Catalogue 348 (May 2–4, 1996), lot 120. This example has a large cut on the reverse.

12. Auctions: Bank Leu 45 (May 26, 1988), lot 132; *Classical Numismatic Review* 20, 1 (1995), lot 104.

13. Auctions: Bank Leu 13 (April 29, 1975), lot 130; *Numismatic Fine Arts* 5 (February 23–24, 1978), lot 81.

14. An additional specimen, apparently not from the 1973 Iraq hoard, has been reported in a Swiss collection: Nicholas Duerr, "Neues aus Babylonien," *Schweizer Münzblätter* 14 (1974): 34. Another unpublished medallion is now in a private U.S. collection. Its weight and die axis have been reported to me as 15.98 and 3:00 (→); it seems to have been struck from dies Obv1 and RevA.

15. First published in ibid., p. 36 (d). This specimen passed from a private collection in Austria to an auction in Bâle: *Monnaies et medailles* 64 (January 30, 1984), lot 99, and later, via Spink, to the ANS.

16. Bank Leu 13 (April 29–30, 1975), lot 131; later in the Viscount Wimborne Collection, then Sotheby's (April 4, 1991), lot 43, then Numismatic Fine Arts 27 (December 4–5, 1991), lot 51, and Sotheby's / NFA (October 26, 1993), lot 36.

17. *Coin Hoards* 1 (1975), no. 38, photo 6. This medallion has a cut across the obverse.

18. Reported as on the market in Duerr, "Neues aus Babylonien," p. 34 and 36 (c). See also Nicolet-Pierre, "Monnaies," p. 402.

19. Duerr, "Neues aus Babylonien," 36 (b). This medallion traveled from a private collection in the Middle East to successive auctions: Numismatic Fine Arts 5 (February 23–24, 1978), lot 82 (purchased by the late William Wahler); Numismatic Fine Arts 25 (November 29, 1990), lot 82.

20. See *Coin Hoards* 1 (1975), no. 38, photo 7.

21. In commerce, as published in Price, "Circulation," p. 70 (no. 18) and his pl. 15.

22. See Price, "Circulation," p. 70 (no. 21).

23. Duerr, "Neues aus Babylonien," 36 (a). From a private collection in the Middle East, this specimen passed via Bank Leu to the ANS in April 1974.

24. Ibid., 36 (2), from a private collection.

25. Price, "Circulation," p. 70 (no. 24) and pl. 15.

26. Bank Leu 13 (April 29–30, 1975), lot 132. See also Nicolet-Pierre, "Monnaies," p. 402.

27. This example has only been partially published, the picture printed by Price, "Circulation," pl. 15 (no. 26) being in fact the BN specimen (E/C 1) rather than this example in commerce. This error aside, Price does provide the weight (p. 70) and curators at the ANS have confirmed the die-linkage, attributing this medallion to a private collection in Britain: *Annual Report of the ANS*, 1990, p. 9.

28. Spink 71 (November 1989), lot 48; see also *Annual Report of the ANS*, 1990, p. 9 with photograph. This specimen has a test cut on the obverse.

SOME POSSIBLE FORGERIES OF THE LARGE MEDALLION

No.	Marks	Weight	Axis	Obverse	Reverse	Disposition
F1	–[1]/AB	?	?	F1	FA	Banaras Hindu University Col.[2]
F2	–/AB	41.18	?	F1	FA	Calcutta Museum 13902[3]
F3	–/AB	?	?	F1	FA	unknown[4]
F4	–/AB	?	?	F1	FA	unknown[5]
F5	–/AB	?	?	F1	FA	unknown[6]
F6	Ξ/AB	40.98	?	F2	FB	unknown[7]
F7	Ξ/?	40.06	↑	F3	FC	H. Berk black cabinet[8]
F8	Ξ/?	42.28	↗	F4	FD	H. Berk black cabinet
F9	Ξ/[9]	41.48	↑	F4	FE	F. Kovacs black cabinet[10]

1. Since many forgeries were based upon the Franks medallion (E/A 1) on which the letter Ξ is not visible, this marking is lacking.

2. Illustrated in A. K. Narain, "Alexander and India," *Greece and Rome* 12 (1965): pl. 1, fig. 3a and 3b; listed in the unpublished catalogue of T. P. Verma (1965).

3. Published by S. P. Basu, *The Second Supplementary Catalogue of Coins to Volume 1* (Calcutta: Indian Museum, 1977), p. 35 and pl. 7, photo 2.

4. A photograph of this unpublished specimen, once part of the H. L. Haughton collection, is preserved in the ANS archives.

5. Said to have been donated to the Bibliothèque nationale (accession Y6431) in 1926 by Jouveau-Dubreuil: Paul Bernard, "Le monnayage d'Eudamos, satrape grec du Pandjab et 'maître des éléphants,'" in *Orientalia Iosephi Tucci Memoriae Dicata*, ed. G. Gnoli and L. Lanciotti, 1: 65–94 (Rome: Istituto italiano per il Medio ed Estremo Oriente, 1985), pp. 68–69, n. 11.

6. This forgery passed through the hands of Kabul merchants in the 1960s; a plaster cast has been kept in the forgery trays of the Bibliothèque nationale.

7. Published in *Classical Numismatic Review* 15, 3 (1990): lot 1; recently called into question by some numismatists, though listed as genuine by Price, "Circulation at Babylon in 323 B.C.," in *Mnemata: Papers in Memory of Nancy M. Waggoner*, ed. William Metcalf, pp. 63–72 (New York: American Numismatic Society, 1991), p. 70 (no. 9A). See *Bulletin on Counterfeits* 17, 1 (1992): 14–15. The forged dies of this piece were copied from the genuine medallion auctioned by Bank Leu in 1988 (App. A, E/A 9).

8. This and the next unpublished forgeries have modified the obverse design with an extended ground line.

9. This specimen shows a complex monogram composed of the Greek letters *eta* (H), *delta* (Δ), and *iota* (I).

10. This specimen, aged with acids, has added the ethnic ΑΛΕΞΑΝΔΡΟΥ to the reverse.

APPENDIX C

THE 1973 IRAQ HOARD

	Duerr[1]	*Coin Hoards*[2]	Price[3]	Van Alfen[4]
Lot A				
Regular Decadrachms		4+	8	
Alexander Tetradrachms	~700	114+	large no.	
Lot B				
E/A "Decadrachms"	small no.	3+	7[5]	
E/B "Tetradrachms"		7+	11	
E/C "Tetradrachms"		1	3	
Lion Staters: No inscription			22	
Lion Staters: Mazeus			20	
Lion Staters: Other	~700	12+	64	
Owl Imitations	~400	159	161	163
Hierapolis Shekel			1	
Sardis Siglos		1	1	
Philip II			1	
Uncertain Drachms			2	
Cos			1	

1. Data kindly provided by Michel Duerr, September 21, 2001.

2. Data compiled from *Coin Hoards* 1 (1975), no. 38; 2 (1976), no. 49; 3 (1977), no. 22; 8 (1994), no. 188.

3. Martin Price, "Circulation at Babylon in 323 B.C.," in *Mnemata: Papers in Memory of Nancy M. Waggoner*, ed. William Metcalf, pp. 63–72 (New York: American Numismatic Society, 1991).

4. A careful study devoted to one portion of the hoard is P. G. van Alfen, "The 'Owls' from the 1973 Iraq Hoard," *American Journal of Numismatics* 12 (2000): 9–58, which includes Price's two "uncertain" drachms.

5. Price includes one medallion that is probably a forgery (see App. B, F6).

SELECT BIBLIOGRAPHY

Listed below are all works cited in the text and notes with the exception of numismatic auction catalogues, standard classical sources such as Plutarch and Arrian, and other well-known literary works by such authors as Shakespeare and Kipling.

Abbot, James. "Some Account of the Battle Field of Alexander and Porus." *Journal of the Asiatic Society of Bengal* 17 (1848): 619–33.

———. "Addendum on the Battlefield of Alexander and Porus." *Journal of the Asiatic Society of Bengal* 18 (1849): 176–77.

Abbott, Jacob. *The History of Alexander the Great.* New York: Harper & Brothers, 1848.

Adcock, F. E. *The Greek and Macedonian Art of War.* Berkeley: University of California Press, 1957.

Adriani, Achille. *La tomba di Alessandro: Realtà, ipotesi e fantasie.* Rome: "L'Erma" di Bretschneider, 2000.

Alder, Garry. *Beyond Bokhara: The Life of William Moorcroft, Asian Explorer and Pioneer Veterinary Surgeon.* London: Century, 1985.

Alfen, Peter G. van. "The 'Owls' from the 1973 Iraq Hoard." *American Journal of Numismatics* 12 (2000): 9–58.

Anderson, A. R. "Bucephalus and His Legend." *American Journal of Philology* 51 (1930): 1–21.

Arnold-Biucchi, Carmen. "I decadrammi nel mondo greco: Monete o medaglie?" *Rivista italiana di numismatica e scienze affini* 95 (1993): 243–50.

Badian, Ernst. "Alexander the Great and the Unity of Mankind." *Historia* 7 (1958): 425–44.

———. "The Eunuch Bagoas: A Study in Method." *Classical Quarterly* 8 (1958): 144–57.

———. "Alexander the Great and the Loneliness of Power." *Journal of the Australasian Universities Language and Literature Association* 17 (1962): 80–91.

———. "The Death of Philip II." *Phoenix* 17 (1963): 244–50.

———. "Alexander the Great, 1948–67." *Classical World* 65 (1971): 37–56, 77–83.

———. "The Deification of Alexander the Great." In *Ancient Macedonian Studies in Honor of Charles F. Edson*, ed. H. J. Dell, pp. 27–71. Thessaloniki: Institute for Balkan Studies, 1981.

———. "Alexander the Great between Two Thrones and Heaven: Variations on an Old Theme." In *Subject and Ruler: The Cult of the Ruling Power in Classical Antiquity*, ed. Alastair Small, pp. 11–26. Ann Arbor: University of Michigan Press, 1996.

———. "Two Numismatic Phantoms: The False Priest and the Spurious Son." *Arctos* 32 (1998): 45–60.

———. "A Note on the 'Alexander Mosaic.'" In *The Eye Expanded: Life and the Arts in Greco-Roman Antiquity*, ed. Frances B. Titchener and Richard F. Moorton, Jr., pp. 75–92. Berkeley: University of California Press, 1999.

Banerji, J. N. "The Obverse Device of Some Decadrachms with Alexandrian Association." *Journal of the Numismatic Society of India* 12 (1950): 118–20.

Basu, S. P. *The Second Supplementary Catalogue of Coins to Volume I.* Calcutta: Indian Museum, 1977.

Baynham, Elizabeth. "Who Put the 'Romance' in the Alexander Romance? The Alexander Romance within Alexander Historiography." *Ancient History Bulletin* 9, 1 (1995): 1–13.

———. *Alexander the Great: The Unique History of Quintus Curtius.* Ann Arbor: University of Michigan Press, 1998.

Bellinger, A. R. "The Coins from the Treasure of the Oxus." *American Numismatic Society Museum Notes* 10 (1962): 51–67.

———. *Essays on the Coinage of Alexander the Great.* New York: American Numismatic Society, 1963.

Bellinger, A. R., and Marjorie Barlincourt. *Victory as a Coin Type.* 1962. Reprint, Rockville Center, N.Y.: Durst, 2001.

Bernard, Paul. "Le philosophe Anaxarque et le roi Nicocréon de Salamine." *Journal des Savants*, January–June 1984: 3–49.

———. "Le monnayage d'Eudamos, satrape grec du Pandjab et 'maître des éléphants.'" In *Orientalia Iosephi Tucci Memoriae Dicata,* ed. G. Gnoli and L. Lanciotti, 1: 65–94. Rome: Istituto italiano per il Medio ed Estremo Oriente, 1985.

———. "Le temple du dieu Oxus à Takht-i Sangin en Bactriane: Temple du feu ou pas?" *Studia Iranica* 23 (1994): 81–121.

———. "Greek Geography and Literary Fiction from Bactria to India: The Case of the Aornoi and Taxila." In *Coins, Art, and Chronology: Essays on the Pre-Islamic History of the Indo-Iranian Borderlands,* ed. M. Alram and D. Klimburg-Salter, pp. 51–98. Vienna: Österreichischen Akademie der Wissenschaften, 1999.

Berry, Burton Y. *A Numismatic Biography.* Lucerne: C. J. Bucher, 1971.

Berve, Helmut. *Das Alexanderreich auf prosopographischer Grundlage.* 2 vols. Munich, 1926. Reprint, Salem, N.H.: Ayer, 1988.

Berzunza, Julio. "A Digression in the *Libro de Alexandre:* The Story of the Elephant." *Romantic Review* 18 (1927): 238–45.

Bevan, E. R. "Alexander the Great." In *The Cambridge History of India,* ed. E. J. Rapson, 1: 309–46. Cambridge, 1922. Reprint, Delhi: S. Chand, 1962.

Bieber, Margarete. *Alexander the Great in Greek and Roman Art.* Chicago: Argonaut, 1964.

Bigwood, J. M. "Aristotle and the Elephant Again." *American Journal of Philology* 114 (1993): 537–55.

Boon, George. "Counterfeit Coins in Roman Britain." In *Coins and the Archaeologist,* ed. John Casey and Richard Reece, pp. 102–88. 2d ed. London: Seaby, 1988.

Bopearachchi, Osmund. *Monnaies gréco-bactriennes et indo-grecques: Catalogue raisonné.* Paris: Bibliothèque nationale, 1991.

———. "Grand trésors récents de monnaies pré-sasanides trouvés en Afghanistan et au Pakistan." *International Numismatic Newsletter* 24 (1994): 2–3.

———. "Récentes découvertes de trésors de monnaies pré-Sassanides trouvés en Afghanistan et au Pakistan." *Cahiers numismatiques,* September 1994: 7–14.

———. "Découvertes récentes de trésors indo-grecs: Nouvelles données historiques." *Comptes rendus de l'Académie des inscriptions et belles-lettres,* April–June 1995: 611–29.

Borza, Eugene. "The Royal Macedonian Tombs and the Paraphernalia of Alexander the Great." *Phoenix* 41 (1987): 105–21.

———. *In the Shadow of Olympus: The Emergence of Macedon.* Princeton: Princeton University Press, 1990.

Borza, Eugene, and J. Reames-Zimmerman. "Some New Thoughts on the Death of Alexander the Great." *Ancient World* 31 (2000): 22–30.

Bosworth, A. B. *A Historical Commentary on Arrian's History of Alexander.* Vols. 1 and 2. Oxford: Clarendon Press, 1980, 1995.

———. *Conquest and Empire: The Reign of Alexander the Great.* Cambridge: Cambridge University Press, 1988.

———. *From Arrian to Alexander: Studies in Historical Interpretation.* Oxford: Clarendon Press, 1988.

———. *Alexander and the East: The Tragedy of Triumph.* Oxford: Oxford University Press, 1996.

Bothmer, Dietrich von, et al. *Wealth of the Ancient World: The Nelson Bunker Hunt and William Herbert Hunt Collections.* Fort Worth, Tex.: Kimbell Art Museum, 1983.

Briant, Pierre. *Alexander the Great: Man of Action, Man of Spirit.* New York: Abrams, 1996.

———. *Histoire de l'empire perse de Cyrus à Alexandre.* 2 vols. Leiden: Nederlands Instituut voor het Nabije Oosten, 1996.

Burn, A. R. *Alexander the Great and the Hellenistic World.* 2d ed. New York: Collier Books, 1962.

Burstein, Stanley. *Graeco-Africana: Studies in the History of Greek Relations with Egypt and Nubia.* Athens: Aristide Caratzas, 1995.

Camp, L. Sprague de. *An Elephant for Aristotle.* New York: Doubleday, 1958.

Caprino, C., et al. *La colonna di Marco Aurelio.* Rome: "L'Erma" di Bretschneider, 1955.

Carlsen, Jesper, et al., eds. *Alexander the Great: Reality and Myth.* Rome: "L'Erma" di Bretschneider, 1993.

Carney, Elizabeth. *Women and Monarchy in Macedonia.* Norman: University of Oklahoma Press, 2000.

Carson, R. A. G. *Coins of the Roman Empire.* London: Routledge, 1990.

Cary, George. *The Medieval Alexander.* Cambridge: Cambridge University Press, 1956.

Cavaignac, E. "À propos de la bataille d'Alexandre contre Porus." *Journal asiatique* 203 (1923): 332–34.

Cawkwell, George. *Philip of Macedon.* London: Faber & Faber, 1978.

Caygill, Marjorie. "Franks and the British Museum." In *A. W. Franks: Nineteenth-Century Collecting and the British Museum,* ed. Marjorie Caygill and John Cherry, pp. 51–129. London: British Museum Press, 1997.

Chabouillet, Anatole. "L'Eucratidion." *Revue numismatique,* 1867: 382–415.

Chugg, Andrew. "The Sarcophagus of Alexander the Great?" *Greece and Rome* 49, 1 (2002): 18–26.

Clain-Stefanelli, Elvira. *Numismatic Bibliography*. Munich: Battenberg, 1984.

Clarke, Edward. *The Tomb of Alexander: A Dissertation on the Sarcophagus Brought from Alexandria and Now in the British Museum*. Cambridge: Cambridge University Press, 1805.

Cohen, Ada. *The Alexander Mosaic: Stories of Victory and Defeat*. Cambridge: Cambridge University Press, 1997.

Coin Hoards. 8 vols. London: Royal Numismatic Society, 1975–94.

"A Coin of Eucratides." *American Journal of Numismatics* 14 (1879): 18–20.

Creasy, Sir Edward. *Decisive Battles of the World*. 1852. Reprint, New York: D. Appleton, 1898.

Cubelli, Vincenzo. "Moneta e ideologia monarchica: Il caso di Eucratide." *Rivista italiana di numismatica e scienze affini* 95 (1993): 251–59.

Cunningham, Alexander. "Relics from Ancient Persia in Gold, Silver, and Copper." *Journal of the Asiatic Society of Bengal* 50 (1881): 151–86.

Curiel, Raoul, and Daniel Schlumberger. *Trésors monétaires d'Afghanistan*. Paris: Klincksieck, 1953.

Curtis, John. "Franks and the Oxus Treasure." In *A. W. Franks: Nineteenth-Century Collecting and the British Museum*, ed. Marjorie Caygill and John Cherry, pp. 228–49. London: British Museum Press, 1997.

Dalton, O. M. *The Treasure of the Oxus*. 3d ed. London: British Museum Press, 1964.

Darwin, Charles. *The Formation of Vegetable Mould, through the Action of Worms, with Observations on Their Habits*. London: Murray, 1881. Reprint, New York: D. Appleton, 1896.

———. *The Expression of the Emotions in Man and Animals*. 1872. 3d ed. Oxford: Oxford University Press, 1998.

Davis, Norman, and Colin Kraay. *The Hellenistic Kingdoms: Portrait Coins and History*. London: Thames & Hudson, 1973.

Delbrück, Hans. *Warfare in Antiquity*. Vol. 1 of *History of the Art of War*. 1920. Reprint, Lincoln: University of Nebraska Press, 1990.

Develin, R. D. "The Murder of Philip II." *Antichthon* 15 (1981): 86–99.

Devine, A. M. "The Battle of Gaugamela: A Tactical and Source-Critical Study." *Ancient World* 13 (1986): 87–116.

———. "The Battle of Hydaspes: A Tactical and Source-Critical Study." *Ancient World* 16 (1987): 91–113.

———. "The Macedonian Army at Gaugamela." *Ancient World* 19 (1989): 77–80.

Dietrich, Erwin. "Fälscher und Fälschungen." *Helvetische Münzen-Zeitung* 22, 10 (1987): 423–31.

"Dr. Schliemann at Burlington House." *The Times* (London), March 23, 1877, p. 10.

Druce, G. C. "The Elephant in Medieval Legend and Art." *Archaeological Journal* 76 (1919): 1–73.

Duerr, Nicholas. "Neues aus Babylonien." *Schweizer Münzblätter* 24 (1974): 33–36.

———. "Ein 'Elephantenstater' für Porus." In *Actes du 8ème Congrès international de numismatique, New York–Washington, septembre 1973*, 2 vols., ed. Herbert A. Cahn and Georges Le Rider (Paris: Association internationale des numismates professionnels, 1976). 1: 43.

———. "New Porus Commemoratives." Translated by A. Ilsch. *Numismatic Digest* 2 (1978): 4–7.

Dupree, Louis. "Einige Bemerkungen zur Schlacht am Jhelum (326 v. Chr.)." In *Aus dem Osten des Alexanderreiches: Völker und Kulturen zwischen Orient und Okzident: Iran, Afghanistian, Pakistan, Indien*, ed. Jakob Ozols and Volker Thewalt, pp. 51–56. Cologne: DuMont, 1984.

Edmunds, Lowell. "The Religiosity of Alexander." *Greek, Roman and Byzantine Studies* 12 (1971): 363–91.

Ellis, J. R. *Philip II and Macedonian Imperialism*. Princeton: Princeton University Press, 1976.

———. "The Assassination of Philip II." In *Ancient Macedonian Studies in Honor of Charles F. Edson*, ed. H. J. Dell, pp. 99–137. Thessaloniki: Institute for Balkan Studies, 1981.

Engels, Donald. *Alexander the Great and the Logistics of the Macedonian Army*. Berkeley: University of California Press, 1978.

Evans, Joan. *A History of the Society of Antiquaries*. Oxford: Oxford University Press, 1956.

Fears, J. R. "Pausanias, the Assassin of Philip II." *Athenaeum* 53 (1975): 111–35.

Ferrill, Arther. "Alexander in India." *Military History Quarterly* 1 (1988): 76–84.

Foss, Clive. *Roman Historical Coins*. London: Seaby, 1990.

Fraser, P. M. *Cities of Alexander the Great*. Oxford: Clarendon Press, 1996.

Fredricksmeyer, Ernest. "Alexander, Midas, and the Oracle of Gordium." *Classical Philology* 56 (1961): 160–68.

———. "Alexander and the Kingship of Asia." In *Alexander the Great in Fact and Fiction*, ed. A. B. Bosworth and E. J. Baynham, pp. 136–66. Oxford: Oxford University Press, 2000.

French, Roger. *Ancient Natural History*. London: Routledge, 1994.

Freud, Sigmund. *The Standard Edition of the Complete Psychological Works of Sigmund Freud*. Edited by James Strachey. Vol. 6: *The Psychopathology of Everyday Life* [1901]. New York: Norton, 1976.

Fuller, J. F. C. *The Generalship of Alexander the Great*. New Brunswick, N.J.: Rutgers University Press, 1960. Reprint, New York: Da Capo Press, 1989.

Gardner, Percy. "New Coins from Bactria." *Numismatic Chronicle* 19 (1879): 1–12.

———. "Coin of Agathocles, with Types of Alexander." *Numismatic Chronicle* 20 (1880): 181–91.

———. "Coins from Central Asia." *Numismatic Chronicle*, 3d ser., 1 (1881): 8–12.

———. *The Coins of the Greek and Scythic Kings of Bactria and India in the British Museum*. London, 1886. Reprint, Chicago: Argonaut, 1966.

———. "New Greek Coins of Bactria and India." *Numismatic Chronicle* 7 (1887): 177–81.

———. "Henry Schliemann." *Macmillan's Magazine*, April 1891, pp. 474–80.

———. *New Chapters in Greek Art*. Oxford: Clarendon Press, 1926.

———. *Autobiographica*. Oxford: Basil Blackwell, 1933.

Gay, Peter. *Freud: A Life for Our Time*. New York: Norton, 1988.

Ginouvès, René, ed. *Macedonia from Philip II to the Roman Conquest*. Princeton: Princeton University Press, 1994.

Goukowsky, Paul. "Le roi Pôros, son éléphant et quelques autres." *Bulletin de correspondance héllenique* 96 (1972): 473–502.

———. *Essai sur les origines du mythe d'Alexandre*. Vol. 1. Nancy: Université de Nancy, 1978.

Gould, Stephen J. *Hen's Teeth and Horses' Toes*. New York: Norton, 1983.

Green, Peter. "Caesar and Alexander: *Aemulatio, imitatio, comparatio*." *American Journal of Ancient History* 3 (1978): 1–26.

———. *Alexander of Macedon, 356–323 B.C.* Berkeley: University of California Press, 1991.

Grierson, Philip. *Numismatics*. Oxford: Oxford University Press, 1975.

Gunderson, Lloyd. *Alexander's Letter to Aristotle about India*. Meisenheim am Glan: Anton Hain, 1980.

Hahn, Johannes. *Alexander in Indien, 327–325 v. Chr.* Stuttgart: Jan Thorbecke, 2000.

Hamdy Bey, O., and T. Reinach. *Une nécropole royale à Sidon*. Paris: Leroux, 1892.

Hamilton, J. R. "The Cavalry Battle at the Hydaspes." *Journal of Hellenic Studies* 76 (1956): 26–31.

————. "The Letters in Plutarch's *Alexander.*" *Proceedings of the African Classical Association* 4 (1961): 9–20.

————. "Alexander's Early Life." *Greece and Rome* 12 (1965): 117–24.

————. *Plutarch, "Alexander": A Commentary.* Oxford: Clarendon Press, 1969.

Hammond, N. G. L. "The End of Philip." In *Philip of Macedon*, ed. M. Hatzopoulos and L. Loukopoulos, pp. 166–75. Athens: Ekdotike Athenon, 1980.

————. *Alexander the Great: King, Commander and Statesman.* 1980. 2d ed. Bristol, U.K.: Bristol Press, 1989.

————. "Arms and the King: The Insignia of Alexander the Great." *Phoenix* 43 (1989): 217–24.

————. *Sources for Alexander the Great: An Analysis of Plutarch's "Life" and Arrian's "Anabasis Alexandrou."* Cambridge: Cambridge University Press, 1993.

————. *Philip of Macedon.* Baltimore: Johns Hopkins University Press, 1994.

————. *The Genius of Alexander the Great.* Chapel Hill: University of North Carolina Press, 1997.

————. "Cavalry Recruited in Macedonia down to 322 B.C." *Historia* 47 (1998): 404–25.

Hammond, N. G. L., and G. T. Griffith. *A History of Macedonia.* Vol. 2: *550–336* B.C. Oxford: Clarendon Press, 1979.

Head, Barclay Vincent. "The Earliest Graeco-Bactrian and Graeco-Indian Coins." *Numismatic Chronicle* 6 (1906): 1–16.

————. *Historia Numorum.* 1887. 2d ed. Oxford: Clarendon Press, 1911. Reprint, London: Spink & Son, 1963.

Heckel, Waldemar. *The Marshals of Alexander's Empire.* London: Routledge, 1992.

Hill, Sir George Francis. *Catalogue of Greek Coins in the British Museum: Arabia, Mesopotamia, Persia.* London: British Museum Press, 1922.

————. "Decadrachm Commemorating Alexander's Indian Campaign." *British Museum Quarterly* 1 (1926–27): 36–37.

————. "Greek Coins Acquired by the British Museum." *Numismatic Chronicle*, 5th ser., 7 (1927): 204–6.

————. *Ancient Greek and Roman Coins: A Handbook.* London, 1899. Reprint, Chicago: Argonaut, 1964.

Hogarth, David G. *A Wandering Scholar in the Levant.* 2d ed. London: Murray, 1896.

Hollstein, Wilhelm. "Taxiles' Prägung für Alexander den Grossen." *Schweizerische Numismatische Gesellschaft* 68 (1989): 5–17.

Holt, Frank. "The Hyphasis 'Mutiny': A Source Study." *Ancient World* 5 (1982): 33–59.

————. "The So-Called Pedigree Coins of the Bactrian Greeks." In *Ancient Coins of the Graeco-Roman World*, ed. W. Heckel and R. Sullivan, pp. 69–91. Waterloo, Ontario: Wilfrid Laurier University Press, 1984.

————. "Alexander's Settlements in Central Asia." *Ancient Macedonia* 4 (1986): 315–23.

————. "The Missing Mummy of Alexander the Great." *Archaeology* 39 (January/February 1986): 80.

————. *Alexander the Great and Bactria: The Formation of a Greek Frontier in Central Asia*. Leiden: Brill, 1988.

————. "Spitamenes against Alexander." *Historikogeographika* 4 (1994): 51–58.

————. "Alexander the Great and the Spoils of War." *Ancient Macedonia* 6 (1999): 499–506.

————. "Alexander the Great Today: In the Interests of Historical Accuracy?" *Ancient History Bulletin* 13, 3 (1999): 111–17.

————. "Mimesis in Metal: The Fate of Greek Culture on Bactrian Coins." In *The Eye Expanded: Life and the Arts in Greco-Roman Antiquity*, ed. Frances B. Titchener and Richard F. Moorton, Jr., pp. 93–104. Berkeley: University of California Press, 1999.

————. *Thundering Zeus: The Making of Hellenistic Bactria*. Berkeley: University of California Press, 1999.

————. "The Death of Coenus: Another Study in Method." *Ancient History Bulletin* 14, 1–2 (2000): 49–55.

————. "Dead Kings Are Hard to Find." *Saudi Aramco World* 52, 3 (2001): 10–11.

Hopkirk, Peter. *The Great Game: The Struggle for Empire in Central Asia*. New York: Kodansha International, 1992.

Houghton, Arthur, and Andrew Stewart. "The Equestrian Portrait of Alexander the Great on a New Tetradrachm of Seleucus I." *Schweizerische Numismatische Rundschau* 78 (1999): 27–35.

Hoving, Thomas. *Making the Mummies Dance*. New York: Simon & Schuster, 1993.

Jenkins, G. K. "A Group of Bactrian Forgeries." *Revue numismatique* 7 (1965): 51–57.

————. *Ancient Greek Coins*. 2d ed. London: Seaby, 1990.

Justinus, Marcus Junianus. *Epitome of the Philippic History of Pompeius Trogus: Books 11–12, Alexander the Great*. Translated by J. C. Yardley. Commentary by Waldemar Heckel. New York: Oxford University Press, 1997.

Kahn, Paul, ed. *The Secret History of the Mongols*. Boston: Cheng & Tsui, 1998.

Kaiser, Wilhelm. "Ein Meister der Glyptik aus dem Umkreis Alexanders des Grossen." *Jahrbuch des Deutschen Archaeologischen Instituts* 77 (1962): 227–39.

Kantorowicz, Ernst. "Gods in Uniform." *Proceedings of the American Philosophical Society* 105 (1961): 368–93.

Keynes, John Maynard. *A Treatise on Money.* Vol. 2. New York: Harcourt, Brace, 1930.

Kulak, Miroslaw. "Bitwa Aleksandra Wielkiego z Porosem nad Rzeka Hydaspes." *Meander* 43 (1988): 229–41.

Lahiri, A. N. *Corpus of Indo-Greek Coins.* Calcutta: Poddar Publications, 1965.

Lane Fox, Robin. "Text and Image: Alexander the Great, Coins and Elephants." *Bulletin of the Institute of Classical Studies* 41 (1996): 87–108.

Lane-Poole, Stanley. *Coins and Medals: Their Place in History and Art.* London, 1885.

Le Rider, Georges. "Antimène de Rhodes à Babylone." *Bulletin of the Asia Institute* 12 (1998): 121–40.

———. *La naissance de la monnaie: Pratiques monétaires de l'Orient ancien.* Paris: Presses universitaires de France, 2001.

Leo, Archipresbyter. *The History of Alexander's Battles: Historia de preliis, the J1 Version.* Translated with an introduction and notes by R. Telfryn Pritchard. Toronto: Pontifical Institute of Mediaeval Studies, 1992.

Litvinsky, Boris, and Igor Pichikyan. "Handles and Ceremonial Scabbards of Greek Swords from the Temple of the Oxus in Northern Bactria." *East and West* 49 (1999): 47–104.

———. *Ellinisticheskiy khram Oksa v Baktrii (Iuzhnyi Tadzhikistan)* [The Hellenistic Temple of the Oxus in Bactria (South Tajikistan)]. 2 vols. Moscow: Vostochnaya Literatura, 2000.

Lloyd, Alan. "Philip II and Alexander the Great: The Moulding of Macedon's Army." In *Battle in Antiquity*, ed. A. Lloyd, pp. 169–98. London: Duckworth, 1996.

Longpérier, Adrian de. "Trésor de Tarse." *Revue numismatique* 13 (1868): 309–36.

Lunt, James. *Bokhara Burnes.* London: Faber & Faber, 1969.

Mackay, James. *Key Definitions in Numismatics.* London: Frederick Muller, 1982.

Macrory, Patrick. *The Fierce Pawns.* Philadelphia: Lippincott, 1966.

———, ed. *Lady Sale: The First Afghan War.* Hamden, Conn.: Archon Books, 1969.

Manti, Peter. "The Macedonian Sarissa, Again." *Ancient World* 25 (1994): 77–91.

Markle, Minor. "The Macedonian Sarissa, Spear, and Related Armor." *American Journal of Archaeology* 81 (1977): 323–39.

Marsden, E. W. *The Campaign of Gaugamela.* Liverpool: Liverpool University Press, 1964.

Mattingly, Harold, et al., eds. *Coins of the Roman Empire in the British Museum.* 2d ed. London: British Museum Press, 1968.

Mayhew, Henry. *London Labour and the London Poor.* Vol. 2. London: Griffen, Bohn, 1851.

Meyer, Karl, and Shareen Brysac. *Tournament of Shadows: The Great Game and the Race for Empire in Central Asia.* Washington, D.C.: Counterpoint, 1999.

Meyer, Michael. *The Alexander Complex.* New York: Times Books, 1989.

Miller, M. C. J. "The 'Porus' Decadrachm and the Founding of Bucephala." *Ancient World* 25 (1994): 109–20.

Mitchiner, Michael. *The Origins of Indian Coinage.* London: Hawkins, 1973.

———. *Indo-Greek and Indo-Scythian Coinage.* Vol. 1. London: Hawkins, 1975.

Moorehead, Caroline. *Lost and Found: The 9,000 Treasures of Troy.* New York: Penguin Books, 1994.

Mørkholm, Otto. "Athen og Alexander den Store, Fra bystat til guddomeligt Kongedømme." *Nationalmuseets Arbeidsmark* (1974): 89–95.

———. *Early Hellenistic Coinage.* Cambridge: Cambridge University Press, 1991.

Morrisson, Cécile. *La numismatique.* Paris: Presses universitaires de France, 1992.

Narain, A. K. "Alexander and India." *Greece and Rome* 12 (1965): 155–65.

Neuffer, Eduard. "Das Kostüm Alexanders des Grossen." Diss., Giessen, 1929.

Nicolet-Pierre, Hélène. "Monnaies 'à l'éléphant.' " *Bulletin de la Société française de numismatique* 33 (1978): 401–3.

———. "Argent et or frappés en Babylone entre 331 et 311 ou de Mazdai à Séleucos." In *Travaux de numismatique grecque offerts à Georges Le Rider,* ed. Michel Amandry and Silvia Hurter, pp. 285–305. London: Spink, 1999.

Noe, Sydney. *A Bibliography of Greek Coin Hoards.* 2d ed. New York: American Numismatic Society, 1937.

Norris, James. *The First Afghan War, 1838–1842.* Cambridge: Cambridge University Press, 1967.

Nylander, Carl. "Darius III—the Coward King: Point and Counterpoint." In *Alexander the Great: Reality and Myth,* ed. Jesper Carlsen et al., pp. 145–59. Rome: "L'Erma" di Bretschneider, 1993.

Oikonomides, Alcibiades N. "Decadrachm Aids in Identification of Alexander." *Coin World International,* November 25, 1981: 31–32.

———. "Scholarship, Research, and The Search for Alexander." *Ancient World* 4 (1981): 67–89.

Oldach, David, et al. "A Mysterious Death." *New England Journal of Medicine* 338 (1998): 1764–68.

Padover, Saul, ed. *A Jefferson Profile*. New York: John Day, 1956.

Pandey, Deena. "The Hydaspese-Battle Commemorative Medal of Alexander the Great—A Fresh Approach." *Journal of the Numismatic Society of India* 33 (1971): 1–7.

Parke, H. W. *Greek Mercenary Soldiers*. 1933. Reprint, Chicago: Ares, 1981.

Payne, Martha. "Alexander the Great: Myth, the Polis, and Afterward." In *Myth and the Polis*, ed. Dora Pozzi and John Wickersham, pp. 164–81. Ithaca, N.Y.: Cornell University Press, 1991.

Pearson, C. "Alexander, Porus, and the Panjab." *Indian Antiquary* 34 (1905): 253–61.

Pearson, Lionel. *The Lost Histories of Alexander the Great*. London: American Philological Association, 1960.

Pichikyan, Igor. "Rebirth of the Oxus Treasure: Second Part of the Oxus Treasure from the Miho Museum Collection." *Ancient Civilizations* 4 (1997): 306–83.

Pollitt, J. J. *Art in the Hellenistic Age*. Cambridge: Cambridge University Press, 1986.

Powers, Edward. *War and Weather*. 2d ed. Delavan, Wisc.: E. Powers, 1890.

Prakash, Buddha. *History of Poros*. Patiala: Punjabi University Press, 1967.

Price, Martin. "The 'Porus' Coinage of Alexander the Great: A Symbol of Concord and Community." In *Studia Paulo Naster Oblata*, vol. 1: *Numismatica Antiqua*, ed. S. Scheers, pp. 75–85. Leuven: Peeters, 1982.

———. "Circulation at Babylon in 323 B.C." In *Mnemata: Papers in Memory of Nancy M. Waggoner*, ed. William Metcalf, pp. 63–72. New York: American Numismatic Society, 1991.

———. *The Coinage in the Name of Alexander the Great and Philip Arrhidaeus*. 2 vols. London: British Museum Press, 1991.

Radet, Georges. "Alexandre et Porus: Le passage de l'Hydaspe." *Revue des études anciennes* 37 (1935): 349–56.

Rapson, E. J., ed. *The Cambridge History of India*. Vol. 1. Cambridge, 1922. Reprint, Delhi: S. Chand, 1962.

"A Rare Bactrian Decadrahm *[sic]*." *American Journal of Numismatics* 22 (October 1887): 40.

Rice, Anne. *Servant of the Bones*. New York: Knopf, 1996.

Rice, Ellen. "The Glorious Dead: Commemoration of the Fallen and Portrayal of Victory in the Late Classical and Hellenistic World." In *War and Society in the Greek World*, ed. John Rich and Graham Shipley, pp. 224–57. London: Routledge, 1993.

Riginos, Alice. "The Wounding of Philip II of Macedon: Fact and Fabrication." *Journal of Hellenic Studies* 114 (1994): 103–19.

Roberts, Moss, ed. *Three Kingdoms: A Historical Novel.* Berkeley: University of California Press, 1999.

Robinson, Charles A., Jr. *The History of Alexander the Great.* Vol. 1. Providence, R.I.: Brown University, 1953. Reprint, Chicago: Ares, 1996.

———. "The Two Worlds of Alexander." *Horizon* 1 (1959): 28–59.

Robson, Brian. *The Road to Kabul: The Second Afghan War, 1878–1881.* London: Arms & Armour Press, 1986.

"Roman Villa at Abinger, Surrey." *The Times* (London), February 18, 1878, p. 7.

Romm, J. S. "Aristotle's Elephant and the Myth of Alexander's Scientific Patronage." *American Journal of Philology* 110 (1989): 566–75.

Rouille, G. *Promptuaire des médailles des plus renommées personnes qui ont esté depuis le commencement du monde, avec brève description de leurs vies et faicts, recueille des bons auteurs.* 2 vols. Lyon, 1553.

Sallet, Alfred von. *Münzen und Medaillen.* Berlin: W. Spemann, 1898.

Satchell, J. E., ed. *Earthworm Ecology from Darwin to Vermiculture.* London: Chapman & Hall, 1983.

Schreider, Helen, and Frank Schreider. "In the Footsteps of Alexander the Great." *National Geographic* 133 (January 1968): 1–65.

Schubert, Rudolf. "Die Porusschlacht." *Rheinisches Museum für Philologie* 56 (1901): 543–62.

Scullard, H. H. *The Elephant in the Greek and Roman World.* Ithaca, N.Y.: Cornell University Press, 1974.

Settis, Salvatore. "Alessandro e Poro in *Campis Curculionis.*" *La parola del passato* 23 (1968): 55–75.

Sinha, B. C. *Studies in Alexander's Campaigns.* Varanasi: Bhartiya Publishing House, 1973.

Smith, Federica. *L'immagine di Alessandro il Grande sulle monete del regno (336–323 a.C.).* Milan: Ennerre, 2000.

Smith, R. R. R. *Hellenistic Royal Portraits.* Oxford: Clarendon Press, 1988.

Spencer, Frank. *The Piltdown Papers, 1908–1955.* London: Oxford University Press, 1990.

Stauffer, D. E. "Die Londoner Dekadrachme von 324 und die Ideenpolitik Alexanders." *Jahrbuch für Numismatik und Geldgeschichte* 2 (1950–51): 132.

Stein, Sir Aurel. "The Site of Alexander's Passage of the Hydaspes and the Battle with Poros." *Geographical Journal* 80 (1932): 31–46.

Stewart, Andrew. *Faces of Power: Alexander's Image and Hellenistic Politics.* Berkeley: University of California Press, 1993.

Stoneman, Richard. *Alexander the Great.* New York: Routledge, 1997.

————, ed. *Legends of Alexander the Great.* London: J. M. Dent; Rutland, Vt.: C. E. Tuttle, 1994.

Svoronos, Joannes. *Christodoulos the Counterfeiter.* Athens, 1922. Reprint, Chicago: Ares, 1975.

Tarn, Sir William Woodthorpe. *Alexander the Great.* 2 vols. Cambridge: Cambridge University Press, 1948.

Thompson, Margaret. "Paying the Mercenaries." In *Festschrift für Leo Mildenberg: Numismatik, Kunstgeschichte, Archäologie = Studies in Honor of Leo Mildenberg: Numismatics, Art History, Archeology,* ed. Arthur Houghton et al., pp. 241–47. Wetteren, Belgium: NR Editions, 1984.

Thompson, Margaret, Otto Mørkholm, and Colin Kraay, eds. *An Inventory of Greek Coin Hoards.* New York: American Numismatic Society, 1973.

Traill, David. *Schliemann of Troy: Treasure and Deceit.* New York: St. Martin's Press, 1995.

Trousdale, William, ed. *War in Afghanistan, 1879–1880: The Personal Diary of Major General Sir Charles Metcalfe MacGregor.* Detroit: Wayne State University Press, 1985.

Troxell, Hyla. *Studies in the Macedonian Coinage of Alexander the Great.* New York: American Numismatic Society, 1997.

United States Senate. *Hearings before the Committee on Foreign Relations: Environmental Modification Techniques.* Washington, D.C.: Government Printing Office, 1979.

Veith, Georg. "Der Kavalleriekampf in der Schlacht am Hydaspes." *Klio* 8 (1908): 131–53.

Vermeule, Cornelius. "Alexander the Great, the Emperor Severus Alexander and the Aboukir Medallions." *Revue suisse de numismatique* 61 (1982): 61–72.

Waller, John. *Beyond the Khyber Pass.* New York: Random House, 1990.

Walsh, John. *Unraveling Piltdown: The Science Fraud of the Century and Its Solution.* New York: Random House, 1996.

Warner, S. L. "Freud the Mighty Warrior." *Journal of the American Academy of Psychoanalysis* 19, 2 (1991): 282–93.

Westing, Arthur, ed. *Environmental Warfare: A Technical, Legal, and Policy Appraisal.* London: Taylor & Francis, 1984.

Whitehead, R. B. "The Eastern Satrap Sophytes." *Numismatic Chronicle,* 6th ser., 3 (1943): 60–72.

Wilson, David. *The Forgotten Collector: Augustus Wollaston Franks of the British Museum.* London: Thames & Hudson, 1984.

Wimmel, Kenneth. *The Alluring Target: In Search of the Secrets of Central Asia.* Washington, D.C.: Trackless Sands Press, 1996.

Wirth, Gerhard. "Alexander und Rom." In *Alexandre le Grand: Image et réalité*, ed. Ernst Badian, pp. 181–221. Geneva: Fondation Hardt, 1976.

Wolohojian, A. M., ed. *The Romance of Alexander the Great by Pseudo-Callisthenes.* New York: Columbia University Press, 1969.

Wood, John. *A Journey to the Source of the River Oxus.* London: John Murray, 1872.

Wood, Michael. *In the Footsteps of Alexander the Great.* Berkeley: University of California Press, 1997.

Worthington, Ian. "Alexander and 'the Interests of Historical Accuracy': A Reply." *Ancient History Bulletin* 13, 4 (1999): 136–40.

———. "How 'Great' Was Alexander?" *Ancient History Bulletin* 13, 2 (1999): 39–55.

INDEX

Abbott, Jacob, 2

Abdalonymos, 5

Abdur Rahman, 31, 33

Abinger Hall, Surrey, 23, 25, 48

Abisares, 51n10

Abulites, 105–7, 144–46

Acesines River (modern Chenab), 49

Achaemenids: dynasty, 73; empire, 8. *See also* Persia/Persian Empire

Achilles, 7–8, 71

Afghanistan, 13–14, 28–35, 41, 86–87

Afghan War, First, 30, 32

Afghan War, Second, 31

Agamemnon, 7; mask of, 69

Agathocles, 46

Ajax (Greek hero), 49, 78

Ajax (Indian elephant), 78

Albania, 9

"Alexander Keraunophoros," 123–24, 151

Alexander Mosaic, 22, 71, 120–21, 126–27, 129; and elephant medallions, 130–31, 133–34, 162; modern interpretations of, 131–34

Alexander Sarcophagus, 5, 126–27, 133

Alexander the Great: Abulites and, 105–7, 146; apotheosis/divinity of, 1, 11, 68, 98, 112, 124, 134, 152–55, 163–65; challenges Indian archer, 135; coinage (regular) of, 39, 70, 90, 92–93, 96, 111, 122, 140–42, 145; Diogenes and, 85; elephant hunts of, 103; image on elephant medallions, 42–43, 45, 48, 53–54, 61–63, 68–71, 73, 89, 91, 97–100, 102, 104, 107, 123–24, 126, 134–35, 138–39, 151, 155; legends and legacy of, 1–6, 24, 27, 29, 44, 46; military equipment of, 118–21, 123, 131, 134; modern views of, 6, 21–22, 107–8, 111–17, 131–33, 151, 162; Plautus and, 83; Porus and, 15–16, 49–60, 71–80, 82, 84, 94, 99–101, 109–10, 129–30, 136, 149–53, 160; reign of, 9–18; sources on, 18–22, 110–11; Taxiles' monetary gift to, 104; Timoleon in Sicily and, 157–58; tombs and coffins attributed to, 4–5, 22, 26; Zoroastrianism and, 36. *See also* Bucephalus

Alexandria, Egypt, 3, 5, 11

American Numismatic Society, 39, 92, 104; acquisition of elephant medallions, 70, 94

Amorites, 157

Anaxarchus, 152

ancus (elephant goad), 98, 102, 128, 131, 137

Antonine Column, 159
Anuphis, 159
Apelles, 123–24, 151
Apis bull, 11
Apollonius of Tyana, 78
Aral Sea, 28
archaeology/archaeologists, 22, 40, 43, 56, 78, 88, 105; indebted to worms, according to Darwin, 24–25. *See also* Schliemann, Heinrich; Takht-i Sangin; Vergina
archer/archers: Indian, 50, 135, 154, 163–64; on elephant medallions, 93–94, 99–100, 102–3, 108, 134, 136, 139, 149. *See also* elephant (bowman type)
Aria, 106
aristeia (military awards), 146–49, 154, 156, 164
Aristobulus, 21, 59, 74, 83–84, 136, 153
Aristotle, 8, 15, 20–21; knowledge of elephants, 80
Arnold-Biucchi, Carmen, 104
Arrian of Nicomedia, 18, 21–22, 69, 111, 148; on Abulites, 106; on elephant hunts, 99, 103; on Gaugamela (battle), 73, 75–76; on Hydaspes (battle), 73–74, 77, 79, 150; on Indians, 101–2, 135; on Porus's retreat, 54–55, 57–59, 62, 75
Artaxerxes, 13
Asia Minor, 10–11, 140–41
Assyrians, 157
Athenian-style coins, 92, 96, 141
Athens/Athenians, 8–9, 17, 80, 110
Attic standard, 141
Augustine, Saint, 1
Aurelius, Marcus, 159, 161
awards, military. See *aristeia*
Ayab Khan, 31

Babylon/Babylonia, 16–17, 24, 93, 109, 141, 146, 149, 164; attribution of elephant medallions to, 63, 68, 91, 98, 100–101, 104, 145; Iraq hoard (1973) found at, 92, 140, 147; lion staters from, 93, 104, 141, 145
Bactria/Bactrians, 28, 53, 114, 150, 164; elephant medallions and, 42–46, 77, 91; *Epigoni* recruited from, 17; invaded by Alexander, 13–14, 127; Oxus Treasure and, 37, 45–46
Badian, Ernst, 110–11, 113–14, 132–33
Bagoas, 113
Banerji, J. N., 68–69, 71
Bank Leu, 94–95
Beirut, 89–90
Bellinger, Alfred, 90
Bernard, Paul, 88, 101–3, 105
Berry, Burton Y., 70
Bessus, 13
Bibliothèque nationale, 45, 87; acquisition of elephant medallions, 94, 97
Bosworth, A. B., 74, 107–11, 115
bowman. *See* archer/archers
Britain/British, 24, 26, 30–35, 76, 112
British Archaeological Association, 25
British Museum, 4, 39, 43, 53, 92; Franks and, 27, 37, 41–42, 84, 87; Iraq hoard and, 94; Oxus Treasure and, 38, 41; second elephant medallion and, 60, 120–21
Brydon, Dr. William, 30
Bucephala, 99, 104
Bucephalus: death of, 58, 80, 99, 136; elephant medallions and, 103–5, 126–28, 133
Bukhara/Bukharans, 29–35, 40, 45
Burnes, Sir Alexander, 30–31
Burton, Captain Francis Charles, 34–35

Caesar, 1, 3
Calcutta, Indian Museum of, 86–87
Caligula, 3
Callataÿ, François de, 140
Callisthenes, 21; death of, 15
Canaanites, 156–58
Carthaginians, 81, 157–58

Cassander, 132

Cathay, 112

Cavagnari, Sir Pierre Louis Napoleon, 30

Central Asia, 5, 13, 27, 36, 73; "Great Game" in, 29–30, 32; nomads from, 109

Champollion, Jean-François, 4

Chares, 21

chariots: Canaanite, 156, 159; Carthaginian, 158; depicted on elephant medallions, 94, 99–100, 108, 118, 136–37, 139, 149, 154–55; Greek, 125; Indian, 19–20, 50, 52, 74, 136–37, 153–54, 163–64; Persian, 72, 131–32. *See also* elephant (chariot type)

Charlemagne, 1

Charles the Bold, 81

China/Chinese, 37, 160

chlamys (cavalry cloak), 121

Christians, 159

Christodoulos, Constantine, 86

Chrysostom, St. John, 3

Cleitarchus, 21

Cleitus, 15

Climax, Mt., 10, 164

Clytemnestra, 69

Cohen, Ada, 131

coins/medals/medallions: distinction between, 39n37; manufacture of, 62–66. *See also* die linkage; forgeries; monogram/control mark

Craterus, 52, 150

Creasy, Sir Edward, 112, 114

cuirass (breastplate), 121, 125

Cunningham, General Sir Alexander, 37

Curtius Rufus, Quintus, 18–19, 22, 75; on Bagoas, 113; on Hydaspes (battle), 58–60, 69, 81, 137, 153, 155; on Taxiles, 60, 104; part of Vulgate tradition, 21

Dahae, 150

Dante, 1

Danube River, 9

Darius III, 84, 91, 129, 146; Alexander Mosaic and, 22, 71, 130–33; Porus and, 49, 75–76; war of, with Alexander, 11, 13, 72–73, 75–77

Darwin, Charles, 37, 48, 85, 112; study of earthworms, 23–27, 36, 47, 56, 161, 164

David, King, 157

Demanhur hound, 140

Demaratos of Corinth, 158

Demosthenes, 8

die linkage, 66, 70, 103, 140, 144

Diodorus of Sicily, 18, 57, 75; part of Vulgate tradition, 21

Diogenes of Sinope, 85

Dost Muhammed, 30

Drangiana, 106

Dryden, John, 2

Duerr, Nicholas, 92–96

earthworms: archaeology and, 23–27, 36, 38, 47, 56, 161, 164

Ecbatana, 100

Edmunds, Lowell, 71

Egypt/Egyptians, 9, 11, 13, 21, 53, 70, 159; Herodotus and, 80; Schliemann and, 26

Eisenhower, Dwight D., 1

Ekkehard of Aura, 19–20

elephant (Alexander type), 97, 117

elephant (bowman type), 95, 97, 102, 110, 117, 140, 144

elephant (chariot type), 97, 102, 105–6, 117, 140, 144, 146n16

elephant medallions, 96, 98, 111, 117, 139, 161–62, 165; die axis of, 65, 70, 93, 143–44; large (decadrachms), 53, 68, 70, 73, 77, 84, 88, 90, 93–110, 118–34, 155; overstrikes and, 65, 143; size of mintage, 139–41; small (tetradrachms), 93–95, 97, 99–110, 134–38, 154–55; weights of, 141–43

elephants: Abulites and, 106; anatomy of, 102, 128; commemorated in India, 78; considered exotic in West, 80–82; deployed in Battle of Gaugamela, 72, 76; deployed in Battle of the Hydaspes River, 15, 19–20, 49–50, 52, 56–59, 74–75, 79–80, 84, 101–2, 154–55, 163–64; given to Alexander, 55; hunting of, 99, 103; nomads and, 44; Plautus and, 82–84; shown on large medallions, 42, 48, 54, 56, 61, 63, 67, 69, 75, 79, 83, 89, 94, 98, 104, 108, 126, 128–29, 131, 138–39, 155; shown on small medallions, 93–95, 99–103, 108, 134, 137–39, 150–51, 155. *See also* Ajax (Indian elephant); elephant medallions; Hannibal

England, 37, 112. *See also* Britain/British

Environmental Modification Techniques, Convention against, 160

Epigoni ("Successors"), 17

Eucratides the Great, 44–46, 48, 54, 64, 91

Eudamos, 101, 105

Evans, Joan, 40

Evans, Sir John, 40

exhibitions: Search for Alexander, 95; Wealth of the Ancient World, 95

Exiles' Decree, 17, 108

Ezekiel, 157

Farrer, Thomas Henry, 23, 25

Firdausi, 76

forgeries, 85–90, 95

Franks, Sir Augustus Wollaston, 27, 37, 39–43, 87–88, 112, 165; and Franks Medallion, 44, 46, 48, 53, 59, 70, 84, 89, 120, 144

Freud, Sigmund, 2

Fuller, J. F. C., 52

Gardner, Percy, 43–48, 53–54, 63, 89, 111, 146, 165

Gaugamela, Battle of, 13, 72–73, 77, 79,

84, 91, 119, 127, 129, 146, 163; Porus and, 49, 75–76

Gaza, 11

Gedrosia, 105

Gedrosian Desert, 16, 147

Genghis Khan, 159–60

Gettysburg, 78

Ghilzais, 32–34

Ghulan Muhammud, 29

Gladstone, Willaim, 26–27, 47

Gordian Knot, 11, 128, 152

Gordium, 10, 164

Gordius, 11

gorget (neck guard), 118–19

Goukowsky, Paul, 98

Granicus River, Battle of, 10, 119, 127, 163

"Great Game," 30, 35

Greece/Greeks, 7–10, 13, 15–17, 44, 47, 49, 61, 69, 71, 77, 79–81, 84–86, 99–102, 108–10, 112, 125, 157–58, 163; numismatics and, 39, 48, 53, 70, 98, 128, 141; settlers in Central Asia, 29, 36, 114

Green, Peter, 153

Halicarnassus, 10

Hamilton, J. R., 106

Hammond, Nicholas, 99–100, 103

Handel, George Frederick, 2

Hannibal, 49, 52, 81

Haranpur, 50

Head, Barclay Vincent, 53–63, 68, 165

Hector, 49

Heliocles, 44

helmet, 78; shown on elephant medallions, 54, 61–63, 71, 89, 98, 102, 118–20, 123, 125, 131

Henry III, 81

Hephaestion, 16, 148

Hercules (Herakles), 8, 71

Hermitage Museum, 123

Herodotus, 20, 76, 80

Hill, Sir George Francis, 60–63, 143

Himalayas, 49
Hindu Kush Mountains, 15
Hogarth, David, 52, 86
Hollstein, Wilhelm, 104–5
Homer/Homeric, 7, 26, 49, 69, 71, 91,
    118, 134, 136, 162
Hydaspes River (modern Jhelum), 49, 51,
    55, 59, 80, 99, 164; Battle of, 15,
    51–56, 59, 62, 71–75, 77–79, 81–82,
    91, 100–101, 126–27, 129, 135, 146,
    148, 150–56, 158, 162
Hydra, 14
Hyphasis River, 16–17, 129, 155, 163

India, 53, 79, 83, 91, 148–49, 164; Alexan-
    der and, 9, 15–16, 19, 73, 76–77,
    98–99, 103, 109–10, 131, 146–47,
    162–63; Apollonius and, 78; coinage
    of, 104n29, 149n25; forgeries in,
    86–87; military forces of, 15–16, 19,
    49–52, 73–75, 93, 99–101, 105–9, 125,
    129, 134–39, 145, 150, 153–54; mod-
    ern, 29–30, 40, 42, 71, 112
Indian Ocean, 16
Indus, 16, 55, 148
International Numismatic Commission, 96
Ionnina Museum, 118
Iran, 13, 60
Iraq, 13, 84; hoard from (1973), 92–97,
    101–2, 110, 141, 146–47
Iron Maiden (rock band), 6
Isaiah, 157
Isocrates, 8
Israel, 13
Israelites, 156–57, 159
Issus, Battle of, 11, 73, 163
Istanbul, 5
Italy, 70, 82–84
Ithaca, 26

Jagdalak, 30, 33
Jalalabad, 33, 35
Jamugha, 159
Jefferson, Thomas, 2

Jhelum, 50
Jordan, 13
Joshua, 157
Justin, 18–19, 75; part of Vulgate tradi-
    tion, 21

Kabul, 30–33, 87
Kaiser, Wilhelm, 71
Kandahar, 31
Kantorowicz, Ernst, 70–71
Karkacha caves, 33
Khiva, 29
Khobadian, 31
Khullum, 37, 40–41, 43
Khyber Pass, 35
Kipling, Rudyard, 30, 34, 112
Kishon, Battle of, 156, 158
Kokcha River, 28
kothornos (leggings), 121
Krimisos River, Battle of, 157–58
Kuwait, 13
kyrbasia (Persian headgear), 61, 98

Lane Fox, Robin, 105–6
Lane-Poole, Stanley, 39
Langdon, John, 2
Lebanon, 5, 13, 70
Leonnatus, 148
Libyan desert, 11
lightning. *See* thunderbolt/lightning
London, 24, 27, 30, 39, 47, 61, 70, 95
Louis IX, 2
Louis XIV, 81
Louvre, 4
Lucian of Samosata, 59

Macedonia/Macedonians, 54, 112, 125;
    Alexander as king of, 1, 20, 53, 132,
    151, 155, 164; army of, 9–11, 14–17,
    49–52, 55, 58, 72–75, 77–78, 98–101,
    109–10, 127, 129, 131, 133–36, 150,
    153–55, 161; society and culture of,
    7–8, 119–23, 134
Macriani, 3

Maiwand, Battle of, 31
Malli, 16, 148
Malraux, André, 4
Mauretania, 53
Mazaeus, 104
medallion. *See* coins/medals/medallions; elephant medallions
Megiddo, 156
mercenaries, 10, 17
Mercury, 159
Meroes, 73, 75, 150
Mesopotamia, 9, 16, 67, 73, 147, 149
Miletus/Milesians, 10, 110
Miller, M. C. J., 103–5
Mitchiner, Michael, 77, 79
Molière, 82
Mongols, 160
monogram/control mark, 42, 61, 63–64, 89–90, 93–94, 105–6, 117–18, 144–45, 146n16
monsoon, 15–16, 49–50, 148, 152, 155, 163; Defense Department and, 160. *See also* storms
Moorcroft, William, 27
Mycenae, 26, 69

Napoleon I, 1, 4
Napoleon III, 3, 45
Narain, A. K., 87
Nearchus, 21, 148
Nectanebo II, 4
Neisos gem, 71, 123
Neptune, 158–59. *See also* Poseidon
Nereid, 5
New Carthage, 158
Newton, Sir Charles, 47
New York, 8, 39, 42, 70, 92, 95
Nicaea, 75, 104, 151
Nicolet-Pierre, Hélène, 92, 97–98
Niffer (ancient Nippur), 67
Nike/Victory: on elephant medallions, 62–63, 73, 89–90, 104, 123, 134, 151, 155; on Roman coinage, 161; on Sicilian coinage, 125. *See also* Nicaea

Nile River, 27
Numismatic Fine Arts, 95
numismatics/numismatists, 42, 45, 48, 56, 60, 62, 64, 71–72, 76–77, 79, 87, 90, 94–95, 99–100, 110, 114, 125, 128, 142, 149, 155, 161–62; congresses, 68, 92; development of, 38–39, 53, 66, 85–86, 88, 111, 138–39

Octavian/Augustus, 3
Odysseus, 26
Oikonomides, Alcibiades, 98, 100, 103
Old Testament, 156–57
Olympia, 47
Olympias, 8, 163
Olympus, 9
Omphis/Ambhi, 55. *See also* Taxiles
Onesicritus, 21, 126, 148
Opis Mutiny, 17
Ora, 148
Oxus River (modern Amu Darya), 27–29, 31, 36, 42
Oxus Treasure, 29, 31, 35–37, 40–45, 53–54, 94, 96; forgeries and, 86, 88

Pakistan, 15
Pamir Mountains, 28
Pandey, Deena, 72–76, 79, 146
Paris, 39, 45, 87, 92, 94–95, 97
Parmenion, 15, 73
Patala, 16
Paul III (Pope), 2
Pauravas, 49
pelte (shield), 99, 121
Perdiccas III, 7
Persepolis, 100
Perseus, 135
Persia/Persian Empire: Alexander and, 9–11, 13, 15, 61, 72, 77, 119, 130–33; coinage of, 98, 135, 147–48; Philip II and, 8–9; Porus and, 49. *See also* Achaemenids; Darius III; helmet; *kyrbasia*; women; Zoroastrians
Persian Gulf, 16

Peshawar, 29, 32–33, 35–37
Petrarch, 38
Peucestas, 148
Philip II, 7–11, 126–27, 162
Philip V (king of Spain), 2
Philostratus, 77–78
Philotas, 15
Phrataphernes, 106
Piltdown Man, 85, 88
Plautus, 82–84
Plutarch of Chaeronea, 18, 57, 75, 79,
    111, 153; on Abulites' money, 105–7;
    on Alexander's helmet, 118–19; on
    Bagoas, 113; on Timoleon, 158
Polybius, 158–59
Pompeii: Alexander Mosaic from, 22, 71,
    120, 130; painting in House of the Vet-
    tii, 123
Pompey the Great, 3
Porus, 91, 102, 130–31, 135, 138–39; al-
    legedly shown on small medallions,
    93–94, 135; campaign of, against
    Alexander, 15–16, 48–53, 69, 71–74,
    77, 99–101, 107–9, 133, 136–37, 146,
    148–55, 163; commemorates battle,
    78; Darius and, 75–76; death of, 164;
    description of, 129; elephant of,
    79–80, 84; in medieval historio-
    graphy, 19–20, 82; Taxiles and, 55–
    58, 60, 62; Taxiles' brother and,
    58–59
Poseidon, 112, 157. *See also* Neptune
Prakash, Buddha, 71
Priam, 69
Price, Martin, 92, 96–97, 99–105, 107,
    110, 140–41, 149–51
proskynesis (ritual obeisance), 15
Ptolemy, 21, 74, 136, 154
Punjab, 49, 54, 101, 146, 149
Pyrgoteles, 68

quiver, 134
Qunduz, 31
Qunduz River, 28

Rawalpindi, 29, 35–37, 88
Rhône River, 52
Rice, Anne, 6
Rome/Romans, 18, 25, 37, 39, 77, 79, 85;
    elephants and, 49, 80–82; wars of, and
    divine intervention, 157–59, 161
Rosetta Stone, 4
Roxane, 14
Royal Numismatic Society, 95–96
Russia/Russians, 30–31, 35–36

St. Petersburg, 30
Samarkand, 29, 31
sarissa (Macedonian spear), 121–22, 126,
    128–30, 132–33
Sarpedon, 157
scepter, 121–23, 161
Schliemann, Heinrich, 26–27, 37, 39, 47,
    67, 69, 136
Scipio (Africanus), 158–59
Scythians, 150
Seh Baba, 30, 33–34
Settis, Salvatore, 82–83
Shakespeare, William, 5, 23, 78n25, 82
Shuja, Shah, 30
Shuker Ali, 29
Sicily, 125, 157–58
Side, 140
Sidon, 5, 126, 133
Sisera, 156–57, 159
Siwah, 11
Smith, R. R. R., 124
Society of Antiquaries, 27, 37, 47, 61
Sogdiana/Sogdians, 13, 17, 114, 127, 150
Song of Deborah, 157
Sotheby's, 95
South Asia, 13, 32, 73
South Kensington Museum (Victoria and
    Albert Museum), 35
South Tajikistan Archaeological Expedi-
    tion, 36
Spain, 3, 53, 158
Sparta, 8
Spitamenes, 14

Stasanor, 106
Stauffer, D. E., 68, 70
Stewart, Andrew, 105, 130–31, 133
storms: warfare and charismatic leadership in, 152–64. See also monsoon
Strabo, 101
Susa, 17, 100, 105–6, 145–46, 148–49
swords, 78, 123, 125, 132; makhaira, 120; xiphos, 120
Syria, 13, 53, 141

Tajikistan, 13
Takht-i Kuwad, 31
Takht-i Sangin, 35–37, 120n9
Tarn, Sir William Woodthorpe, 112–16, 149, 151
Tarsus, 3, 86
Taxila, 55, 78, 100
Taxiles, 91, 109, 125; ally of Alexander, 55, 60, 100, 104–5, 150; enemy of Porus, 55–58, 60–62, 75
Tesinka Pass, 33
Tezin Valley, 34
Thebes, 9
Theophilos, 119
Therapontigonus, 83
thunderbolt/lightning: on elephant medallions, 42–43, 54, 63, 69, 122–24, 131, 134, 151–54, 164; and Israelites in battle, 157; on Neisos gem, 71, 123; and Romans in battle, 159, 161; shown in "Alexander Keraunophoros," 123. See also monsoon; storms
Timoleon, 157–58
Trogus, Pompeius, 18–19; part of Vulgate tradition, 21
Trojan War, 7, 69

Troy, 26, 69
Trump Taj Mahal Casino Resort, Atlantic City, 5–6
Tryphon of Apamea, 157
Turkestan, 28
Turkey, 13, 70
Turkmenistan, 13
Tyre, 11

Uzbekistan, 13

Vakhsh River, 28
Vergina (ancient Aegae), 119–21
Verma, T. P., 87
Victory (goddess). See Nike/Victory
Vietnam War, 160
Vulgate tradition, 21, 55, 77, 80, 113, 129, 154

Waggoner, Nancy, 92–93, 96–97, 104
Wazi ad-Din, 29
William the Conqueror, 52
women: Macedonian, 8; Persian, 14, 17
Wood, Captain John, 27
Wood, Michael, 115
World War, Second, 113
Worthington, Ian, 115

Xenophilos, 105–7, 144–46
Xenophon, 57

Yueh-Chi, 44, 101n20

Zeus/Zeus-Ammon, 42, 122; Alexander and, 11, 43, 78, 107, 112, 122–24, 134, 151–53, 163
Zoroastrians, 35–36

HELLENISTIC CULTURE AND SOCIETY

*General Editors: Anthony W. Bulloch, Erich S. Gruen, A. A.
Long, and Andrew F. Stewart*

I. *Alexander to Actium: The Historical Evolution of the Hellenistic Age*, by
Peter Green

II. *Hellenism in the East: The Interaction of Greek and Non-Greek
Civilizations from Syria to Central Asia after Alexander,* edited by
Amélie Kuhrt and Susan Sherwin-White

III. *The Question of "Eclecticism": Studies in Later Greek Philosophy*, edited
by J. M. Dillon and A. A. Long

IV. *Antigonos the One-Eyed and the Creation of the Hellenistic State*, by
Richard A. Billows

V. *A History of Macedonia*, by R. Malcolm Errington, translated by
Catherine Errington

VI. *Attic Letter-Cutters of 229 to 86 B.C.*, by Stephen V. Tracy

VII. *The Vanished Library: A Wonder of the Ancient World*, by Luciano
Canfora

VIII. *Hellenistic Philosophy of Mind*, by Julia Annas

IX. *Hellenistic History and Culture*, edited by Peter Green

X. *The Best of the Argonauts: The Redefinition of the Epic Hero in Book One of Apollonius' Argonautica,* by James J. Clauss

XI. *Faces of Power: Alexander's Image and Hellenistic Politics,* by Andrew Stewart

XII. *Images and Ideologies: Self-definition in the Hellenistic World,* edited by A. W. Bulloch, E. S. Gruen, A. A. Long, and A. Stewart

XIII. *From Samarkhand to Sardis: A New Approach to the Seleucid Empire,* by Susan Sherwin-White and Amélie Kuhrt

XIV. *Regionalism and Change in the Economy of Independent Delos, 314-167 B.C.,* by Gary Reger

XV. *Hegemony to Empire: The Development of the Roman Imperium in the East from 148 to 62 B.C.,* by Robert Kallet-Marx

XVI. *Moral Vision in* The Histories *of Polybius,* by Arthur M. Eckstein

XVII. *The Hellenistic Settlements in Europe, the Islands, and Asia Minor,* by Getzel M. Cohen

XVIII. *Interstate Arbitrations in the Greek World, 337–90 B.C.,* by Sheila L. Ager

XIX. *Theocritus's Urban Mimes: Mobility, Gender, and Patronage,* by Joan B. Burton

XX. *Athenian Democracy in Transition: Attic Letter-Cutters of 340 to 290 B.C.,* by Stephen V. Tracy

XXI. *Pseudo-Hecataeus, "On the Jews": Legitimizing the Jewish Diaspora,* by Bezalel Bar-Kochva

XXII. *Asylia: Territorial Inviolability in the Hellenistic World,* by Kent J. Rigsby

XXIII. *The Cynics: The Cynic Movement in Antiquity and Its Legacy,* edited by R. Bracht Branham and Marie-Odile Goulet-Cazé

XXIV. *The Politics of Plunder: Aitolians and Their* Koinon *in the Early Hellenistic Era, 279–217 B.C.*, by Joseph B. Scholten

XXV. *The Argonautika*, by Apollonios Rhodios, translated, with introduction, commentary, and glossary, by Peter Green

XXVI. *Hellenistic Constructs: Essays in Culture, History, and Historiography*, edited by Paul Cartledge, Peter Garnsey, and Erich Gruen

XXVII. *Josephus's Interpretation of the Bible*, by Louis H. Feldman

XXVIII. *Poetic Garlands: Hellenistic Epigrams in Context*, by Kathryn J. Gutzwiller

XXIX. *Religion in Hellenistic Athens*, by Jon D. Mikalson

XXX. *Heritage and Hellenism: The Reinvention of Jewish Tradition*, by Erich S. Gruen

XXXI. *The Beginnings of Jewishness*, by Shaye D. Cohen

XXXII. *Thundering Zeus: The Making of Hellenistic Bactria*, by Frank L. Holt

XXXIII. *Jews in the Mediterranean Diaspora from Alexander to Trajan (323 BCE–117 CE)*, by John M. G. Barclay

XXXIV. *From Pergamon to Sperlonga: Sculpture and Context*, edited by Nancy T. de Grummond and Brunilde Sismondo Ridgway

XXXV. *Polyeideia: The Iambi of Callimachus and the Archaic Iambic Tradition*, by Benjamin Acosta-Hughes

XXXVI. *Stoic Studies*, by A. A. Long

XXXVII. *Seeing Double: Intercultural Poetics in Ptolemaic Alexandria*, by Susan A. Stephens

XXXVIII. *Athens and Macedon: Attic Letter-Cutters of 300 to 229 B.C.*, by Stephen V. Tracy

XXXIX. *Encomium of Ptolemy Philadelphus,* by Theocritus, translated with an introduction and commentary by Richard Hunter

XL. *The Making of Fornication: Eros, Ethics, and Political Reform in Greek Philosophy and Early Christianity,* by Kathy L. Gaca

XLI. *Cultural Politics in Polybius' Histories,* by Craige Champion

XLII. *Cleomedes on the Heavens: Physics and Astronomy in Later Stoicism, A Translation of Cleomedes' Caelestia,* by Robert B. Todd and Alan C. Bowen

XLIII. *History as It Should Have Been: Third Maccabees, Historical Fictions, and Jewish Self-Fashioning in the Hellenistic Period,* by Sara Raup Johnson

XLIV. *Alexander the Great and the Mystery of the Elephant Medallions,* by Frank L. Holt

XLV. *The Horse and Jockey from Artemision: A Bronze Equestrian Monument of the Hellenistic Period,* by Seán Hemingway

Compositor:	Binghamton Valley Composition, LLC
Text:	10/15 Janson
Display:	Janson
Printer and binder:	Maple-Vail Manufacturing Group